Robert Grieve

Narragansett and Mount Hope Bays

Picturesque Narragansett

Robert Grieve

Narragansett and Mount Hope Bays
Picturesque Narragansett

ISBN/EAN: 9783337091316

Printed in Europe, USA, Canada, Australia, Japan

Cover: Foto ©Andreas Hilbeck / pixelio.de

More available books at **www.hansebooks.com**

Narragansett and Mount Hope Bays.

PICTURESQUE

NARRAGANSETT

AN ILLUSTRATED GUIDE

TO THE

Cities, Towns and Famous Resorts of Rhode Island.

WITH A SKETCH OF THE

CITY OF FALL RIVER, MASS.

Third Edition.

By ROBERT GRIEVE.

The Preface.

IN PRESENTING A NEW EDITION OF PICTUR-
ESQUE NARRAGANSETT, WE OFFER NO APOL-
OGY. THE UNDOUBTED EXCELLENCE OF THE
WORK, AMPLE WITHOUT BEING TRIVIAL IN ITS
DETAILS, ACCURATE, BUT NEITHER DULL NOR
DRY, THOROUGH BOTH AS TO HISTORY AND
DESCRIPTIVE MATTER, WITH THE LENGTH OF
TIME WHICH HAS ELAPSED SINCE THE ISSUE
OF THE LAST EDITION, IS SUFFICIENT REASON
FOR A REPUBLICATION. THE TEXT HAS BEEN
CAREFULLY REVISED, AND ITS MANY PEN-
SKETCHES VERIFIED AND CONFORMED TO
THE MOST RECENT CHANGES AND IMPROVE-
MENTS. SPECIAL CARE HAS BEEN GIVEN TO
THE MANUFACTURING AND BUSINESS INTER-
ESTS. WE TRUST THE GUIDE MAY PROVE A
SOURCE OF PLEASURE AND PROFIT TO BOTH
THE CITIZEN AND THE INQUIRING STRANGER.

The Publishers.

CONTENTS.

SILVER SPRING.

H. P. BLISS, Proprietor.

Open from June 20th until Sept. 20th.

Shore Dinners Served from 12.30 till 5 P. M. each day.

EXCEPT SUNDAY.

Bowling Alley and Billiard Room.

Communication by Two Lines of Boats and by Providence, Warren & Bristol Railroad.

BEAUTIFUL, PICTURESQUE SILVER SPRING! Language has been exhausted
in expressing its attractions. Its distant and near views of landscape and
water, city and village, are beyond comparison. The spires and
domes of Providence across the water to the northwest, Rocky
Point to the south, and intervening shores of wondrous
beauty, all along the line of vision.
But its chief attraction is the method by which it is conducted. Its quiet Sundays enjoyed by boarders and cottagers, and the MORALE of its week-
day atmosphere give it a standing of which no other
place of its kind can boast.

LIST OF ILLUSTRATIONS.

RIVER VIEWS.

Providence

PART FIRST.

CHAPTER I.

The City of Providence.

THE chief city in an active community of more than five hundred thousand people within and near the state lines of Rhode Island, peculiarly fortunate in location, and the second in importance among the famous cities of New England. Providence has attained a fame world-wide as an enterprising manufacturing and commercial centre. Its industries are great in number and diversified in character. Its growth and expansion in wealth and population in recent years has been constant. Since the close of the Rebellion it has more than doubled in population, and the Providence of to-day is quite different from the city of that time. Then it seemed a large town with rather provincial character-

WEYBOSSET STREET, LOOKING TOWARDS WESTMINSTER.

istics; now it is really a modern city with much of a cosmopolitan appearance. This progress has been accompanied by the development of its manufactures

2

in all lines, by the formation of a magnificent school system, by the establishment of
libraries, the laying out of parks, increased
opportunities in all directions for literary
and artistic culture, and with other widen-
ing avenues for intellectual, moral, and
material advancement.

Located at the head of navigation on the
northwestern arm of Narragansett Bay, the
city is built in the valleys of the Moshassuck and Woonasquatucket rivers, and on
the adjacent hills to the north, east, and
west, which rise from the confluence of
these rivers with the arm of the bay known
as the Providence River. On the east of
the Providence River the hills rise almost
from the water's edge to an altitude of about
two hundred feet at the highest point, falling away by a more gradual descent eastward to the Seekonk River, a mile distant.
On the west side much of the land originally was low and was overflowed by every
rise of the tide, but beyond this marsh to
the west the land rose abruptly fifty to seventy feet high, spreading out into a large
plateau extending west and south which is
now nearly all occupied by business blocks
and residences to the western and southern
limits of the city. The steep western elevations having been graded to a gently inclined plane, the lower level nearest the
river naturally became the business centre
of the city, while the higher levels to the
east and the northern and western plateaus
have been mostly appropriated for house-
lots for mansions and dwellings.

The first chapter of the history of Providence is very romantic. Roger Williams,
a clergyman, with five or six companions,
settled on the eastern bank of the river in
the spring of 1636, and named the place
"Providence," because he considered the
"supreme deliverer" had guided their selection. Previous to this Roger Williams
had preached in Plymouth and Massachusetts Bay colonies, but had been tried and

PROVIDENCE—FROM THE HARBOR.

THE GREAT STORM OF 1815.

Westminster Street. Market Square.

(From an Old Painting in Possession of the Rhode Island Historical Society.)

found guilty of holding certain opinions distasteful to the leaders of the latter colony. To avoid being sent back to England he fled to the wilderness, and in the course of a few months settled Providence, in whose institutions he caused to be embodied the principle of the right of private judgment—"soul liberty," as he called it—for which he had contended and suffered in Massachusetts. The spirit thus infused by the founder has always continued as a leading characteristic of the people, and although at times it has degenerated into indifference, as a whole it has been a broad and intelligent toleration. Roger Williams has been given a high place in the temple of fame as being the first to apply in practice one of the highest conceptions of free government.

In 1649 Providence was incorporated as a town; in 1708 the population was 1,446; in 1800, 7,614, and since that period the growth has been continuous. In 1832 it was incorporated as a city, and had then a population of about eighteen thousand. The population in 1885 was 118,070. Portions of Cranston were annexed to Providence in 1868 and 1873, and portions of North Providence in 1767, 1873, and 1874. The annexations since 1868 have brought in large additions to the city's population. The growth of the city has been mainly owing to the development of the cotton industry, which was introduced by Samuel Slater in 1793 at Pawtucket, but Providence being the natural centre of operations became the depot of supplies, and many auxiliary industries grew up within her borders, such as the making of machinery, engines and mill supplies of all kinds. The factories on all the streams in the state and on some in adjacent territory had their offices in Providence and made all their commer-

THE LIPPITT MANSION, HOPE STREET.

THE GREAT BRIDGE AND WESTMINSTER STREET.

cial exchanges there. Coincident with the development of the cotton manufacture the woolen industry grew and flourished, and at present amounts to about one-third of the former in capital invested and extent of business.

Many of the places of historic interest in Providence are connected with Roger Williams. One of the most interesting of these is Slate Rock, at the foot of William Street, on the east side of the city, from which, tradition says, an Indian greeted the pioneer and his companions with the salutation " What Cheer," as they were passing in their canoe along the bank of the Seekonk, and the story has been held in such respect that the scene is depicted on the city's seal. Near the western entrance to Roger Williams Park is a small enclosure containing the graves of some of the early members of the Williams family, and overlooking the lake is the Betsey Williams House, built about the middle of the last century.

No monument marks the grave of the founder of these plantations: in the rear of a barn, on the hillside on Bowen Street, the spot where he is said to have been interred is now a kitchen garden. The spring of water that induced the first settlers to land, around which they built their first rude houses, and which was in use until the middle years of this century cannot now be located without more research than the passing traveler can spare. The historical points of undoubted authenticity are few. The location of the camp of the French allies of the American patriots in the Revolution, on the heights at the extremity of Camp Street, is quite definitely known; the remains of Revo-

THE FIRST BAPTIST MEETING-HOUSE.
On North Main Street.

lutionary fortifications at Fort Hill, East Providence, and on the heights at Field's Point can yet be readily traced, and Sabin's Inn, on the northeast corner of Planet and South Main streets, where the plans for the capture of the *Gaspee* were laid at the time of the Revolution, is still standing and in use as a dwelling-house. The oldest building in the city is supposed to be the Whipple house, on Abbott Street near North Main, said to have been built about 1659. A more noteworthy structure, however, is the old brick house at Nos. 537 and 539 North Main Street, which was built by Deputy-Governor Elisha Brown about 1760, and was originally a third longer than at present. The Tillinghast house, corner of South Main Street and Chickenfoot Alley was erected in 1710. Stephen Hopkins' house built about 1750, was moved early in the century to its present location on Hopkins Street. All of these houses are still in use, although some of them have been altered from their original form. The John Brown house on the southeast corner of Power and Benefit streets, built in 1786, and at present the residence of Professor William Gammell, is a good specimen of the architecture of that period, as is also the brick building on the southwest corner of Elizabeth and North Main streets, which was built about the same time.

A number of public buildings date back to those early years, among them being the State House, built in 1759; the Friends' Meeting-House, a plain wooden edifice adjoining the State House on North Main Street, built in 1727; the Board of Trade Building, Market Square, erected as a public market in 1773, and since altered several times. The First Baptist Church on North Main Street, erected in 1775, is still one of the most beautiful ecclesiastical edifices in the city. University Hall, the middle building of Brown University fronting the campus on Prospect Street, was built in 1770.

Located upon the original Roger Williams home lot, southeast corner of Bowen and Benefit streets, stands a substantial, old-fashioned, but beautiful house, known as the Sullivan Dorr Mansion, within whose walls Thomas W. Dorr, the leader of the Dorr Rebellion, died. The reputed grave of Roger Williams was in the garden plat to the east of the house.

PROVIDENCE, FROM PROSPECT TERRACE, CONGDON STREET.

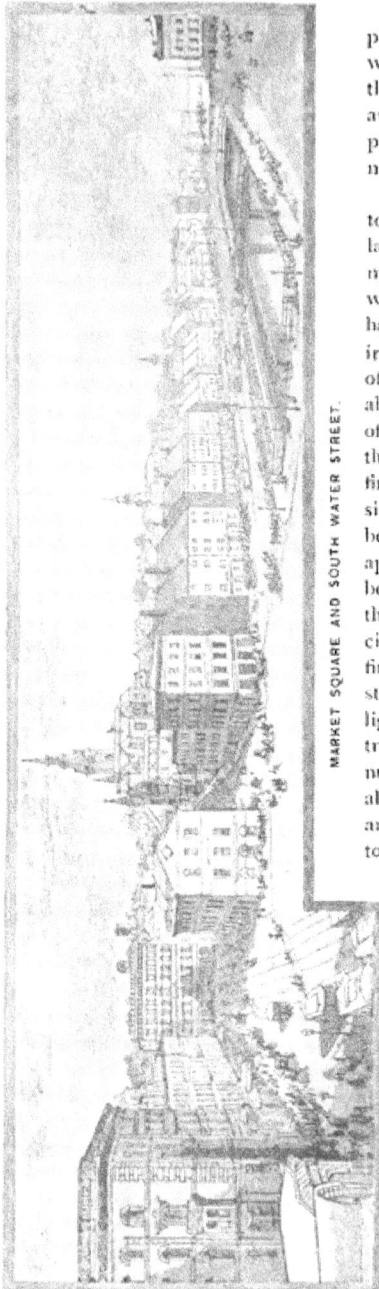

MARKET SQUARE AND SOUTH WATER STREET.

There are many other buildings and places, especially on the east side, about which traditions of the past linger, but the old landmarks are rapidly passing away, and less attention is paid to the preservation of the knowledge of the memorials of the past than is creditable.

In the city of to-day there is much to interest and instruct the visitor. Of late years great improvements have been made by replacing old-fashioned, low wooden structures with substantial and handsome edifices of brick, stone and iron. Within the past year this form of improvement has been more noticeable than ever before, a large number of new buildings having been erected on the principal streets, and a number of fine buildings which formerly were considered among the best in the city have been remodeled and improved vastly in appearance. These improvements have been made chiefly on Westminster Street, the main artery of the business of the city. The entire city is usually kept in fine condition; its drainage is good, its streets are well paved, clean, well lighted, and many of them lined with trees, forming in summer beautiful avenues, and altogether, it is a delightful abiding place, beloved by its inhabitants, admired by strangers, and a place to be desired as a home.

On account of its rivers Providence has many bridges, there being thirty-eight in all. Some of the largest of these, however, are over the railroads, which enter the city along the lines of the river valleys, and over which streets are carried from hill to hill. The best known of the bridges are those connecting the east and west sides of the Providence River, namely, Great Bridge, 160 feet wide, Crawford Street Bridge, and the Point Street Bridge, the last a fine structure with a draw for the passage of vessels. Providence and East

Providence are connected by two fine bridges over the Seekonk, namely, the Red Bridge and the new Washington Bridge, the latter the largest in the state, and both have draws to allow the passage of vessels to and from Pawtucket.

The city is noted for its excellent horse-car system. All the lines are owned and operated by the Union Railway Company, and they start from a common centre, the Great Bridge, at the foot of Westminster Street, and traverse the city from that point in

THE CITY HALL, EXCHANGE PLACE.

all directions. By means of these lines every locality in the city and immediate vicinity can easily be reached. The views obtained from the cars on many of the routes are of a continual succession of pleasant residences, some embowered in trees, or with well-kept lawns, some of elegant architecture, and many unpretentious homes, all contributing to the harmony of the scene. Many of the streets through which the cars run are lined with trees, and the effect in summer is very beautiful. The entire length of track in the city is fifty-four miles, number of cars, 275, and the routes fifteen.

Providence is an important railroad centre. Six roads enter the city, all but one of which are directly connected elsewhere at important points with the railroad system of the country, and they have connecting branches diverging from the main lines, thereby reaching nearly every village and hamlet in the state. The entire length of the lines in the state is a fraction over 318 miles, averaging nearly one linear mile to every three square miles of territory. For years the terminal facilities in the city have been inadequate, and various attempts have been made through the city government to have them improved, but up to the present nothing practical has been effected. A committee of expert engineers, appointed by Mayor Robbins in accordance with a resolution of the city council, made a report last April, and the probability is that their plan, or some modification of it, will be adopted. The outlook for increased facilities

THE BOARD OF TRADE BUILDING,
Market Square.

and for a settlement of the vexed question of proper accommodations, both for freight and passenger, is also rendered much more hopeful from the fact of the consolidation of the Boston & Providence Railroad with the Old Colony system last April, and of the Providence & Worcester with the New York, Providence & Boston Railroad early in May of this year. Instead of the question brought up by the demands for better accommodations being divided by the interests of five or six corporations, these consolidations simplify the matter very much by concentrating the business in the hands of not more than three, the Old Colony, the New York, Boston & Providence, and the New York & New England, and the rivalry, even although without malice, between these great concerns, will necessarily ensure vast improvements. The magnitude of the changes in comtemplation will necessitate a long time for their completion, and probably the new stations and approaches, even if the present plan is adopted, cannot be completed in less than two years. On account of the unsettled condition of affairs, and in view of the experience of the past, it cannot be assumed that the proposed plan will be put in execution in the shape in which it has been presented, and consequently a detailed account would be useless in this connection. One thing, however, is certain : the time has come for improvements ; the railroads are prepared, the city is prepared, and the public are tired of the endless discussions, and are willing to accept any reasonable plan.

In its facilities for commerce by sea Providence has great advantages, which have, however, not been utilized in recent years as their importance demand. The Providence River at Fox Point and the Seekonk at India Point unite with the bay, there forming the harbor, which is a

THE STATE HOUSE, NORTH MAIN STREET.

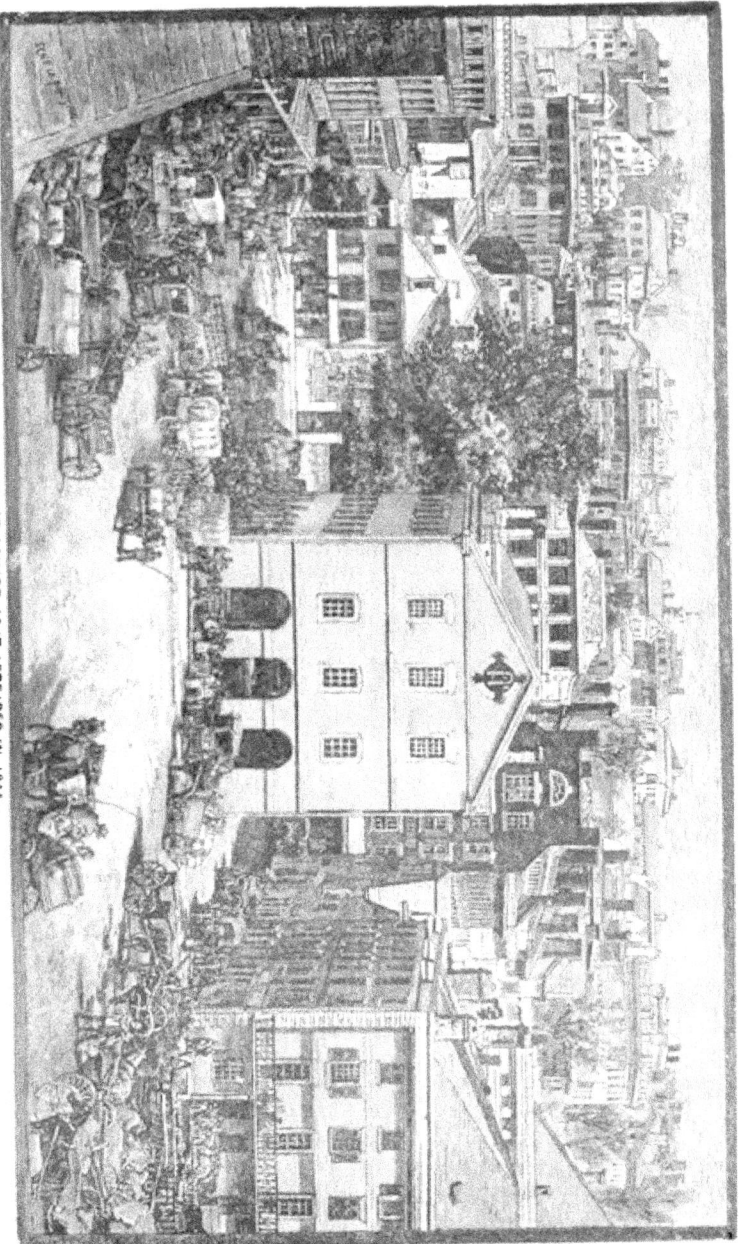

MARKET SQUARE AS IT APPEARED IN 1844.

Old Coffee House.   Manufacturers' Hotel, the Old   The Old City Building.   Franklin House.   Hoppin Building.
Stage Rendezvous.   Franklin Hall.

THE HOMŒOPATHIC HOSPITAL, PROVIDENCE.

safe and commodious basin, inclosed from the winds by high bluffs on all sides, and from which there is a channel to the ocean through the bay, deep and wide enough for the largest vessels.   There is, however, no foreign commerce worth mentioning.   Only an occasional merchant vessel, with a stray consignment of goods arrives, whose appearance is such a rarity that a long newspaper article is usually written about each one.   There are three important coastwise lines of steamers: the Providence and Stonington Steamship Line to New York; the Providence, Norfolk and Baltimore Steamship Line, and the Winsor Line to Philadelphia, all of which have their wharves on the harbor, from Fox to India Point.   There are three lines of steamers plying to places on the bay: the Fall River and Providence line, to Bristol and Fall River; the Continental Steamboat Company, to Newport, Rocky Point, the shore places, and the islands; and the Shore Transportation Company, to the east-side shore places.   The *George W. Danielson*, a small, but seaworthy propeller, runs from Providence to Block Island during the winter: in the summer it connects at Newport with the boats of the Continental Steamboat Company, and makes daily trips to Block Island. · One of the boats of the Fall River and Providence line makes several trips a

week to Block Island, affording opportunity for a continuous passage and return
in one day. A small steamer, the *Queen City*, runs regularly to Seaconnet
Point in the summer, making a round trip every day, and during the summer
another small steamer also runs to the point. Besides these, a small freight
steamer, the *William Marvel*, runs to Fall River.

Rhode Island is a manufacturing state, and Providence the headquarters.
A great proportion of the actual manufacturing is done within the city limits, and
the business offices of all the large concerns with factories near or remote in the
state, and even in adjoining districts in Connecticut and Massachusetts, are
located here. The principal industries are the cotton and woolen manufacture. According to the state census for 1885 — which, however, the superintendent says, on account of the failure to reply to his queries, does not fully
show the extent of the business — the number of establishments engaged in
the manufacture of cotton was 93, with an invested capital of $21,154,255,
and a product for that year of $21,771,504; those engaged in the woolen man-
ufacture were 34, with a capital of $8,568,450, and a product of $18,983,634.

RESIDENCE OF B. B KNIGHT, ESQ., BROAD STREET.

rubber goods in Provi-
dence, Bristol, and Woon-
socket. The total amount
of capital invested, according to census returns of
1885, was $59,616,229, in
2,393 establishments, em-
ploying 71,695 persons, to
whom were paid in wages
$23,353,099; the materials
used were valued at $48,-
271,448, and the product
for the year was $95,452,-
085.

The best points of obser-
vation for a general view
of the city, from its out-
skirts, are the summit of
Camp Street on the north-
east, which gives a fine
view of the whole city and
a large area of its environs
to the east and north; from
Mount Pleasant, northwest
of Olneyville, the highest

THE COUNTY COURT HOUSE.
Corner of Benefit and College Streets

Next in importance, judged by the
amount of capital invested, are the
print-works, followed in the order
given, by metals and metallic
goods, gas-works, machines and
machinery, paper and paper
goods, jewelry, building, silverware, rubber and elastic goods.
The cotton factories are located
on the rivers of the state, as are
also the woolen factories, but a
number of the former and a large
proportion of the latter, are in the
city and immediate vicinity.
Metals and metallic goods and
machines and machinery are manufactured chiefly in Providence
and Pawtucket, paper in Pawtucket and East Providence, jewelry and silverware in Providence,

THE SOLDIERS' AND SAILORS' MONUMENT.
Exchange Place.

RESIDENCE OF JOHN M. AUSLAN, ESQ.

point in that section, where an excellent view of the east and west sides and far down the harbor and bay may be obtained, and from Mount Neutaconkanut, near the southwest city line, in Johnston, which, though one of the least known and visited, is really one of the finest points from which to overlook the entire city and its surroundings, and secure splendid views, especially at a fair sunset hour. This elevation is said to be 296 feet above the sea level at its highest point. All of these "outlooks" can be readily reached by the horse-cars; Camp Street summit and Mount Pleasant by the routes so named, and Mount Neutaconkanut by the Plainfield Street route. From the site of the old reform school, on Tockwotton Heights, overlooking the harbor, a fine view down the bay can be obtained, and when the city has laid out this spot as a park, as is contemplated, the beauty of the scene ought to make it a favorite "breathing" place. An easily accessible place from which the business portion of the city can be viewed is the top of the tower of the City Hall. This is open to the public, and visitors are expected to register their names. Since the opening of the building, in 1873, an average of about three thousand persons per year have looked out on the city from this lofty place. The interior of the dome contains the batteries and apparatus for the city's fire alarm system, all of which are open to public inspection.

The Public Parks in Providence are eighteen in number, the majority of which are small inclosures. Of these the most important is Roger Williams Park. Blackstone Park, on the east side of the city, is a wooded ravine of much natural beauty, extending from Butler Avenue to the Seekonk River. The Cove Promenade is a narrow strip of land, with trees and grass plots, which borders and surrounds the Cove, a circular, walled basin, about a mile in circumference, in the centre of the city. Dexter Training Ground, between Cranston and High streets, in the western part of the city, is an open lot deeded to the city many years ago, by Ebenezer Dexter, to be used as a training-field by the militia. It is now rarely used for this purpose, but it makes a very pleasant small park, and its surroundings are beautiful.

Roger Williams Park is the people's popular place for public recreation. It is located on the southern border of the city adjoining Cranston, and is much the largest public park of the city, containing about one hundred and ten acres of land and water. This land was originally given by the great Indian sachems, Canonicus and Miantonomi, to Roger Williams in token of their good will and esteem for the founder of our state. It was bequeathed to the city by Betsey Williams (a direct descendant and heir of her great ancestor, Roger, in the sixth generation) for a public park, and was accepted by the city in November, 1872.

RESIDENCE OF COL. R. H. I. GODDARD, HOPE STREET.

THE FIRE IN THE DANIELS BUILDING. PROVIDENCE

THE ATHENÆUM.
Corner of Benefit and College Streets.

on the condition that it should contain a statue of Roger Williams, and be called the "Roger Williams Park." A fine bronze statue of Roger Williams, standing on a granite base, designed and executed by Franklin Simmons, sculptor, of Rome, was dedicated here October 16, 1877, with imposing ceremonies and a very excellent and eloquent oration by Professor J. L. Diman. This monument cost $22,000, and subsequently another granite monument to the memory of Betsey Williams was erected in the ancient Williams Cemetery, in the park, at a cost of $500. The grounds of the park are artistically laid out with beautifully diversified walks and drives, smooth green lawns, turfy-slopes, and shady groves. Crystal Lake, flowing quite a large area of the park, is one of its chief beauties, and affords opportunities for rowing in summer, or skating in winter, that are largely taken advantage of by the young people of the city. Within the past year or two, the lake has been doubled in size by digging out an adjacent marsh, and during the past winter and spring another large addition has been made in the same manner, so that now the lake is in reality a chain of three separate bodies of water encircled by grassy banks and pleasant woods. The graceful swans and other water-fowl on the lake, and groups of animals and birds about the grounds, the delightful shady nooks and quiet rural retreats, and the additional attractions that are constantly added, have greatly advanced the park in the public favor, and it now has more visitors and admirers than ever be-

HIGH SCHOOL SUMMER AND POND STREETS.

CRYSTAL LAKE, AT ROGER WILLIAMS PARK.

fore.   The "What Cheer Cottage," the charming restaurant and resting-place at the park, will be conducted again this season by Mr. James W. Cooper, with every possible improvement to make it pleasant and attractive to visitors and patrons, and sustain its high reputation.

Prospect Terrace.— The finest point for the visitor to obtain a panoramic view of the city is this elevated and airy esplanade, located on Congdon Street.   It is the most convenient, accessible, and popular observatory, located near the centre of trade and travel. The citizen of Providence always takes his guest and guides the stranger to the "Terrace" with the feeling that there they can secure a more pleasing and satisfactory view of the city than from any other point within its boundaries. Directly in the foreground we look down upon a wilderness of roofs, far below us, out of which the stately spire of the First Baptist Church lifts itself against the sky.   Farther away in the middle

THE BETSEY WILLIAMS HOUSE,
Roger Williams Park.

PROMINENT BUSINESS MEN OF PROVIDENCE.

ELISHA H. ROCKWELL.
Providence Agent of the Providence, Norfok & Baltimore Steamship Company.

WILLIAM S. HAYWARD,
Of the Firm of Rice & Hayward.

ST. JOHN'S EPISCOPAL CHURCH, NORTH MAIN STREET.

distance to the right, are the sandy slopes of Smith's Hill. A little more to the
left our line of vision crosses the Woonasquatucket valley, with its busy workshops. Rising from the valley on the left are the abrupt barriers of Federal
Hill. Directly before us, lifting itself above all surrounding structures, is the
Federal Street school building. Moving still further to the left, the eye becomes
bewildered amid the confused and varied mass of architectural structures, nearer
and more remote, that crowd upon the vision. From this point may be seen
many of the larger and handsomer buildings of the city with far better effect
than close at hand, such as the cathedral and other leading churches, the gas
reservoir, the Rhode Island Hospital, and other commanding points. During
the fall of 1887 it was discovered that the wall of the terrace had begun to project outward, and it was feared that it might in time fall on the houses below on
the slope of the hill, so during the winter of '87–'88 the masonry was taken apart
and built up anew, and in the summer of 1888 the terrace was again in good and
safe condition.

THE DORR MANSION, BENEFIT STREET,

Located upon the original Roger Williams Home Lot. Roger Williams was buried in what is now the Garden Plot of the House also the House in which Thomas W. Dorr died. Now the residence of Samuel Ames.

THE ARSENAL, BENEFIT BETWEEN THOMAS AND MEETING STREETS.

The Pawtuxet River.— Within the past five years the stretch of the Pawtuxet River from the village of Pawtuxet for several miles up stream, even to the Pettaconsett Pumping Station, and beyond to Pontiac, has become a favorite place for rowing and picnic parties by the young people of the city, on moonlight evenings, summer afternoons, and holidays. The river meanders between grassy banks which here rise in a steep hillside and there slope away in a meadow; at one place the stream is overhung by stately trees, at another fringed by tangled shrubbery. It hardly follows a straight course for half a mile, and as a consequence the point of view is constantly changing, the effect of which is further increased by the diversified character of the banks. Several bridges cross the river, two of them being railroad bridges, and it adds much to the scenic effect to see a lighted train dash across one of them while the spectators are rowing slowly on the river below. What idyls, what romances, are here enacted " in the glimpses of the moon "— who can say ? Certainly they are many, for the romantic surroundings, the music of the oars, the spell of the woods, the voices of the air, and the presence of eyes that speak responsive to each other, all contribute to heighten the charm and to bring out the latent and perhaps unavowed sentiment. Along the river are numerous spots where parties can enjoy a picnic, and many persons have already discovered these "woodland dells and mossy banks," and have availed themselves of their good fortune in recent seasons. The river is reached by the Pawtuxet line of horse-cars, and boats can be readily obtained at the boat-houses near the village.

The city's water supply is pumped from the river at Pettaconsett, three miles above Pawtuxet, by powerful engines, which force the water into the Sockanosset Reservoir, on the heights about a mile west of the river. The system was put in successful operation November 30, 1871.

Walks About Town.—A former resident returning after an absence of twenty-five or thirty years would hardly recognize Westminster Street, and would look in vain about the city for many of its ancient but vanished land-marks, but would find in every direction marked evidences of improvement, and every way he turned some new object of interest would arrest his attention. He would especially notice the immense and elegant Narragansett Hotel on Broad and Dorrance streets, and the Hotel Dorrance on Westminster Street, new

THE PROPOSED HOME OF THE YOUNG MEN'S CHRISTIAN ASSOCIATION,
Jackson and Westminster Streets.

BROWN UNIVERSITY—SOME OF ITS NOTED BUILDINGS.

PROMINENT BUSINESS MEN OF PROVIDENCE.

FITZ JAMES RICE,
Founder of the Rice & Hayward Industry.

WILLIAM TINKHAM.
President and Superintendent of the Providence and Springfield Railroad, and Manufacturer.

THE RHODE ISLAND HISTORICAL SOCIETY'S CABINET
Waterman Street.

and luxurious homes for the traveler and sojourner, so unlike those of his day. On Exchange Place he would find the magnificent new City Hall with its generous approaches, and would be impressed with the grandeur of its lofty, artistic walls of enduring granite.

The Soldiers' and Sailors' Monument standing directly in front of the new City Hall, erected by the state to the memory of the soldiers of the War of the Rebellion, attracts the attention of all visitors, while opposite, at the eastern end of Exchange Place, is the heroic equestrian statue of General Burnside which was dedicated with imposing ceremonies July 4, 1887.

When our returned townsman finds himself upon the "Great Bridge" as it used to be called, he perceives that it is very much broader and more substantial than in the olden time. It has the reputation of being the *widest* bridge in the world. It was once the only connecting link between the eastern and western sides of the river. But he observes that now a series of bridges, both above and below, span the stream and divide the unceasing current of travel that flows over them.

Nor has the improvement been confined to .the West Side. North Main Street has been widened and straightened, and with its handsome business

THE BURNSIDE STATUE.

blocks and substantial pavements, wears an aristocratic appearance, worthy the most ancient street of the city. Ascending College Street, he discovers that where once stood the time-worn Town-House, now in its fair proportions rises the County Court House. With the gray walls of the staid Athenæum on his right, he climbs the hill to the University where he also sees many works of industry in the form of new buildings and other improvements.

But will the stranger please accept our guidance to some of the most noted and leading points of interest to visit here and there throughout the city. Leaving Narragansett Hotel and passing up Broad Street, from Dorrance to Richmond Street we get a view of the widest street in the city. A little farther on the music of falling water is heard and the eye refreshed with the sight of the tossing, sparkling plumes of the Abbott Park Place fountain. The fine edifice with colonnaded front, next beyond the fountain, is the Beneficent Congregational Church, one of the historic churches of the city. A little way down Chestnut Street, to the left, stands the Chestnut Street M. E. Church, the oldest Methodist Church in the city, and directly across Broad Street stands the handsome brick Central Baptist Church, one of the oldest of that denomination.

Passing on up Broad Street we soon reach the Union Congregational Church, with its lofty spire, and turn to the right into Summer Street, where we find the city High School building, facing on three streets, and in close proximity an intermediate school building of picturesque design. Passing on to High Street, we turn again to the right, and move eastward to the junction of High and Westminster streets, near which is the new Cathedral, with its magnificent proportions, and its grand and imposing façade. Directly in front of this splendid edifice, at the junction of the two streets, the monument to the late Mayor Thomas A. Doyle will be erected, and across the square at the corner of Westminster and Jackson streets, fronting the Cathedral, the proposed new block of the Young Men's Christian Association is now in process of construction.

PROMINENT BUSINESS MEN OF PROVIDENCE.

DR. WILLIAM GROSVENOR, OF PROVIDENCE.
A Distinguished Manufacturer.

LYMAN KLAPP,
Founder of the Union Oil Company of Providence and New Orleans.

From this point we gain a fine view of Westminster Street, all of which may be seen at a glance. With its incessantly moving forms and changing colors, it is a perfect kaleidoscopic view in perspective. What a lively, busy scene it is! Far enough away to catch only the hum of its traffic, we can see the forms of men and women moving up and down the pavement, crossing and recrossing from one

PROMINENT BUSINESS MEN OF PROVIDENCE.

THOMAS J. HILL,

Founder of the Providence Machine Company, and Manufacturer.

side of the street to the other, while a crowd of vehicles of every description is in constant motion. Half-way up the street the tall, dark, tapering spire of Grace Church breaks the monotony of the sky-line on the right; upon the left the scene is varied by the lofty towers of the Butler Exchange, or perhaps from the flag-staff surmounting the Hotel Dorrance may float upon the morning air the bright colors of our national banner.

But we must not linger, so down the street we go, becoming ourselves a part of the picture we have been contemplating. We reach the lower end of

PROVIDENCE, FROM SMITH'S HILL.—THE COVE IN 1858.

the street, and stop for a moment at the Atlantic building near the junction of Westminster and Weybosset streets, to point out to our visitor the only bit of resemblance to Boston, which our city can boast. From our station, looking directly into Weybosset Street, beyond the Post-Office, there is presented in the narrowness of the street, the lofty blocks on either side, and the closing up and disappearance of the street in its curving lines, a strong suggestion of likeness to some of the narrow

B. B. KNIGHT,
Of the Manufacturing Firm of B. B. & R. Knight.

and winding by-ways of Boston, in the neighborhood of Court Street and Cornhill.

From Crawford Street Bridge, looking south, in the early morning or near the sunset hour, especially when the condition of the atmosphere is favorable, very fine views of the harbor and upper bay, with quite effective and picturesque effects, may be easily obtained, or turning north-

WILLIAM H. HOPKINS,
Of the Firm of Hopkins, Pomroy & Company.

EXCHANGE PLACE.

ward as pleasing pictures of the business section of our city will gratify the visitor.

For an enjoyable stroll, and to give the visitor and sight-seer the best views of the principal buildings and prominent features of the east side of the city, let us start from the old City Hall, now the Board of Trade Rooms, on Market Square, and passing up North Main Street, we soon come to Waterman Street, at which corner we find the venerable First Baptist Church, with its cool, green lawn, surrounded with its ancient elms. It is the oldest church edifice in the city, and one of the finest specimens of church architecture. Its tall, symmetrical spire never fails to excite the admiration of the cultured observer. In this old church the commencement exercises of the University have been held for a long succession of years.

Keeping up the street we have the State Normal School building confronting us, and as we cross Benefit Street, looking either way along this shaded avenue, we notice its many fine old mansions. Southward, through the leafy arches, we catch a glimpse of the First Congregational Church spire, the picturesque outline of the County Court House, and the brown stone façade of the Central Congregational Church, with its twin turrets. Still following up Waterman Street to the right, we pass on either side delightful residences, and reach the hill-top at the junction of Waterman and Prospect streets. Across the way are the classic grounds and structures of Brown University; directly in front stands the new Library Building of the University (the gift of the late John Carter Brown), one of the finest in the world; next east is the cabinet of

JOHN AUSTIN, ESQ.,
President of the High Street Bank.
Founder of the Austin Gold Refinery.

4

the Rhode Island Historical Society, with its rare collection of books, relics, and historical souvenirs open to visitors daily in the season. Waterman Street stretches thence eastward to the Seekonk River, along which, and on its parallel and intersecting streets in this favorite section of the city, the visitor will find many most charming private residences, with generous surroundings, adorned with shrubbery and flowers, fountains and statuary. We turn northward and take our way along Prospect Street, marking the tokens of wealth and ease on either side. Following Prospect as far as Barnes Street, and then going east we make Hope Reservoir, from the commanding site of which we gain a broad outlook. To the eastward are the pleasant grounds of Dexter Asylum and the Friends' School, which is one of the notable and honored landmarks of the city; to the north and northwest the view widens out over the town and far away to the blue ranges of the open country.

There are in Providence eighty-four church edifices and more than ninety societies that meet for religious worship, about ten of whom hold their services in hired halls. There are thirteen Baptist Churches, nine Congregational, twelve Episcopal, five Free Baptist, ten Methodist Episcopal, five Colored Methodist, fourteen Roman Catholic, three Unitarian, two Universalist, and two Presbyterian, besides ten of various other denominations. Many of the churches are elegant structures and add much to the beauty of the city. The most interesting from a historical point of view is the First Baptist Church on North Main Street already mentioned. St. John's Episcopal Church stands next in historical importance. It is a handsome stone edifice further up North Main Street, and stands near the spot where the first settlement was made. The largest and most imposing church edifice in the city is SS. Peter and Paul's Cathedral on High, near the head of Westminster Street, which was dedicated with imposing ceremonies July, 1887. Other edifices in the central portion of the city are Grace Church, on Westminster Street, the First Universalist, corner Greene and Washington streets; Westminster Congregational, Mathewson Street, and directly opposite the Mathewson Street M. E. Church; Central Baptist, corner High and Burrill streets, and across the square on Broad Street the Beneficent Congregational; further up Broad Street is the Union Congregational, a beautiful brick structure; All Saints' Memorial, Episcopal, corner High and Stewart street, is a beautiful building of gothic architecture; a short distance away is the Stewart Street Baptist Church. On the east side are many fine churches, the most noticeable of which are St. Stephen's, Episcopal, George Street, near Thayer; Hope Street M. E. Church, corner Power and Hope streets; St. Joseph's Catholic Church, corner Hope and Arnold streets; First Congregational, Benefit, corner Benevolent Street. The older churches in the city are nearly all plain structures, but those erected in recent years are more elaborate and much better specimens of architecture. The Episcopal churches are nearly all very beautiful buildings, and the Roman Catholic churches are remarkable for their substantial character, as well as for their architectural excellence.

It has always been a matter of uncertainty as to where Roger Williams was buried. Tradition has it that his remains were interred on the estate at the corner of Benefit and Bowen streets where the Sullivan Dorr house, so called, now stands, and which was at one time the residence of Thomas W. Dorr, the leader of the rebellion of 1842. There was a small graveyard here in the rear of the existing barns, and these graves were opened in 1860 under the direction of Stephen Randall, a descendant from Mercy, the youngest daughter of Roger Williams. In this lot an orchard had been growing for many years. When the grave supposed to be that of Roger Williams was opened "a singular incident was discovered. The root of an apple tree had turned out of its way to enter in at the head. Following the position of the body to the thighs it divided and followed each leg to the feet, tender fibres shooting out in various directions. By nature's promptings it had taken up the chemical deposits of the body and turned them into blossoms and fruit." These quoted words are from an article by an official of Brown University who is an authority on local history. In the cabinet of Brown University this root can be seen to this day, appropriately labeled.

Having thus briefly noticed the more important points of interest in the city, and given the visitor a " starter," we shall leave him to make his own way to the many other features of local interest which it is not necessary to enumerate here, and which will be indicated for his benefit in the Stranger's Guide.

On the night of February 15-16, 1888, Providence was visited by one of the most disastrous fires in its history. At 11.45 P. M., on Wednesday the 15th, the alarm rang out and shortly after midnight the fire had enveloped the Chace block, a large, towering brick edifice on the corner of Eddy and Fountain streets, and despite the efforts of the fire department, the flames spread until the whole section bounded by Union, Washington, Eddy, and Fountain streets, was ablaze. On this territory there were a number of large buildings, the whole covering more than twelve acres of ground in the most central portion of the city. The flames leaped from building to building until by 3 A. M. on Thursday morning, the 16th, there was no hope of saving any of the structures within the limits already mentioned, and the efforts of the firemen were expended to saving the adjoining buildings across the street from the doomed section.

When daylight came the scene was one of desolation and ruin such as is seldom witnessed, but the effect in many respects was not only beautiful, but grand. The front of the Aldrich House was still standing, and the water from the firemen's hose had frozen on it in all manner of fantastic shapes, making a picture that was both weird and beautiful, and transforming the structure into a veritable ice palace, in which shape, as the weather was very cold, it endured for days, and while in this condition numerous photographs of it were taken. Our illustrations on page 47 show to great advantage this phenomenon as well as many other views of the ruins. The entire loss by this fire was about $500,000, which was only partly covered by insurance. One of the most serious losses was the entire destruction of the " Proprietors' Records," the documentary evidences and plans of the original land titles in the city and " Providence Plantations." They were in an iron-bound box in the office of Henry Staples & Company, in the Chace block, Eddy Street.

Just after midnight Saturday morning, February 18th, it was discovered that the well-known Theatre Comique, corner of Orange and Weybosset streets, was on fire. Although the department responded immediately, the flames had gained such headway—the building being of wood, old and dry—that all efforts to stay their progress were futile until the entire interior of the edifice and of an adjoining wooden building, the Telegraph House, had been consumed. The loss by this fire was about $25,000, partly covered by insurance.

Again on Sunday afternoon, February 19th, were the citizens of Providence startled by a call of fire, the third in four days. This time it was the Daniels & Cornell building, on Custom House Street, where the fire was supposed to have started about three o'clock in a water closet on the third floor, and had run up the shaft and also ascended the stair well. The fire soon obtained a strong headway on the upper floor in the large printing establishment of J. A. & R. A. Reid, and belched forth from the windows on the Custom House Street side in tongues of flames reaching half-way across the street. Such was the fierceness of the fire, that it was feared the magnificent collection of engravings which had been the accumulations of years, as well as the plates of a number of costly books published by the firm, would be destroyed. Next morning, however, it was found that while the fire had completely wrecked the establishment, the cuts and plates, although damaged to a considerable extent, were practically safe. The fire had not damaged the building much below the upper floor, but the damage by water on the lower floors was very great.

WILLIAM T. NICHOLSON,
Founder of the Nicholson File Works.

Notes on some of the Industries of the City.—One of the most favorably known and important of the iron industries in the city of Providence, and one having a history of more than half a century, is that of the Providence Machine Company, of which Thomas J. Hill is the president and treasurer. These works have occupied an extensive site on Eddy Street for the last forty years. They are bounded on the west by Eddy Street, on the north by Crary Street, on the east by that extensive tract of water frontage and land, known to all Rhode Islanders as "Hill's Wharf," on the south by the American Screw Company's buildings, and have always been known locally as "Hill's Machine Shop." From these works have been sent forth machines representing the highest type of every stage of improvement made in cotton and woolen machinery, and their product to-day is abreast of every demand of the modern manufacturer. The establishment throughout is now, and long has been, one of the most complete and perfect in New England. The works were established and developed by Mr. Thomas J. Hill, and their history forms only one of the incidents in his varied and eminently successful business career. Mr. Hill was born in Pawtucket, in 1805, and early in life he engaged in mechanical pursuits. In 1830 he came to Providence and took charge of a machine shop in connection with the steam mill then owned by Samuel Slater. In 1834 Mr. Hill and Mr. Slater formed a partnership under the name of the Providence Machine Company. In 1835 Mr. Slater died, and Mr. Hill conducted the business alone, and built it up to such an extent that in 1845 the present extensive buildings were erected. In 1846 Mr. Hill became the sole proprietor. A charter for a corporation had been secured in 1867 and in 1874 a company was organized with Mr. Hill as president and treasurer ; his son, Mr. Albert Hill, secretary ; and Mr. Geo. J. Hazard, the present active manager, as agent.

The works have been continuously prosperous from the first. The present manufactures of the company tax the works to their full capacity, and comprise cotton roving frames, combers and lap machines, worsted drawing, slubbing and roving frames, and worsted spinning and twisting frames. About three hundred hands are employed on the different branches of the work, which are carried on in separate buildings adapted to the purpose. The main building covers an area of 60 x 220 feet and is three stories in height ; the pattern building is 40 x 80 feet, and the blacksmith shop 40 x 100 feet. All parts of the machines are made by the company, including castings and wood work, and all the machinery made is finished in the most substantial and thorough manner. Mr. Hazard, the manager, is a thorough machinist and gives every part of the work his personal supervision. He has been with the company since 1854 — with the exception of an interval of four years when he was engaged with the Providence Tool Company in manufacturing rifles — and has advanced from the position of an apprentice to that which he now holds.

Besides his connection with this, his original and pet enterprise, Mr. Hill has been very extensively engaged in other manufacturing ventures throughout New England. In 1867 he organized the Rhode Island Malleable Iron Works and founded the village known as "Hill's Grove," about seven miles from this city ; and in 1875 he started a cotton mill there of 20,000 spindles which he named the Elizabeth mill in honor of his wife.

PICTURESQUE NARRAGANSETT.

Now-a-days the necessity of and the benefit resulting from insurance are
so well recognized that the only question is the reliability of the companies
carrying the policy and the business character and trustworthiness of the agency
through which it is negotiated. Mr. F. A. Waldron, Jr., having had an experience of twenty years in this city in the insurance business, established an agency
in 1887 at 33 Westminster Street, and represents the following first-class companies: German American, of New York, with a capital of $1,000,000, gross
assets $5,286,249, and net surplus over and above all indebtedness $2,112,138;
Fireman's Fund Insurance Company, of San Francisco, Cal., with a capital
of $1,000,000, gross assets $2,181,925, and a net surplus of $367,568; the
Merchants' Insurance Company of Newark, N. J., with a capital of $400,000,
gross assets of $1,312,031, and net surplus of $467,249. Besides representing
these companies which take fire risks, Mr. Waldron is the agent for the Travelers' Life and Accident Insurance Company, Hartford, Conn., the largest and
strongest accident insurance company in the world, which has a paid up capital
of $6,000,000, assets of over $9,000,000, a reserve of $7,000,000, and a surplus
of $2,000,000. Mr. Waldron's experience equips him excellently for the posi-
tion he now occupies, and the standing of the companies he represents guarantees insurance of the highest reliability. The agency can at any time be called
up by telephone, the number being 1688, and Mr. Waldron's post-office box
is 1481.

The oldest joint stock fire and marine insurance company in New England,
and the sixth oldest in the world is the Providence Washington Insurance
Company. It is the largest concern of the kind in Rhode Island. The company under its present name dates from 1817, when the Providence and the
Washington Insurance companies united their business and their names. The
first of these companies was organized in 1799, and the other in 1800. They
had done a prosperous business before this consolidation, and since then it has
been continually increasing and extending, now having agents scattered
throughout the United States. The cash capital at present is $400,000, and
the assets on January 1st, 1888, were $1,116,858.70. The offices of the com-
pany are at 20 Market Square, in the Providence Washington building, formerly known as the What Cheer building, and now owned by this company.
Since its organization the company has only had four presidents: first, Richard
Jackson, father of Governor Jackson; second, Sullivan Dorr; third, John
Kingsbury; and fourth, the present incumbent, J. H. DeWolf. The present
secretary is J. B. Branch, and assistant secretary, George E. Bixby. The
directors have always been men prominently identified with the business and
manufactures in the state. The names of the present board, who are eminently
men of the highest business position and character, are as follows: Rowland
Hazard, J. H. De Wolf, Wm. Grosvenor, Jr., Wm. Ames, Henry J. Steere,
F. W. Carpenter, R. I. Gammell, E. Philip Mason, Royal C. Taft, Eugene
W. Mason, John S. Palmer.

THE GREAT FIRE OF '88 IN THE ALDRICH HOUSE DISTRICT.

Ruins from Eddy Street.
Aldrich House as an Ice Palace.
Aldrich House at 1.30 A. M.

Ruins from the City Hall.
Bird's-eye View of the Ruins
Shattuck's Exchange.

The Ruins from Fountain Street.
Union and Washington Streets.
Cove and Fountain Streets; 1.30 A. M.

The building of steam engines has been an important industry in the city of Providence for more than fifty years, in fact many of the chief improvements have been the inventions of local mechanics and manufacturers. In 1821, John Babcock began to build engines after the general pattern of Boulton & Watts, and his machines were put in to run cotton mills and print works in the city and its neighborhood. The works that Mr. Babcock then established have had a continuous existence from that time, and the present Providence Steam Engine Company is the historical descendant of the early concern. The firm of Bartlett & Thurston succeeded John Babcock, and in 1843-4 Noble T. Greene became a member. After various changes, in 1863 the concern was organized as a corporation under the state laws, and named the Providence Steam Engine Company. Rathbone Gardner is president and treasurer, and T. W. Phillips manager and secretary.

From 1861 to 1884 these works were very largely engaged in the manufacture of marine engines and boilers. During the war of the Rebellion the company constructed many such engines for the United States government, successfully putting in operation two engines for sloops of war of three thousand tons each, three in double-ender gunboats designed for river service, and supplied more

THE IMPROVED GREENE ENGINE.

than three thousands tons of boilers, besides furnishing steam steering apparatus and steam windlasses. When the government began to construct its own boilers for furnishing high pressures, the company supplied them with the steam riveting machines required. The company was among the earliest builders of compound engines, one of which has been in successful operation at the Hope Pumping Station in this city for the past twelve years, night and day.

The company makes a specialty of constructing the Improved Greene Engine. The original automatic cut-off engine was known as the "Sickle's Cut-off," and this company was the first and sole builders for land use. The next engine of this type to come into use was the Corliss,— soon followed by the Greene, which was built at these works under a royalty until its manufacture was enjoined by Geo. H. Corliss for alleged infringement of his patent. On the expiration of the Corliss patent in 1869, this company purchased the

Greene patent, revised the engine,
retaining all the valuable features
of the original Greene, eliminating
the defects, and substituting new
and valuable improvements which
they have patented. They are now
the sole builders, and the engine as
now constructed is as nearly perfect as the science of the times will
permit. It is built for 100 lbs.
steam, and is run from 80 to 100
revolutions per minute -- the latter
for electric lighting, for which purpose it is particularly adapted on
account of its fine regulation.
Since they commenced its construction, the works have been run
full time and extra hours, and its
manufacture is now simply a question of the capacity of the works
to produce it.

THE CHESTNUT STREET M. E. CHURCH.

Better and less noisy methods
of celebrating the national holiday
have come into vogue in recent
years, and at private outdoor gath-
erings in the summer the practice of illumination on many occasions is becoming common. These facts, with the growing taste for decoration, at times of
public or private celebration, has created more of a uniform demand for the
classes of merchandise required to produce these effects. The only place in
Rhode Island that makes an exclusive specialty of this description of goods is the
Rhode Island Toy & Firework Company, 23 Weybosset Street, F. C. Ferrin,
Manager. They keep all kinds of fireworks and decorating goods for celebrating
and political purposes, and their stock of Chinese and Japanese lanterns for illu-
minating purposes is very extensive. Lines of supplies for political campaign
purposes are carried in large quantities, and a special effort will be made this
presidential year to meet the demand; the only thing in this line the company
does not deal in is uniforms. They manufacture a large proportion of their
goods in another state, and also import all their foreign goods themselves, by
these means being enabled to sell to greater advantage than other dealers possibly can. This season a special invoice of 40,000 Japanese lanterns have been
imported. For the winter and holiday trade the firm imports large quantities
of Christmas goods — toys, albums, fancy articles, china ware, etc. A large assortment of sporting goods is always in stock, and the company are agents for
Reach's base ball supplies. The store at Weybosset Street is occupied for sale
purposes, but on Peck Street the company has two extensive floors for storage.

The art of photography has attained a high degree of perfection in Providence, and among the leading and most popular studios is the one established by Mr. H. Q. Morton at 75 Westminster Street. He began in this city in 1873, and has sustained a rapidly increasing business ever since. As an artist he has an enviable reputation, and by his untiring energy and determination to secure all of the latest improvements, and to do only the best work, he still continues to receive a patronage unexcelled by any photographer in New England. At one time he had made engagements for sittings for every fifteen minutes from 8 to 5 o'clock daily for three weeks in advance, which is more than most artists have ever realized, and which bespeaks for him an ability to produce work in every way satisfactory to the public. His rooms are supplied with every implement ever invented necessary to develop the camera's finest results, either in card photographs, cabinets, panels, or large portraits. During the busy season he employs about twenty assistants. In addition to the above, Mr. Morton has completed and equipped a studio at Block Island at an expense of several thousand dollars, which he opens to the *bon ton* patronage of that noted summer resort during the months of July and August, and has also opened rooms at 81 Westminster Street, Providence. In his particular department he has, by enduring enterprise, added very materially to the business growth of the city.

Probably the historical successor of the old-time inn, where the fathers of the village assembled to gossip over the events of the day with each other and with the passing traveler, is the modern first-class hair-dressing establishment, where the genial but loquacious knight of the shears and the razor not only sharpens his steel implements, but, by interesting converse, "sharpeneth the countenances of his friends" of the great public. At no place in the city of Providence do business and professional men assemble in larger numbers or come in such a continuous stream, as at the hair-dressing rooms of W. J. Nichols, 26 Market Square. They are centrally located, being near the chief business section of the city. None but the best men are employed, eleven chairs being continuously in use, while an extra chair is in reserve. The establishment is first-class in every respect, and is not only the largest in the city of Providence, but in New England. In addition to the tonsorial features, a number of perfectly appointed bath-rooms are connected with the establishment.

One of the most important branches of the jewelry manufacture is the refining and smelting of the worked-over material, "sweepings," and refuse of jewelry shops. Formerly these "sweepings," as all this class of refuse is technically called, were thrown away as useless, but the invention of methods for the extraction of the gold and silver demonstrated the fact that the manufacturers had been wasting valuable material, and now the processes have been brought to such perfection that nearly everything is saved. This business has been developed to its highest perfection in Providence by John Austin, at 74 and 76 Clifford Street, where he has in operation the most complete jewelers' smelting

THE REFINING WORKS OF JOHN AUSTIN, ESQ.

works for waste that contains gold and silver, in the country, and probably in
perfection of appointment and effectiveness of operation unequaled anywhere.
Mr. Austin has been in this business since 1857, starting originally as a
workman. In 1862 he began business on his own account, on Dorrance Street,
and moved to his present location in 1863. Until within five years ago the
business consisted entirely of refining " sweeps," which were shipped in the
refined state all over this country and abroad, chiefly to Paris and London.
But on account of a variety of circumstances, Mr. Austin realized that he
would have to do his own smelting, and accordingly with the assistance and
advice of skilled foreign workmen, he was enabled to develop a system of
smelting that has resulted in making his establishment second to none in this
line anywhere, and by this means all the zinc, copper, and lead which were
really thrown away when the " sweeps " were shipped, are saved and utilized
at home. With the present facilities an average of one and a quarter tons of
" sweeps " can be smelted per hour. The development of the processes has
been mainly the result of Mr. Austin's own study and experiments, and they are
now so perfect as to be extremely simple and economical in practice, so that at
his establishment much more work and better results are obtained for a corre-
sponding outlay of time and labor than at any other similar place in the country.

PROVIDENCE STEAM CAPSTAN WINDLASS,
NEW STYLE.

The city of Providence has many special lines of manufacture, but none are more interesting than one conducted on the banks of the Seekonk River, corner of Waterman and East River streets, near the Red Bridge, in a peaceful neighborhood, quite away from the hum of business. Here, in commodious quarters, the American Ship Windlass Company constructs steam windlasses, steam capstans, improved hand windlasses and capstans, and these machines have been and are of such approved merit that they are in general use in the best class of vessels, both in the government and merchant service. Attention is exclusively devoted to the construction of these machines, the methods of operation, the tools and appliances, and as a result the machines themselves have all been brought to a very high degree of perfection. The demands of modern commerce require large vessels, and the labor of weighing the anchors of these monster crafts as compared with the former class of vessels is such that the steam windlass is a necessary adjunct,

WORKS OF THE AMERICAN SHIP WINDLASS COMPANY.

while its use saves much time and labor, as by its means two men can often accomplish work formerly requiring twenty or twenty-five. A majority of the steel and iron ships built in the last twelve years on the Atlantic coast and the great lakes are provided with this windlass, and seven-eighths of all the vessels of the country have them in use to-day.

OFFICE AND WAREHOUSE OF RUMFORD CHEMICAL WORKS, SOUTH WATER STREET, PROVIDENCE.

When Roger Williams was banished from Massachusetts, he first landed on the east side of the Seekonk River, near the present village of Rumford, in East Providence, R. I.

In these later days Rumford has attained a position of no little importance, by reason of the location there in 1854, of the famous Rumford Chemical Works, a corporation organized by Professor E. N. Horsford, of Cambridge, Mass., and his associates. The spot — once a barren waste — is now covered with fertile fields. Mr. Horsford was then Rumford Professor in Harvard University, and in honor of this professorship and of its founder, Count Rumford, the works take their name. The products of the works are known as Professor Horsford's chemical preparations. They are "Horsford's Cream Tartar Substitute," "Horsford's Bread Preparation," "Rumford Yeast Powder," "Horsford's Phosphatic Baking Powder," "Horsford's Acid Phosphate," "Horsford's Anti-Chlorine," and "Horsford's Sulphite," besides general and special chemicals.

The product has been increased lately by a new manufacture, namely, a sparkling beverage which has been named "Phosa." It is prepared from Horsford's acid phosphate and pure fruit juices, and is a delightful, healthful, and refreshing drink.

The works and their productions are of national importance, and they may indeed be considered as one of our national industries.

As an instance of the high estimation in which these productions are held by scientific men, we subjoin an extract from a personal letter from Baron

54 PICTURESQUE NARRAGANSETT.

Liebig, the greatest known chemist in the world, to the inventor, Professor E. N. Horsford:

> "ROYAL BAVARIAN ACADEMY OF SCIENCE, MUNICH, July, 1868.
> "I have satisfied myself of the purity and excellence of your bread preparations. I consider this invention as one of the most useful gifts which science has made to mankind! It is certain that the nutritive value of the flour will be increased ten per cent. by your phosphatic bread preparations, and the result is precisely the same as if the fertility of our wheat fields had been increased by that amount. What a wonderful result is this!"

———

To most persons mechanical processes are particularly interesting, and this is especially so in regard to such as deal with the materials of every day life. For this reason the grinding of grain has always been an unfailing source of pleased attention, and since it was one of the first of industries it has been celebrated in song and story, by many of the greatest writers of the age. "Ho! the dusty miller," — his mill on the river bank by the falls, was always the centre of trade, of gossip, and has been made the scene of many a romance. Now-a-days the opportunities for observing an old fashioned-grist mill are rare, but the modern mills are far more wonderful with their improved machinery. The mill of the Arlington Hay and Grain Company, Anthony Corcoran, manager, on corner Cranston Street and Depot Avenue, near the horse-car barn, is one of the most perfectly appointed of modern grist mills. It is equipped with Westinghouse boiler and engine of 60 horse-power, has automatic conveyors for grain to every story of the building, and is supplied with coolers and all modern appliances for handling grain. There are facilities for grinding 60 bushels of grain per hour, and the elevators will unload from cars twenty bushels per minute. One hundred bushels of corn in the ear can be ground in one hour by the Sullivan Cracker in use in the mill. For economy in handling, efficient management, and eligible situation, the mill has no superior, and on account of these advantages the patrons have the benefit of the lowest prices. The company, like the ancient millers, grind grain for customers, and do it promptly with satisfaction to all concerned. Besides their mill business the company also deals in hay, straw, salt, coal, wood, and grain of all kinds, and in addition to their main establishment already mentioned, have a branch store at 290 Broadway, Olneyville. Their telephone call number is 3816-2.

———

Until comparatively few years ago there was no distinct profession of dentistry, but every medical man, whether skilled in that line or not, was a dentist, his practice of the art, however, consisting mainly of extracting teeth ;• but with the subdivision of labor and the establishing of specialties in very recent time, dentistry has become a distinct profession, and from being merely devoted to the pulling of teeth, now deals more with their general care and preservation. Continuous advances have also been made for a number of years past in the use of anæsthetics, in methods of filling, dealing with sensitive teeth, and the making and fitting of artificial teeth. No practitioner of this noble and necessary profession has striven more earnestly to keep abreast of all these modern improvements than W. H. Tillinghast, D. D. S., 220 Westminster Street, Providence, in whose elegantly appointed, convenient, and roomy apartments the patient will be certain of the best care, skill, and treatment, and can also be sure that the methods employed are those which experience and the latest research has demonstrated to be the best.

No concern
in Providence
has acquired a
wider or better
reputation for ef-
fective machines
in their own line
than Volney W.
Mason & Co.
Their specialties
are hoisting ma-
chinery, friction
pulleys, and
clutches. The
excellence of
these appliances
is shown by the
fact that this
company re-
cently fitted up

THE RHODE ISLAND HOSPITAL.

sixty-one hoisting machines, shafting, etc., in the New York Central and Hudson River Railroad Company's hay depot, New York, being the most extensive
collection of hoisting machinery ever assembled and operated in one establishment. Illustrated and described in the *Scientific American*, April 21st, 1888.
They took the contract for the erection of these machines against all competition,
and completed it in sixty days. Elevators of various kinds are also made, and
many separate appliances that go with the peculiar class of machines made.
The firm makes a point of carrying in stock a full line of wire rope for elevators,
transmission, and rigging purposes, and are the only parties in Providence carrying such a stock.

———

To establish a business, and by glowing advertisements and well-filled and
gaudy show windows to hold the patronage of the public for a year or more,
is comparatively easy, but the man of enterprise who succeeds for upwards of
two decades in carrying a gradually increasing business year after year, selling
to regular patrons, is the representative merchant — the one who must enjoy the
better class of patronage. We find such the case in the career of the millinery establishment located at 166 Westminster Street, Providence, which was founded in
1868 by A. Rhodes, whose name is well-known throughout the city and state from
the fact that under his efficient management it has become one of the leading
millinery houses of the state, and enjoys a patronage from the city and surrounding towns unsurpassed by any establishment in New England. The secret of
Mr. Rhodes' success is generally ascribed to his system of buying first-class
goods in the belief that customers appreciate a trade which will give them last-
ing satisfaction rather than pay their money for cheap goods, saving perhaps
a few cents on the purchase, but by far the more costly in the end.

THE WORKS OF THE NICHOLSON FILE CO.

Probably no better illustration of the skill and enterprise of native mechanics can possibly be cited than that afforded by the history of the Nicholson File Company. Mr. William T. Nicholson, a native of Pawtucket, and all his life engaged in the construction of intricate machinery, developed during and soon after the Civil War a series of machinery for the construction of files. Previous to that time file making by machinery had not been a success, but Mr. Nicholson made a very eminent success. The works, which are undoubtedly the largest of their kind in the world, are located near the heart of the city upon a plat of four acres of land, two-thirds of which is covered by substantial brick buildings, devoted entirely to the production of files, rasps, and filers' tools. The officers of the company are: W. T. Nicholson, president; Stephen Nicholson, superintendent; Geo. Nicholson, treasurer; and Samuel Nicholson, secretary.

—   —

For the extraction of teeth without pain the new anæsthetic is the best in use. Dr. J. W. Bond, 224 Westminster Street, corner of Mathewson, has had many years' experience, and performs all operations very successfully and satisfactorily, and by its use he has extracted twenty-eight teeth at one sitting with positively no pain. The doctor specially excels in the making of artificial teeth. Particular attention given to preserving the natural teeth, and filling is done in the best manner. The office is fitted up with all the latest appliances, and the whole interior presents an air of general attractiveness.

It is very frequently a question with many of us as to where we can get a good suit of clothes made, and often a few hints about that matter from friends are very seasonable and aid us in making selections. One of the best places in the city, easy of access, well lighted so that the quality and texture of the goods can be inspected to advantage, is the tailoring establishment of H. W. Hudson & Company, on the ground floor of the Narragansett Hotel building, corner of Broad and Dorrance streets.

THE NARRAGANSETT HOTEL,
Corner of Broad, Dorrance and Eddy Streets.

The goods are principally of foreign make, but the best American fabrics are also kept in stock, so that there is always plenty of chance for selection, and the firm caters chiefly to the fine tailoring trade, and do very satisfactory work. In 1879 they started business in the Old Infantry building, but in 1885 moved to their present location, where they have one of the best appointed establishments in the city. From the very beginning their business has constantly increased, necessitating in time their removal, and a continuous increase in the amount of stock carried has been required ever since then.

In these days of change it is pleasant occasionally to find a business that has endured for half a century. Such is the record of that conducted by George Hutchins at 122 and 124 South Main Street, in the Infantry Building. This business was first established in 1838 at No. 9 Westminster Street, where it continued until January 1, 1858, when it was moved to the Howard Building on Westminster Street, but remained there only one year, as that building was burned. For sixteen years thereafter the business was located at corner of Broad and Dorrance Streets. It was removed to Howard building in 1874 and remained there eight years, was then for two years on corner of Westminster and Union Streets, and for the past six years has been at its present location. The business increased continually from 1850 to 1875, a period of twenty-six years, in the last named year reaching the fine sum of a quarter of a million dollars. Most of the time since 1850 the stock carried has included crockery, china, glass, gas fixtures, silver ware, kerosene, oil and lamp goods. Nearly all the large hotels in the city and state have been furnished from this store, among them the magnificent Narragansett Hotel in this city. The present store is well supplied with all the goods just mentioned and many specialties in those lines, and the cheap rent and the personal attention Mr. Hutchins bestows upon the business enables him to guarantee first-class goods at low prices. He has just added to his stock a new patent oil stove, superior to any now in the market.

5

THE EMPORIUM OF ARNOLD, MILLER & CO.

In a busy city the accessibility of a business establishment is an important consideration, especially if it is a place dealing in supplies of prime importance. The firm of Arnold, Miller & Co., dealers in house furnishing goods, corner High and Summer streets, opposite Dean, are exceedingly well located, being within easy walking distance of families on High, Cranston, and Broad streets, Broadway, Atwell's Avenue, the intersecting streets, and all the western part of the city. They occupy a fine, large, brick building, four stories in height, and every floor is reached by a commodious elevator. A large stock is constantly carried, consisting of full lines of all descriptions of household supplies, fine furniture, kitchen furnishings, refrigerators, stoves, crockery, wooden ware, screens, curtains, oil stoves, and a specialty is made of carpets and oil cloths. Here may also be found in abundance the thousand and one articles necessary to fit out a house, and the customer will find ample convenience and be sure of the most courteous treatment.

The Friends' School, an institution for both sexes, is upon an eminence in the City of Providence, one hundred and eighty-two feet above tide water. Most of the State of Rhode Island and a large district of Massachusetts are in view from its cupola, while the beautiful waters and shores of Narragansett Bay, complete the picture. Moses Brown, of Providence, founded it in 1784. The Yearly Meeting of Friends for New England has the care of it. A thorough, practical education for business life and the most approved preparation for college are furnished. Many universities and colleges receive students from it on certificates, without examination.

The school has a large number of experienced teachers, and, as far as practicable they are specialists, limited to their several departments. Industrial instruction has recently been added. The fine arts receive special attention. Excellent instruction is given in music. It has an astronomical observatory, valuable apparatus for chemical and physical work, and a rich mineral cabinet. The Library contains about six thousand well-selected volumes. A very homelike and agreeable appearance has recently been given to the rooms by the use of large numbers of beautiful pictures and busts. It is lighted with the Edison incandescent electric light. The educational force of an institution of this character is not limited to school hours; it is constant. The great benefits of co-education are everywhere discernible. For particulars address, Augustine Jones, A. M., Friends' School, Providence, R. I.

THE FRIENDS SCHOOL, PROVIDENCE.

THE NEW MASONIC HALL.—WAREROOMS OF HALE & BOSWORTH.
Corner Pine and Dorrance Streets, Providence.

Man's well-being depends upon many agencies. First, he must be clothed. The wearer of a fabric from the plant or the animal seldom gives a thought to the means by which he is properly clad, yet the making ready of these necessities of civilized existence requires the time, thought, and labor of a vast army of workers. The agents who stand between the producer and the consumer are indispensable to both. What hindrance and waste would result if every man must buy cloth, thread, and buttons, and find cutter and maker. The tailor would be embarrassed if he had to procure all his goods from the manufacturer, but he is best served by buying of the merchants who make a specialty of supplying his wants.

Messrs. Hale & Bosworth (George B. Hale and John C. Bosworth) belong to this class of the people's agents, and they deal in foreign and domestic woolens and tailors' trimmings, keeping before their customers the best productions found in home and foreign markets. The business was established January 1, 1882, in Butler Exchange, but is now carried on in the Masonic Hall building, corner of Pine and Dorrance streets, where a large trade, growing larger rapidly, has been built up. Both members of the firm were formerly in the employ of Messrs. James H. Read & Company and are the only members of the old house now in active business. The firm's wareroom measures 85 x 45, and is excellently adapted to the display of goods. There is ample storage room in the basement, and an elevator is devoted exclusively to the firm's business. The firm is favorably known, and finds customers throughout New England.

CAPTAIN W. M. JONES.
Superintendent of the Providence Line.

GEO. A. KILTON.
Providence Agent of the Winsor Line Steamers.

The "Winsor line" of steamers, at first called the "Empire line," and later the "Keystone line," was established to run as freight steamers between Providence and Philadelphia, in 1866, by J. M. Huntington & Company, of Norwich, Conn. In 1872 the line was sold to Henry Winsor, of Philadelphia, by whom a new company was soon afterwards formed and incorporated by the Massachusetts legislature, with the title of the "Boston & Philadelphia Steamship Company," with its shipping port at Providence, transporting the freight received here to Boston and elsewhere by rail.

The new line commenced business here early in 1866, with its first office at the Boston Railroad Company's wharf on India Street, at the foot of Ives. In 1872 the business was removed to the wharf on India, foot of South Main Street. In 1875, because of the great increase of business ample quarters were secured at Ives wharf, where the line now has a water front and a wharfage of 225 feet, with a freight and store-house 225 by 60 feet, with over two acres of yard room and spur tracts connecting with the railroads on India Street; with ample appliances for receipt, quick discharge, and careful storage of freight.

The line at present comprises three large screw steamers: the *Saxon*, 1,500 tons, Captain Wm. M. Swasey; the *Catherine Whiting*, 800 tons, Captain John H. Briggs; the *Aries*, 1,200 tons, Captain John R. Briggs, and the *Tonawanda*, 800 tons, kept at Philadelphia as a spare steamer. One of these staunch and commodious vessels leaves each port every Wednesday and Saturday afternoon. The line receives large freights of manufactured goods, cottons, woolens, hardware, and machinery, and brings back large cargoes of cotton, wool, leather, iron, hides, and other southern and western products. From Philadelphia, the agents forward freight west by the Pennsylvania Railroad, and south by the Ocean Steamship Company to Savannah.

The present officers of the line are as follows: president, Henry Winsor, of Philadelphia; treasurer, Edward Whitney, of Boston; secretary, James Hill, of Boston. Agents: Henry Winsor & Company, at Philadelphia; E. B. Sampson, at Boston. Mr. George A. Kilton has been the Providence agent of this line from 1872 to the present time.

In 1830, not far from its present location, the Phenix Iron Foundry was established. The business of the concern has always been largely in connection with cotton and woolen mills and dyeing, bleaching, and finishing works. Heavy shafting in all its parts, and gearing have been made chiefly for the first two industries mentioned, while for the other three complete machinery has been manufactured. Here in these works have been made the majority of the large calender rolls used in this country, which are constructed of either corn husks, cotton, or paper. Other specialties manufactured are tentering machines for drying and softening cloth including ginghams and velveteens ; mangles of all kinds, hydraulic presses, and a variety of other machines.

A machine shop has always been operated in immediate connection with the foundry. In 1848, the principal owners with others built the Elm Street machine shop, and both establishments were conducted practically by the same management. The machine shops and their connected buildings are on Elm and Butler streets and extend through to South. They have a frontage of eighty feet on Elm, 200 feet on Butler, and eighty feet on South Street, covering the entire lot. There is also a wood working shop on corner of Elm and South street where the patterns and wood work of the establishment are made, and the dimensions of which are 30 x 90 feet. The foundry and offices of the company are on Elm Street east of Eddy. The total area of the entire works is 200,000 square feet.

The first American-made calico printing machine was produced here, and their manufacture still forms a part of the business. For about forty years a friction pulley clutch has been made, which for substantial character for large power has never been excelled.

The concern has recently begun the manufacture of the Nagle power boiler feed pump, which meets a demand long existing for a thoroughly good force pump for the continuous feeding of steam boilers and general mill use for supplying tanks, etc. It is exclusively made at these works. Send for book giving full information.

In a spacious fire-proof building are stored patterns for gears to the value of more than two hundred thousand dollars. These, with patterns for pulleys of all sizes have been accumulating for nearly sixty years. A full list of gears and pulleys has been printed for the use of patrons.

The daily capacity of the foundry for castings is above twenty-five tons. There is no intermission in the daily casting, so that mill owners and others may be sure of the prompt execution of orders.

The capital stock of the company is $140,000. Under a change in the management many improvements have been made and evidences of increased activity are visible in all directions. The present financial manager is Charles R. Earle, who is president and treasurer. Mr. Amos W. C. Arnold, the present agent, has held that position since 1885, and has been in the employ of the company for about fourteen years. He is a practical man in all respects, and his large experience enables him to take advantage of all recent improvements to develop the works to the best advantage. About one hundred and seventy-five men are employed in the entire works.

THE DOCKS, FREIGHT HOUSES AND YARDS OF THE PROVIDENCE, NORFOLK AND BALTIMORE STEAMSHIP COMPANY, INDIA STREET.

THE ALDINE PATENT FIRE-PLACE

The largest marble and granite work, the city of Providence are those of S, ton & Farnum, at 575 High Street. Here at all times can be seen in their extensive sheds all descriptions of monuments, head-stones, mantels, lettering and carving in process of construction Besides this business the firm deals in marble mantels made in imitation of cherry, mahogany, antique oak, and other prevailing fashionable styles, and the imitations are so perfect that even experts cannot detect them by the eye. The firm are also agents for the Aldine patent iron fire-place, which is probably the most effective contrivance for heating and ventilating offices and rooms in use. It is the only open fire-place that can be piped to a chimney, one or more rooms removed from the grate itself. It takes in the cold air from the floor by suction, and emits the heated air from above the grate, while its embodiment of the return draft principle ensures perfect combustion, the whole resulting in a very perfect ventilation of the room.

If you want to get a good article in ice cream, one of the best places to go to is W. H. Doughty & Company's, 79 Fifield Avenue. The firm started business in 1885 rear 989 Eddy Street in a small shop with hand machinery, but business increased so rapidly that next season they removed to their present location, where they operate a six horse-power engine, run three machines, have five teams out retailing their cream, and employ from seven to ten men. Special attention is paid to supplying families, select parties, church festivals, or excursion parties, and orders large or small can be filled at short notice. A prompt response is always made to telephone orders. The firm also makes a specialty of hulled corn in the winter season, and as some of the partners have had an experience in this line extending over twelve years, they can guarantee an excellent article.

A first-class place where ladies could go to have their hair dressed and trimmed without the publicity that is a necessary feature of even the most elegant barbering establishment patronized by gentlemen, has long since been a desideratum in this city. In view of this fact Messrs. Parker & Storm have recently fitted up a ladies' parlor, in a commodious apartment in the basement of the Hotel Dorrance, across the entrance from their gentlemen's establishment. This room is specially devoted to ladies, where they can have the consciousness that they will not be subjected to the scrutiny of a promiscuous company ; it is fitted up elegantly, and three chairs are in constant use. In the gentlemen's department across the passage, six chairs are in use, and every convenience, such as baths, boot polishing, etc., is readily furnished.

THE NINTH ANNUAL RHODE ISLAND CLAM DINNER, TENDERED
WORKS, AT VUE DE L'EAU CLUB, PR(

THE ELECTRICAL FRATERNITY BY THE AMERICAN ELECTRICAL
)ENCE, R. I., ON FRIDAY, AUGUST 12th, 1887.

The manufacture of electrical supplies is conducted on an extensive
scale by the American Electrical
Works, No. 67 Stewart Street, Providence. The business was begun by
Eugene F. Phillips in 1870, with two
braiding machines, which could have
been run on an ordinary office desk.
A steady increase continued until 1878,
when Mr. Phillips associated with him-

AMERICAN ELECTRICAL WORKS.

self Mr. Wm. H. Sawyer, as superintendent of the works, a thoroughly practical electrician, who has made the mysteries of electricity a life study. This
gave a fresh impetus to the business, and in 1882 the concern was incorporated
as the American Electrical Works, with Mr. Phillips as president, and Mr.
Sawyer as secretary and treasurer. Each succeeding year has shown sales much
greater than its predecessor, and the scope of
articles furnished has increased from two or three
styles in 1870 to over one thousand in 1888.
Among these are electric light wire, telephone,
incandescent and electric cordage, magnet wire,
patent rubber covered wire, office and annunciator
wire, lead encased wire, Faraday aerial and un-
derground cables. Orders have increased from a
few pounds in 1870 to ten and twenty thousand at
present, the Faraday cables being ordered in lots
as large as twenty miles at one time, the length
of the latter strung out as single wire would measure 2,000 miles. The
main factory is a four-story brick building with a basement, 121 x 40 feet, with
two Ls, each 65 x 30 feet, while in the rear is a four-story wooden building,
115 x 30 feet, the whole forming a hollow square, in the centre of which is an
engine which operates the entire establishment. A visit to these works will
repay any one interested in electrical matters.

THE VUE DE L'EAU CLUB HOUSE AND GROUNDS

The idea of
pain is inti-
mately associa-
ted with the
mere sugges-
tion of any op-
eration upon
the teeth. But
like any other
science or pro-
fession, won-
derful improve-
ments are being
made in dentis-
try. Dr. Z. T.
Williams, 527
High Street,
corner of
Knight, ex-
tracts teeth free

THE FIRST LIGHT INFANTRY BUILDING,
South Main Street.

of pain. without the use of chloroform, ether, or gas. He can also extract your
teeth and give you a full set the same day, being probably the only man in
Providence who can do this. Such a set he guarantees to fit for ten years. His
new gold-lined vulcanite plates are worth examining. Special attention is
given to treating and saving the natural teeth, and thereby badly decayed and
ulcerated teeth are rendered painless and serviceable for years. Roots crowned
and restored to their original usefulness. All work done by the doctor will be
found to be eminently satisfactory. The office, being at the corner of High
and Knight, is exceedingly well located for a large section of the city.

One of the most enjoyable excursions in the state is a trip up the Woonasquatucket Valley on the Providence and Springfield Railroad, which is only
twenty-three miles in length, and runs for nearly the whole distance on the
bank of the river. alternately crossing and recrossing the stream, but mostly
keeping on the south side. Between Providence and Pascoag, the terminal
station. there are sixteen factory villages. The train speeds along past a continual succession of pleasant scenes consisting of wooded banks, sloping meadows. mills in the hollows. houses among the trees. a church here and there
on high ground, and the river in places stretching out in a wide expanse, held
back by a dam. or in other localities rushing over the rocky bed or pouring
over an artificial waterfall. a bright and laughing stream. Notwithstanding the
many villages. the outlook for the greater part of the distance is on the woods
and fields. The road follows the Woonasquatucket River until beyond Georgiaville. and from thence onward to the terminus follows the valleys of the Tar-
kiln and Clear rivers. The beauty of the country along this road has already
attracted many residents. who, by means of the railroad, live in these scenes of
rural contentment and get to and from their business in the city.

HOTELS.

Narragansett, corner Dorrance and Broad.
Dorrance, corner Dorrance and Westminster.
City, Broad, near Eddy.
Perrin, 127, 129, and 131 Washington, opposite Snow.
Central, 6 to 10 Canal.
Revere, corner Pine and Dorrance.
Ætna, (formerly Freeman), 98 Union.
St. George, 66, 68, and 70 Washington.
Musee, 1 Aborn.
Hopkins, 421 and 423 High.
Mansion House, 159 Benefit.
Bruckers, 261 Westminster.
Girard, Eddy Street opposite City Hall.
Bijou, 60, Union Street.

CHURCHES.

Baptist.

Branch Avenue, Flora, corner Ashton.
Broadway, Broadway, corner Valley.
Central, High, corner Burrill.
Congdon Street, Congdon.
Cranston Street, Cranston, corner Paine.
Ebenezer, Slade building, 65 Eddy.
First, North Main, between Waterman and Thomas.
Fourth, Scott, corner Bacon.
Friendship Street, Friendship, corner Prince.
Jefferson Street, Jefferson, corner Common.
Mt. Pleasant, Academy ave., corner Beaufort.
Roger Williams, Waushuck.
South, Ocean, corner Gallup.
Stewart Street, Stewart, corner Pond.
Union, East, corner John.

Congregational.

Academy Avenue, Mount Pleasant.
Beneficent, Broad, near Chestnut.
Central, Benefit, near College.
Elmwood, Greenwich, corner Oakland.
Free, Richmond, corner Pine.
North, Charles, near H. R. crossing.
Pilgrim, Harrison, near High.
Plymouth, Richardson, near Prairie avenue.
Union, Broad, near Stewart.

Episcopal.

All Saints' Memorial, High, corner Stewart.
Church of the Messiah, High, corner Valley.
Church of the Redeemer, North Main, corner Riley.
Church of the Saviour, Benefit, corner Transit.
Church of the Epiphany, Elmwood, Potter's avenue, near Greenwich.
Christ, Oxford, corner Eddy.
Grace, Westminster, corner Mathewson.
St. James, Gesler, near Courtland.
St. John's, North Main, corner Church.
St. Stephen's, George, near Thayer.
St. Thomas', Douglas ave., near Waushuck.

Free Baptist.

First, Plainfield, Olneyville.
Greenwich Street, Greenwich, cor. West Friendship.
Second, Pond.
Park Street, Park, corner Jewett.
Roger Williams, High, corner Knight.

Methodist Episcopal.

Asbury, Hewes, near North Main.
Broadway, Broadway, corner Ringgold.
Chestnut Street, Chestnut, corner Clifford.
Cranston Street, 441 Cranston.
Harris Avenue, Harris ave., near Broadway.
Hope Street, Hope, corner Power.
Mathewson Street, Mathewson, between Westminster and Washington.
St. Paul's, Potter's avenue, cor. Prairie avenue.

Trinity, Broad, corner Major.
Swedish, Federal, corner Sabin.

Roman Catholic.

Assumption, Potter's avenue, near Cranston.
Cathedral, SS. Peter and Paul, High, corner Fenner.
Holy Name, Jenkins, corner Knowles.
Immaculate Conception, West River.
Pro-Cathedral, Broad.
St. Charles, French Church, Branch Avenue.
St. John's, Atwell's avenue, corner Sutton.
St. Patrick's, State near Smith.
St. Mary's, Broadway, corner Barton.
St. Joseph's, Hope, corner Arnold.
St. Edward's, Geneva.
St. Michael's, Prairie avenue, corner Oxford.
St. Teresa's, Manton avenue.
St. Thomas.
Elmhurst (Convent), Smith.

Unitarian.

First Congregational, Benefit, corner Benevolent.
Olney Street Congregational, Olney, opposite Pratt.
Westminster Congregational, Mathewson, near Westminster.

Universalist.

Ballou Universalist, North, near Orms.
Church of the Mediator, Cranston, corner Burgess.
First, Greene, corner Washington.

Presbyterian.

First, Clifford, near Claverick.
United, Broadway, corner Hicks.

Other Denominations.

Advent Christian Society, Hammond.
African Union, Clayton (colored).
Allen Chapel, A Street (colored).
Bethel, Meeting, near Thayer (colored).
Christian, Broad, corner Fenner.
Christian Mission or Bethel Coffee House, 84 Wickenden.
Church of the Yahveh, Pearl, corner Providence.
Congregation Sons of Israel and David, 98 Weybosset.
Cranston Mission, Baptist, Jackson Avenue.
Doughty's Mission, Advent, Broad, near Prairie Ave.
Ebenezer Primitive Methodist, Franklin Avenue, corner Vale.
Free Religious Society, Blackstone Hall, Washington, corner Snow.
Friends Meeting, North Main, corner Meeting.
Gorton Hall Christian Mission, Potter's Avenue, near Cranston.
Gospel Mission, 114 High.
Lilac Street M. E., 76 Lilac (colored).
Manton Christian Church, Manton avenue, corner Clarkstone avenue.
Mount Zion (colored) Potter's avenue, corner Cranston.
New Jerusalem Church, Broad, corner Linden.
Olivet Mission (colored), Congregational, 10 Cove, room 4.
Pawtucket Avenue Mission, Baptist, Pawtucket ave.
People's Evangelical Church, 161 Oxford.
Pettis Avenue Mission.
Providence Spiritual Association, Blackstone Hall.
Reorganized Church of Jesus Christ, 275 High.
Salvation Army of America, 266 High.
Salvation Army (English), 281 High.
Second Advent, Temperance Hall, Eddy, corner Potter's avenue.
St. Andrew's Mission, Episcopal, Odd Fellows Hall, Mt. Pleasant.
Swedish Baptist Mission, 98 Weybosset.
Swedish Episcopal Mission, Grace Church chapel.
Swedish Christian Association, 79 Weybosset.
Swedish Methodist Mission, Slade Building, Eddy.
Swedish Lutheran, Slade Building, Eddy.
Union Sea and Land Mission, Ashore and Afloat, 108 John.
Union A. M. E., Leorna.
Zion, Gaspee, near Smith (colored).

POINTS OF INTEREST.

Allen's Print Works, Printery and Thurber's Lane.
American Screw Co.'s Works, New England Mills Eddy.
American Screw Co.'s Works, Eagle Mills, Stevens
American Ship Windlass Co., Waterman, corner East River.
Arcade, 76 to 84 Westminster, running through to Weybosset
Armington & Sims Engine Co., Eagle Street.
Arsenal, Benefit, near Meeting.
Athenaeum, Benefit.
Atlantic Mills, Manton Avenue, Olneyville.
Barstow Stove Co., Point, corner Chestnut.
Blackstone Hall, Washington, corner Snow.
Board of Trade, Market square.
Brown & Sharpe Manufacturing Co., Promenade.
Brown University, Prospect.
Brown University Ball Ground, George.
Brown, The John, House, Power, corner Benefit.
Brown, Deputy Governor Elisha, House, 537 and 539 North Main.
Bryant and Stratton Business College, Hoppin Homestead Building.
Builders' Iron Foundry, 22 Codding, near High.
Burnside Monument, Exchange place.
Butler Hospital for the Insane, Swan Point Road, near Butler Avenue.
Butler Exchange, Westminster.
Cathedral, High, corner Fenner.
Charity Building, 3 North Court.
City Hall, Exchange place.
City Machine Co., Harris Avenue, corner Acorn.
Conrad Building, Westminster, corner Aborn.
Corliss Steam Engine Co.'s Works, Charles and Burt.
County Court House, Benefit.
Cove Promenade, rear of Union Passenger station.
Custom House, Weybosset.
Davol Rubber Co., 16 Point.
Dexter Training Ground, Dexter, near High.
Dexter Asylum, Hope.
Dyer's Opera House, Olneyville Square, Olneyville.
Dyerville Manufacturing Co., Dyerville.
Elba Woolen Mills, Butler, corner Elm.
Elizabeth Building, 108 to 106 North Main.
Elmwood Cott on Mills, Mawney and Daboll.
Exchange Place, opposite Union Passenger Depot.
Franklin Foundry and Machine Co., Charles and Randall square.
First Baptist Church, North Main.
First Congregational Church, Benefit.
First Universalist Church, Greene.
Fletcher Manufacturing Co., Back and Charles.
Fox Point Wharf, south end South Main.
Freemason's Hall, Dorrance, Pine and Eddy.
Friends' Boarding School, Hope.
Friends' Meeting House, North Main.
Fuller Iron and Machine Works, South Main, cor. Pike.
Gasometer, Crary (largest dome in the world).
Gas Works, Benefit, corner Pike.
Gas Works, Langley.
Gas Works, Allen's avenue.
Geneva Mill, Douglas Avenue, Geneva.
Gorham Manufacturing Co., North Main, corner Steeple.
Grace Church, Westminster.
Granger Foundry and Machine Co., Gaspee, corner Francis.
Grant Mill, Carpenter, corner Grant.
Harbor Junction Wharf, South Providence.
Harris Steam Engine Works, Park, corner Promenade.
High School, Summer.
Hillside Woolen Mills, Eagle.
Home for Aged Women, Front.
Hope Club House, 6 Benevolent.
Hope Pumping Station and Reservoir, Olney.
Hopkins, Stephen, House, Hopkins.
Hoppin Homestead Building, 277 to 289 Westminster.
Horse Car Depot, foot of Westminster.
Hotel Dorrance, Westminster.
Hoyle Tavern, Junction High and Cranston.
Infantry Armory, South Main.
Laurel dale Chemical Works, Promenade.
B. F. Keith's Gayety Opera House, formerly Low's Grand Opera House, 192 Westminster.
Manton Manufacturing Co., Manton.
Market Square, space around old city building, near Horse Car station.
McWilliams Manufacturing Co., 111 Orange.
Miller Iron Co., Harris Avenue.
Monohansett Mill, Eagle.
Mowry & Goff, English and Classical School, Snow.
Music Hall, Westminster, corner Aborn
Narragansett Boat Club House, Seekonk River, near Red Bridge.
Narragansett Hotel, Dorrance.
New England Butt Co., Pearl, corner Perkins.
Nicholson File Co., 118 Acorn.
Normal School, Benefit, corner Angell.
North Burying Ground.
Nottingham Mills (formerly Steam Mill), 314 Dyer.
Odd Fellows Hall, 97 Weybosset.

Olneyville Square, end High, at western extremity city, on border town of Johnston.
Oriental Mills, Admiral, corner Whipple.
Phenix Iron Foundry, Eddy, corner Elm.
Point Street Bridge.
Post-Office, Weybosset
Prospect Terrace, Congdon.
Providence Dyeing, Bleaching and Calendering Co., 436 Valley.
Providence Institution for Savings, 76 South Main.
Providence Machine Co., 564 Eddy.
Providence National Bank
Providence Opera House, Dorrance, corner Pine.
Providence Steam Engine Co., 373 South Main.
Providence Worsted Mills, Valley.
Randall Square, Junction Charles, Randall, Stevens and Chalkstone Avenue.
Red, or Central Bridge, east end of Waterman, to East Providence.
R. I. Bleach and Dye Works, Eddy, corner Bleachery.
R. I. Club, 171 Broad.
R. I. Hospital, Eddy.
R. I. Locomotive Works, Valley, corner Hemlock.
R. I. School of Design, Westminster.
Richmond Print Works, Valley, corner Eagle.
Riverside Mills, Kilby, near Manton Avenue.
Roger Williams Park, south end city.
Rumford Chemical Works, 175 South Main, and Rumford, East Providence.
Sabin Tavern, The Old, corner Planet and South Main.
Sacred Heart Female Academy, (Roman Catholic), Elmhurst, South.
Sanitary Gymnasium, Aborn.
Saus Souci Summer Garden, Broadway.
Scholfield Commercial College, 174 Westminster.
Silver Spring Bleaching and Dyeing Co., Charles, n. Admiral.
Slate Rock, foot of William, near river bank.
Soldiers' and Sailor's Monument, Exchange place.
State House, North Main.
State Normal School Benefit.
Stedman & Fuller Manufacturing Co., 58 Warren.
Steere Worsted Mill, Wanskuck.
St. Mary's Church, Broadway.
Sullivan Dorr House, corner Benefit and Bowen.
Swan Point Cemetery.
Tillinghast House, The Old, corner South Main and Chickenfoot alley.
Tool Co.'s Works, Wickenden.
Tool Co.'s Works, Burt.
Union Club House, corner Washington and Aborn.
Union Congregational Church, Broad.
Union Oil Co., India near Ives.
Union Passenger Station, Exchange Place.
University Grammar School, cor. College and Prospect.
Valley Worsted Mills, Eagle.
Wanskuck Mills, Branch Avenue, Wanskuck.
Washington Bridge, India Point to East Providence.
Waterman Burial Place, corner Benefit and Waterman.
Weybosset Mills, Valley, corner Oak.
Whipple House, oldest house in Providence, north side Abbott street, near North Main, at North End.
Whitestone Cotton Mill, Cranston, corner Dexter.
Wilkes Barre Pier, East Providence.
Y. M. C. A. new building, corner Westminster and Jackson.

INSTITUTIONS.

Arion Club, (musical), Blackstone Hall.
Art Club, 11 Thomas.
Athenaeum, Benefit, corner College.
Board of Trade, Market square.
Bronson Lyceum, 119 Westminster.
Brown University, Prospect, opposite College
Butler Hospital for the Insane, Swan Point Road, near Butler Avenue.
Children's Friend Society, (Orphan's Home) 47 Tobey
Christian Mission, or Bethel Coffee House, Wickenden
Commercial Club, (business)
Deaf and Dumb School, Fountain, near Aborn.
Dexter Asylum, Hope.
Franklin Lyceum, 62 Westminster.
Friends' School, Hope.
Home for Aged Men, 63 Chestnut.
Home for Aged Women, Front, corner East.
Hope Club, 6 Benevolent.
Irrepressible Society, 81 North Main.
La Salle Academy, Fountain near Broadway.
Mechanics Exchange, 9 Custom House.
Narragansett Boat Club, Seekonk River, foot of Angell.
Providence Association for the Benefit of Colored Children, 29 Olive.
Providence Lying-in Hospital.
Providence Medical Association, 54 North Main.
Providence Press Club, Room 17, 4th floor, Butler Exchange
Public Library, 56 and 57 Snow.
Reform School, at State Farm, Cranston, R. I.
Rhode Island Exchange for Women's Work, 343 Westminster.
Rhode Island Homeopathic Hospital, 181 Olney.
Rhode Island News-dealers Protective Union, 91 Westminster, room 7.

Rhode Island Society for the Encouragement of Domestic Industry, 128 North Main.
Rower Williams Saving Fund and Loan Association, 62 Westminster.
Rhode Island 1 Bible Society, 133 Westminster.
Rhode Island Women's Christian Temperance Union, 14 Butler Exchange.
Rhode Island Historical Society, Waterman.
Rhode Island Hospital, Eddy, near Hospital.
Rhode Island School of Design, 263 Westminster.
Sanitary Gymnasium, Aborn.
Sophia Little Home, Norwood Avenue, Edgewood.
St. Aloysius Orphan Asylum, Prairie Avenue.
St. Xavier Academy, 300 Broad.
St. Elizabeth Home, Atlantic, corner Melrose.
Union for Christian Work, 115 Broad.
Union Club, Washington, corner Aborn.
University Grammar School, cor. College and Prospect.
Veteran Fireman's Association, 98 Westminster.
Women's Educational and Industrial Union, 173 Broad.
Women's Christian Association, Boarding House, 66 Fountain, Branch House, 96 Mathewson.
Women's City Missionary Society.
Women's Christian Temperance Union, 24 Butler Exchange.
Women's Club (R. I.), Conrad building.
Woonasquatucket Library, Atwell's Avenue, cor. Earle.
Workingmen's Home, Earle's Block, South Main, corner James.
Young Women's Christian Temperance Union, Library and Tea Room, 151 Broad.
Y. M. C. A., 276 Westminster, Music Hall Building.

LOCALITIES IN CITY LIMITS.

SOUTH PROVIDENCE.—The southern portion of the city immediately west of the harbor, and included in the present Sixth Ward.

ELMWOOD.—Southwest part of the city, west of South Providence, the main portion of Seventh Ward.

WANSKUCK. — A factory suburb in extreme northwest portion of city.

GENEVA.— A factory suburb west of Wanskuck.

MOUNT PLEASANT.— A considerable elevation covered with residences in western section of city.

OLNEYVILLE.— A name applied generally to the locality centering on square of that name, two miles west from City Hall, a large part of which is across the line in town of Johnston.

NORTH END.—The locality in neighborhood of Randall Square and North Burial Ground.

ARLINGTON.— End of Cranston street, west of Fenner Avenue in town of Cranston, just over the city line.

DYERVILLE — West from Mount Pleasant at extremity of Manton Avenue horse car route.

FIELD'S POINT.— At entrance to Providence Harbor, South Providence.

EAST SIDE.—All that portion of the city lying east of Providence River.

BROOK STREET DISTRICT.— On east side, south of Wickenden Street.

FEDERAL HILL.— So called from the high sandy bluffs along the railroad west of Broadway, and name has been generally applied to this locality.

CEMETERIES.

Grace Church, Trinity Square.
Hebrew Cemetery, Reservoir avenue.
Locust Grove, Elmwood.
North Burying Ground, North Main.
Roman Catholic, Douglas avenue.
Swan Point, Swan Point road.
Oakland, Cranston, just beyond city line, Broad street.
Riverside, adjoins Swan Point, within limits of Pawtucket.
St. Francis, new Catholic, Smithfield avenue, Pawtucket, near Providence line.

AMUSEMENTS.

Amateur Dramatic Hall, South Main, corner Power.
Keith Grand Opera House, Union, near Westminster.
Prov. Opera House, Dorrance, corner Pine.
Sans Souci Garden, Broadway, opp. Jackson.
Westminster Museo, 268 Westminster.

PARKS.

Abbott Park, Broad.
Blackstone, Seekonk River.
Cove Promenade.
Fifth Ward Park (formerly the Proprietors Burial Ground), Friendship, Beacon, and Plain sts.
Franklin Square, Atwell's avenue, corner Bradford.
Prospect Terrace, Congdon.
Rower Williams, south end of city.
Tockwotton Park, site of the old Reform School, Front, corner East, overlooking harbor.
Washington Square, Benefit, corner India.

PUBLIC SCHOOL BUILDINGS.

Providence High School, Summer, corner Pond.

Grammar Schools.

Branch Avenue, junction Charles.
Bridgham Street, near Division.
Candace Street, corner Orms.
Doyle Avenue, near Camp.
Federal Street, Federal, corner Dean.
Manton Avenue, corner Fruit Hill avenue.
Mt. Pleasant, Atwell's avenue and Putnam.
Oxford Street, corner Seymour.
Point Street, corner Plain.
Thayer Street, Thayer and George.
Elmwood, Vineyard Street.

Primary and Intermediate Schools.

FIRST DISTRICT—Benefit Street, corner Halsey; Camp Street, between Cypress and Private; Graham Street; Walling Street.

SECOND DISTRICT—Meeting Street, corner South Court; Thayer Street, corner of Meeting; Arnold Street, corner Brook; East Street, corner Transit; Manning Street.

THIRD DISTRICT—Federal Street, west of grammar school; Fountain Street (occupied in part for ward room purposes and by State for Deaf and Dumb School); Sabin Street, rear of preceding; Carpenter Street, corner Pallas; Harris Avenue, King Street, near Knight; Africa Street, Atwell's Avenue (new) corner Messenger.

FOURTH DISTRICT.—Elm Street; Richmond Street, near Ship; Hospital, corner Borden; Beacon Street.

FIFTH DISTRICT.—Summer Street, corner Pond; Hammond Street; Friendship Street, corner Portland; Warren Street, corner Fuller; Messer Street, corner Willow; Somerset Street.

SIXTH DISTRICT.—Public Street; Eddy Street; Thurber Avenue, corner Plain; Jackson Avenue; Bellevue Avenue; Greenwich Street, junction of Potter's avenue and Greenwich street; Potter's Avenue, corner Brattle; Chester Avenue; Aldrich Street; Harriet Street; Plain Street.

SEVENTH DISTRICT.—Chalkstone Avenue, corner Wayne street; Berlin Street, corner Chalkstone avenue; West River; Manton Avenue Intermediate (in Grammar School building); Julian Street, corner Capron; Admiral Street; Amherst Street, Smith Street, corner Duke, near Chalkstone avenue; Coville Street.

DRIVES.

DRIVE No. 1.—Swan Point Cemetery.—Starting from Market sq., via North Main st., passing the First Baptist Church and State House, to Olney St., Olney st., passing Hope Reservoir and station, to Swan Point road, Swan Point road to Cemetery and Butler Hospital. Returning, via Swan Point road to Butler ave., Butler ave. to Angell st., Angell to Hope, Hope, passing Dexter Asylum and Friends' School, to Reservoir, through Thayer st., to Waterman, Waterman, passing Brown University, to Prospect, Prospect to George, George to Benefit, Benefit, passing Athenæum and Court House, to College st., College st. to Market sq.

DRIVE No. 2.—Swan Point and Pawtucket.—Via drive No. 1 to Swan Point Cemetery, and Swan Point road to Pawtucket, through Pawtucket to East ave., East ave. to Olney st., Olney to North Main, North Main to Market sq.

DRIVE No. 3.—Angell Street and East Side.—Starting from Market sq., via North Main to Waterman, Waterman to Prospect to Angell, Angell to Butler ave., Butler ave to Waterman st., Waterman to Blackstone ave., Blackstone ave. to Glen ave. Returning, via Blackstone ave. to Waterman, Waterman to Hope, Hope to Sheldon, Sheldon to Benefit, Benefit, passing the Athenaeum, Court House, and State House, to North Main st., North Main to Market sq.

DRIVE No. 4.—Broadway, Manton and Chalkstone aves.—Starting from Market sq., via Westminster st. to Aborn, Aborn to Broadway, passing Sans Souci Garden and St. Mary's Church, to Manton ave., Manton ave., through Dyerville, to Chalkstone ave., Chalkstone ave. to Smith st., Smith to North Main, North Main to Market sq.

DRIVE No. 5.—Elmwood and Roger Williams Park.—Starting from Market sq., via Westminster st., to Weybosset, Weybosset to Dorrance, Dorrance, passing Narragansett Hotel, to Pine st., Pine to Broad, Broad to Roger Williams Park, through the Park avenues, to Elmwood ave., Elmwood ave. to Greenwich, Greenwich to Broad, Broad to Weybosset, Weybosset to Westminster, Westminster to Market sq.

DRIVE No. 6.—Broad Street and Pawtuxet.—Starting from Market sq., via Dyer st. to Friendship, Friendship to Broad, Broad to Pawtuxet, Oakland Beach and Rocky Point. Returning, via same.

DRIVE No. 7.—Sockanosset Reservoir, Pumping Station, and State Prison.—Starting from Market sq., via drive No. 6 to Broad st., Broad to Greenwich, Greenwich to Reservoir ave., Reservoir ave. to Sockanosett Reservoir, Sockanosset Reservoir to Pumping Station, Pumping Station to State Prison and Farm. Returning, via Pontiac road to Reservoir ave., Reservoir ave. to Greenwich st., Greenwich st. to Broad, Broad to Weybosset, Weybosset to Westminster, Westminster to Market sq.

DRIVE No. 8.—Broadway, Rocky Hill and Roger Williams Park.—Via drives No. 4 to Plainfield st., Plainfield st. to Rocky Hill road, Rocky Hill Road to Cranston st., Cranston st. to Fenner ave., Fenner ave. to Reservoir ave., Reservoir ave. to Park ave., Park ave. to Elmwood ave., Elmwood ave. to Roger Williams Park, through the park drives to Broad st., Broad to Friendship, Friendship to Richmond, Richmond to Broad, Broad to Weybosset, Weybosset to Westminster, Westminster to Market sq.

DRIVE No. 9.—Broadway, Fruit Hill and Smith St.—Via drive No. 4 to Chalkstone ave., Chalkstone ave. to Fruit Hill ave., Fruit Hill ave. to Fruit Hill, down Smith st. to Park, Park to Gaspee, Gaspee to Cove, Cove to Exchange place and Market sq.

DRIVE No. 10.—Woonasquatuck Valley.—Through Olneyville, via Broadway and Manton aves., or through Atwell's ave. to Manton ave., thence past the villages of Dyerville, Manton, Lymansville, Allendale, Centredale, Graniteville, Graystone, Allenville, to Georgiaville. Returning same way until junction of Chalkstone ave. is reached, then via Drive No. 9.

DRIVE No. 11.—Warwick Shore.—Via drive No. 6, down Broad st. to Silver Hook road, thence to Rocky Point road, turning after some miles into River road, passing thereon Riverdale, Shawomet Beach, River View, Bay Side, and then continuing on to Rocky Point. Returning by Warwick Neck, Old Warwick, Bills Grove, Pontiac, State Farm, Pumping Station, Reservoir ave. and Greenwich st. to the city.

DRIVE No. 12.—Pawtuxet Valley.—Cranston st. to Cranston Print-Works, thence through the county to Natick over the hill to Phenix, then across country to Anthony and Quidnick, and return through villages of Arctic, River Point, and Pontiac, and back to city as per Drive No. 11.

DRIVE No. 13.—Blackstone Valley to Pawtucket via drive No. 2, or through Waterman, Benefit, North Main, and Pawtucket Pike, then through the numerous villages on banks of river; returning same way or through East Providence.

DRIVE No. 14.—Warren and Bristol.—Through East Providence, past Silver Spring, Riverside, across the town of Barrington to Warren and Bristol, returning same way. Or this drive can have for its termination Nayatt Point.

DRIVE No. 15.—Hunt's Mills.—Four miles from Washington Bridge, route through East Providence.

POLICE DEPARTMENT.

Headquarters, City Hall, Exchange Place.
1st District station house, Canal, corner Haymarket.
2d District station house, corner Martin and Ashburton.
3d District station house, Wickenden.
4th District station house, 33 Knight.
5th District station house, Plain, near Lockwood.
6th District station house, Capron, near Julian.

FIRE DEPARTMENT.

Headquarters, City Hall, Exchange place.
Hose Co. No. 1, Exchange Place.
" " 2, North Main.
" " 3, Pond.
" " 4, Mill.
" " 6, Benevolent.
" " 7, Richmond.
" " 9, Atwell's avenue, corner America.
" " 11, Public.
" " 13, Central.
" " 15, Wickenden.
Steamer No. 5, North Main, corner Doyle avenue.
" " 8, Harrison, near High.
" " 10, Burnside.
" " 12, Smith, corner Orms.
" " 14, Putnam.
Hook and Ladder No. 1, Exchange Place.
" " 2, Harrison.
" " 3, Smith.
" " 4, Wickenden.
" " 5, Burnside, corner Public.
" " 6, Atwell's avenue, cor. America.
Protective Co No.1, Exchange Place.
Chemical Engine, No. 1 Richmond.
" " 2, Benevolent.

EXPRESS COMPANIES.

Adams, Dorrance, corner Broad.
Earle & Prew's, 65 Eddy, corner Fulton.
Hopkins Transfer Co., 1 Boston Depot.
International Express Co., 21 Washington Street, opposite City Hall.
New York and Boston Dispatch. 58 Eddy.
New Express Co., 10 Dorrance, corner Broad.
Providence & Worcester R. R. Express Department, 58 Eddy.
Taunton and New Bedford Express, Dorrance, corner Broad.
U. S. and Canada Express Co., 58 Eddy.
United States Express, 144 and 146 Broad.

TELEGRAPH OFFICES.

American Telephone and Telegraph Co., 54 Westminster.
Mutual Union Co., 54 Westminster.
Providence District Messenger Co., 54 Westminster.
Providence Telephone Co., Central Office, Butler Exchange.
Providence Telephone Co., Public Station, 54 Westminster Street.
United Lines Telegraph Co., 16 Westminster.
Western Union Co., 6 Weybosset.
" " " Butler Exchange.
" " " Central Passenger Depot.
" " " Narragansett Hotel.
" " " Fox Point Wharf.
" " " India Point Freight Department.
" " " Wilkes Barre Pier, East Prov.
Mutual Union Branch Office, 1676 High, Olneyville.

DAILY NEWSPAPERS.

Providence Morning Dispatch, 54 Westminster.
Evening Bulletin, 2 Weybosset.
Evening Telegram and Sunday Telegram, No. 7 Weybosset.
Providence Daily Journal, 2 Weybosset.

MILITIA ARMORIES.

Burnside Guards (colored), corner Winter and Cranston streets, near junction of High.
Emmet Guards, 129 Westminster.
First Light Infantry, Infantry Building, South Main.
Horse Guards, 128 North Main.
Meagher Guards, corner Dorrance and Broad, old Infantry building, entrance on Dorrance.
Marine Artillery, State Arsenal, Benefit, near Meeting.
Slocum Light Guard, Broad Street.
United Train Artillery, Canal Street.
Wolfe Tone Guards, 54 North Main.

WHARVES.

Browns. (J. R. White & Sons), India.
Butler's Wharf, opp. 129 Dyer.
Continental Steamboat Co.'s, Dyer.
Clarke's wharf, foot of Dorrance.
Duncan Wharf, 145 Dyer, foot of Peck.
Ferry wharf, Dyer.
Fall River Steamboat Co.'s, opp. 71 South Water.
Fox Point wharf, India.
Gas Co.'s wharf, Langley.
Hill's wharf, Crary.
Ives wharf, India Point.
Lonsdale wharf, India.
Lehigh & Wilkes Barre Coal Co.'s pier, E. Providence.
Providence & Stonington R. R. Co.'s pier, Allen's ave.
Providence Coal Co.'s Wharf, foot of Dorrance.

RAILROADS.

Old Colony, Providence division (formerly Boston & Providence.)
New York and New England.
Providence, Warren & Bristol.
Providence & Springfield.
Providence & Worcester.
New York, Providence & Boston.
Pawtuxet Valley Branch.
Warwick & Oakland Beach.

RAILROAD STATIONS AND STEAM-BOAT LANDINGS.

Union Station, Exchange Place.
Providence & Springfield, Gaspee Street.
Warren & Bristol, Fox Point.
Continental Steamboats, Dyer, foot Bay.
Providence & Fall River Steamers, South Water.
Shore Transportation Steamers, South Water, near Crawford Street Bridge.
New York Steamers, Fox Point.
Norfolk and Baltimore Steamers, Lonsdale Wharf.
Seaconnet Point Steamers, South Water, near Crawford Street Bridge.
Winsor Line Steamers for Philadelphia, Ives Wharf India Street.

STEAMERS.

Continental Steamboat Co., Dyer.
Providence & Fall River Steamboat Co., So. Water.
Providence & New York Steamboat Line, Fox Point.
Providence, Norfolk & Baltimore Steamship Line, Lonsdale wharf.
Shore Transportation Co., South Water, near Crawford Street Bridge.
Winsor's Line for Philadelphia, Ives wharf.

HORSE RAILROADS.

Depot, Weybosset Bridge.

HIGH STREET AND OLNEYVILLE. Color of car, green and white; signal light, green. From Market sq., via Westminster and High sts., to Olneyville; returning via High, Broad, Weybosset and Westminster sts., to Market square.

* GOVERNOR STREET From Market sq. via South Main, Wickenden, Governor, Waterman, Gano, Angell sts., and Butler ave. to Blackstone Park.

* BROOK STREET — From Market Sq., via South Main, Wickenden, Brook, Meeting, and Thayer sts. to Olney st.

PLAINFIELD STREET — From Turk's Head, same as High st. to Olneyville, then via Plainfield st.

MANTON AVENUE.—From Turk's Head, same as High st. to Olneyville, then via Manton ave. to Dyerville.

SWAN POINT CEMETERY.—Governor st. car to Blackstone Park, then via bus through Butler avenue and Swan Point road.

* On the Governor and Brook street routes, continuous round trips are run from Olneyville via High.

ELMWOOD.— Color of car, red and white; signal light, red. From Market Sq., via Westminster, Mathewson, Broad and Greenwich sts. Returning, via Greenwich, Broad, Weybosset and Westminster sts., to Market Sq.

ELMWOOD AND SMITH'S HILL.—From Market Sq., via North Main, Mill, Charles, Orms and Smith sts., to Ruggles st., Smith's Hill.

PRAIRIE AVENUE.—Color of car, straw and white; signal light, blue and white. Via Westminster, Mathewson, Broad, Chestnut, Friendship, Beacon and Point sts., and Prairie ave., to South Providence stable. Return, via Prairie ave., Point, Beacon, Friendship, Richmond, Broad, Weybosset, to Market Sq.

CAMP STREET.— Prairie ave. car from South Providence to Market Sq., then via North Main, Olney, and Camp sts. Return same way.

ELMWOOD AVENUE ROUTE.— Color of car, Pullman; signal light, dark star on white ground. From Market Sq., via South Main, Wickenden, Governor, Waterman and Gano sts. Return same to Market Sq., then via Westminster, Mathewson, Broad, Greenwich sts., and Elmwood ave. to Roger Williams Park.

PAWTUXET—Color of car, straw and white; signal light, straw. From Market Sq., via North Main, Mill, Charles, Randall, North Main sts., and Pawtucket ave., Garden, Main sts., Pawtucket, to corner Broad and Main sts. Returning, via same route to Market Sq.

BRANCH AVENUE.—Color of car, light blue; signal light, blue cross on white ground. From Market Sq., via North Main st., and Branch ave. to Wanskuck. Return same way.

BROAD STREET AND PAWTUXET — Color of car, maroon; signal light, purple. From Market Sq., via Westminster, Mathewson and Broad sts., to South Providence, and via Broad st. to Pawtuxet. Return via Thurber's ave., Broad and Weybosset sts., to Market Sq.

BROADWAY AND OLNEYVILLE.—Color of car, blue and white; signal light, blue. From Market Sq., via Westminster, Jackson sts., and Broadway to Olneyville. Returning, via Broadway, Aborn, Washington sts., Exchange Place and Exchange st. to Market Square.

CRANSTON.—Color of car, red and green; signal light, red and green. From Market Sq., via Westminster, High, and Cranston sts., to stable, and by transfer car to Cranston Print Works. Returning, via Cranston, High, Broad, and Weybosset sts., to Market Sq.

EDDY STREET — Color of car, green and red, signal light, straw. From Turk's Head via Westminster, Mathewson, Broad, Richmond, and Eddy sts., and Thurber's ave., to South Providence stable. Return Thurber's ave., Eddy, Richmond, Broad, Weybosset to Turk's Head.

MOUNT PLEASANT—Color of car, drab; signal light, red, with white star centre. From Market Sq., via Westminster, Jackson, Federal, and Bradford sts., Atwell's ave., and Academy ave. to Mount Pleasant. Return same way to Federal; then via Broadway, Aborn, Washington, Exchange Place, and Exchange st., to Market Sq.

EAST PROVIDENCE.—Color of car, orange; signal light, black crescent on orange. From Market Sq., via South Main, Pike, Traverse, Tockwotton, East Providence Bridge, and Warren ave., Potter st. and Broadway. Return same way; connect at Broadway Six Corners with bus for Rumford and East Providence Centre.

BRISTOL R. R. AND N. Y. BOAT — Color of car, straw and green; signal light white. From Exchange Place via Exchange street, Westminster, Market Sq., South Main. Return same way. Cars connect with all trains, both ways, on the Providence, Warren & Bristol Railroad, leaving Exchange Place.

CHESNUT POINT AND FRIENDSHIP STS.— Color of car, light yellow; signal light, orange and black checks. From Turk's Head, via Westminster, Mathewson, Broad, Chestnut, Bassett, Hospital, Point, Friendship, Broad, Public, Greenwich. Return same way, except through Weybosset instead of Mathewson from Broad st.

RATES OF HACK AND EXPRESS FARE.

Hack Fare.

For each passenger from one place to another within the City, not exceeding one mile, . . 50 cts.
For each additional mile or fraction of a mile, . . 25 cts.
Children from 4 to 12 years of age, if more than one, or accompanied by an adult, ... HALF-PRICE.
Under 4 years of age, ... FREE.
BY THE HOUR, first, ... $2 00
Each subsequent hour, ... 1 50

Baggage.

One Trunk and one Valise, Saddlebag, Portmanteau, bundle, or other articles used in traveling, ... FREE.
Every additional Trunk or other article, . . 10 cts.

Express Fare.

For the transportation of any article weighing not more than 300 lbs., from one place to another within the City, not exceeding one mile, ... 30 cts.
For the transportation of any article weighing as aforesaid, more than one mile, ... 50 cts.
For each additional article weighing as aforesaid, 15 cts.
All distances shall be computed by straight lines on the Map of the City, and each owner or driver having charge of such Hackney Carriage or Express Wagon, shall, at all times, when using the same, have a copy of said Map in said carriage or wagon, which shall be exhibited when demanded.

PAWTUCKET, FROM THE BELFRY OF THE CONGREGATIONAL CHURCH, BROADWAY.

CHAPTER II.

The City of Pawtucket.

VIEW OF NORTH MAIN STREET, PAWTUCKET.

THE second place in point of population in the state of Rhode Island is the city of Pawtucket, which is situated four miles northeast of Providence on the Blackstone River. Pawtucket is an Indian word signifying a fall of water, and was given to this locality because the fresh waters of the Blackstone here meet the tides of Narragansett Bay by being precipitated over rocky ledges. Below the falls, the tidal basin or estuary extends for about five miles to India Point, where it unites with Providence Harbor, and is known as the Seekonk River. It is navigable for vessels of light draught as far as the lowest bridge, a short distance below the falls.

While the name Pawtucket has since the earliest settlement been applied to this locality on both the banks of river, yet only since 1862 has it been the designation of a Rhode Island town. The territory on the eastern bank was originally a part of Massachusetts, and was at first in the town of Rehoboth, and then a portion of Seekonk. In 1828 it was incorporated as a Massachusetts town under the name Pawtucket, and in 1862, by the settlement of the boundary question between Rhode Island and Massachusetts, it was annexed to Rhode Island. The village of Pawtucket on the west side of the river was in the limits of the town of North Providence, and continued in

6

that jurisdic-
tion until
1874, when it
was consoli-
dated with
the town of
Pawtucket on
the east side.
Pawtucket
was incorpo-
rated as a city
by an act
which went
into effect
January 4,
1886. For
some years an
agitation with
that end in
view had
been going
on, and dur-
ing that pe-
riod it was
customary to
call Paw-

VIEW ON MAIN STREET, PAWTUCKET.

tucket "the largest town" in the country, and it was undoubtedly the largest
community in the country governed under the form of a town.

Pawtucket has always been a manufacturing place, and it has been such
because of the natural water-power afforded by the falls.   Twenty-five years
after Roger Williams and his companions had made their settlement in Providence, Joseph Jencks purchased sixty acres of land near Pawtucket Falls, erected
a forge and a saw-mill, and began the manufacture of iron and wooden tools
and implements.   Other industries soon followed, and the place was a work-
shop for the adjoining commercial and agricultural communities.   While Providence owed much of its early growth to the development of commerce, Pawtucket was wholly built up by its manufactures.

The honor of being the place where cotton was first successfully manufactured in the New World by the modern methods invented in England belongs
to Pawtucket.   The machines were erected by Samuel Slater, a young English-
man, who built them without drawings to guide him, wholly from recol-
lection.   At first Slater worked for Moses Brown, of Providence, but subse-
quently he established mills in connection with partners,—his wife's relatives,
the Wilkinsons,—and began the development of an industry that has grown
into the greatest in the state and one of the most important in the country.

The two sides of the river, although in different states until 1862, and under

PAWTUCKET FALLS, IN 1789

separate town governments until 1874, were really one community in business and sentiment, and since their union the progress of the place has been rapid and continuous.

Although the cotton manufacture is chief, there are many other industries, among which are large machine shops, foundries, tanneries, leather belting and lace leather establishments, wadding works, print works, hair cloth mills, dye works, manufactories of doors, blinds, and builders' materials, the manufacture of bolts and screws, lumber and saw mills, box manufactories, spool mills, jewelry shops, paper box shops, paper mills, etc.

The manufacture of cotton cloth is not very extensively carried on in Pawtucket, the majority of the establishments engaged in the cotton industry here making yarns or thread, and as a consequence Pawtucket is probably the most important centre for these branches of the manufacture in the country.

The first bridge built over the river at the falls was a wooden one erected in 1763. This bridge was rebuilt several times, and in 1858 the present substantial stone bridge was erected. A short distance above is an iron bridge erected in 1872, and still further above are two iron bridges, erected respectively in 1868 and 1871, connecting the east side with Central Falls.

Below the Main Street bridge is a high stone bridge which crosses the Seekonk on nine arches from the foot of Division Street. This bridge practically marks the limits of navigation. From it a fine view of the surroundings can be obtained.

Pawtucket has an excellent system of water-works, which were put in operation January 31, 1878, and have since that time satisfactorily supplied with water not only Pawtucket, but also East Providence, Central Falls, and other small places in the neighborhood. There are two reservoirs, one located two and a half miles from the business centre, and 300 feet above tide water. The other is a new reservoir recently built in Cumberland.

The railroad shipments to and from a place are an excellent index of the extent of its business. During the month of December, 1887, the Providence & Worcester Railroad received at its Pawtucket station 4,188 tons of freight and dispatched 3,262 tons, a total of 7,480 tons. December is said to be an average month, November being about the heaviest month in the year for freight; at this rate the amount received and dispatched during the year would be about 100,000 tons. This is outside of any coal, bricks, much lumber, and a great deal of iron in bars, which come by water. The freight received in Pawtucket is lumber, cotton, machinery, and general merchandise in cases. When the Providence & Worcester railroad was first built it was thought that Pawtucket would be nothing but a passenger station, and no freight station was erected until about 1856. In 1858–59 when the present depot master and agent, Mr. D. R. Arnold, came to work for the corporation as agent, he did all the work as clerk, ticket-seller, express agent, etc., and the only other employés about the station were a baggage master and one laborer. There was at the same time only one express wagon and one hack. The whole express business did not amount to more than a dollar a week. In contrast to this, there are now employed between thirty-five and forty men in the freight and passenger business of the railroad, besides those engaged in the express business. The amount of business now done at the Woodlawn station both in passenger and freight is much greater than was done at Pawtucket in 1858.

Central Falls is a portion of the populous community of which the greater part is Pawtucket. This village, as it is sometimes called, although it is not that in reality, is the northwest corner of the place, and proportionally is as populous as any section of like size in Pawtucket. But it is in the town of Lincoln, and consequently is under separate government in local matters. The logic of events will undoubtedly in the future bring it under the jurisdiction of the city of Pawtucket, as its business and other interests are similar. The whole place then will be a city of considerably over thirty thousand inhabitants.

The best way to see Pawtucket is to start from the railroad station. Crossing the tracks from the platform and proceeding down Broad Street, a large, beautiful, brick building on the left attracts attention. This contains the offices, barn, and station of the Pawtucket Street Railway Company, and was built in 1886, the horse car lines being opened for travel November 30, 1886. Continuing down Broad Street, Trinity Square is soon reached, which is formed by the junction of Broad, North Union, and Main streets. On the left, on corner of Broad and Main streets, is the Benedict House, the leading hotel in Pawtucket. It is a large wooden building, with stores on the ground floor. On the other corner, and fronting on North Union Street and Trinity Square, is Sheldon Block, a two-story, wooden structure containing many stores and offices. The Pawtucket *Record*, a weekly newspaper, is published in this building.

Turning to the left around the Sheldon building into Main Street, we enter the principal retail section of the city, from this point until Main Street Square is reached, the street being lined on both sides with dry goods, clothing, grocery, and miscellaneous stores. The first particularly noticeable structure is the new Weeden Block, an artistic looking brick building, which is seen a short distance below on the southeast corner of Main Street and Park Place. Before going further it would be well to make a detour and walk up Park Place, which here enters Main Street. A few steps bring us opposite the Park Place Congregational Church, a fine structure of brick and wood. A little further and Wilkinson Park is reached, which is a triangular piece of ground inclosed with an iron railing, with walks through the centre, lined with trees, and laid out in grass plats. It is bounded by Cross and George streets, and Park Place, on all of which there are beautiful residences. At the upper end of Park Place is St. Paul's Episcopal Church.

Returning to Main Street, and proceeding down that street, Music Hall Building on the right-hand side, is first noticed. This is the largest public building in the city. It was erected in 1880, contains a large hall, much used for dramatic entertainments, fairs, lectures, etc., and

ALONG THE RIVER FRONT, CENTRAL FALLS. – FROM PLEASANT VIEW.

THE CONGREGATIONAL CHURCH.

there are many stores and offices in it. On the left a short distance below is Dexter Block, and with a building intervening, is Dexter Building, on the southwest corner of Main Street and East Avenue. The latter building is of pressed brick and is very finely ornamented in its trimmings, being the most expensive and beautiful structure on the street. It was built soon after the close of the War of the Rebellion. The United States government occupies the front of the first floor for the post-office. In this building are the offices of the Providence County Savings Bank. Across Main Street from the Dexter Building is a plain, old-fashioned looking brick edifice, with stores on the ground floor, and containing the offices of the Pawtucket Institution for Savings.

Main Street here widens out and is called Main Street Square. Out of it to the north runs North Main Street, while to the east Main Street continues. There are several large buildings on the square, the finest and most conspicuous being the combined Miller and Spencer brick block, erected in 1873 and 1874. On the front of this building is a large clock, readily seen when coming down Main Street. This building contains the Pawtucket Free Library. On the square at No. 80 Main Street is the office of the *Evening Times*, Pawtucket's daily paper, established in 1884.

On Main Street Square the fountain presented in 1880 by H. D. Coggeshall, of San Francisco, is located.

Turning into North Main Street a large brick building on the right is seen. Here is published the Pawtucket *Gazette and Chronicle*, first issued as the *Chronicle* in 1825. A short distance further up the street to the right, is the police station building where the District Court is also held. On the south side of the police station is Slater Avenue, a short street leading to a number of factories and workshops in the rear

THE PUMPING STATION.

PAWTUCKET FALLS IN 1886.

between the street and the river. Passing down this street we soon come in sight of the old Slater Mill, erected in 1793, and the first factory for the manufacture of cotton by modern methods in America. The building as seen to-day is a modern looking wooden structure two stories and a half in height, 140 x 40 or 50 feet wide, and is situated on the river bank, the east end being close to the upper falls. Originally the old mill was a small building about forty feet long by twenty wide and two stories in height. It has been enlarged at various times by the addition in all of about eighty feet to its length, and about twenty-five feet to its width, and heightened by a half story. The limits of the original structure can yet be easily discerned through means of the old timbers, which are of oak and are roughly hewn. They are very hard and durable, and when the alterations have been made in the mill the workmen have always found it a difficult task to cut into the staunch old oaken beams. Near by the old mill is a three-story brick building, built by the original firm, Almy, Brown & Slater, and used by them as a retail store at which the country people used to exchange their butter, eggs, and poultry for yarn to be woven at home. This building is now occupied by Lyons Delany & Company as a spice mill. The old mill is still used for its original purpose, and cotton yarns, twines, and thread are manufactured on the first floor. In an adjoining building, in the office of Mr. J. L. Spencer, who operates the cotton machinery in the old mill, are some relics worth seeing. Here is the original lock of the mill door. It is eighteen inches in length, nine broad, set in oak, with an iron key nine inches in length. By turning the key once the bolt is shot out about an inch and a half, and on turning it again it is shot the same length again, making in all about three inches. In the olden time the idea seemed to be that the strength of the lock was in proportion to the weight of the key. There are a few other relics, among them being two spindles of the original machines, with their stands and fixtures.

Returning to North Main Street, let us take the first street to the left, Read Street, and going up the hill we are soon on High Street. Standing on the corner of the two streets and looking north along High Street, is seen, near at hand on the right, the unpretentious structure of the First Methodist Church; while further on to the left the brown steeple of the High School, formerly the church of the Second Baptist Society, but devoted to its present use since about 1874; and still further, on the left, the white steeple of the Church of Our Father, Universalist. Going down the street southward, the First Baptist Church, a beautiful wooden building, with a fine spire, is passed on the right, and then on the left is the substantial brick building erected in 1871 as a town record building, and now used for that purpose and for the city offices. A few steps more, down a steep incline, brings us again into Main Street Square.

Starting out of the square through Main Street to the east, the bridge is soon reached. Looking in either direction it is easy to apprehend the fact that manufacturing is carried on here extensively, as on both sides of the stream are tall buildings and factories built close to the water's edge. Looking north, the falls which give the place its name are seen almost directly under the bridge. They are formed by irregular rocky ledges, and the water boils and foams over them. A short distance above is a dam, and on the bank at its westerly end can be seen the old Slater mill with its belfry. The extensive brick factories below the bridge on the eastern bank are those of Darius Goff & Sons, manufacturers of worsted braid and mohair plushes. The wooden building between these factories and the bridge, was formerly a cotton mill, but paper is now manufactured here. Crossing the bridge to the east side, the foot of Broadway is soon reached. Let us first, however, go up Main Street, and a short walk brings us to the corner of School Street, looking down which on the right hand side is seen a low building with the name Town Hall on the front. This building was used from the creation of the town of Pawtucket in 1862, until the formation of the city, as the place of the town-meetings, and is now used as the voting place for the second ward. The adjoining building, with the words Washington Hall on the front, was the place of worship of the First Free Baptist Society until they erected their present edifice, when they sold it to the town. Just beyond School Street, on Main, is the Trinity Episcopal Church, a picturesque stone building. A few steps further, Main Street runs into Walcott, and this is the region of fine residences, which can be seen in all directions. Our progress from the bridge thus far has been up hill, indicating the excellence of the situation.

Returning towards the bridge, instead of going up Walcott Street, the junction of Walcott and Broadway is soon reached, and between the two streets stands the fine building of the Pawtucket Congregational Church. Turning into Broadway and proceeding up the street a fine view of the river and the

Exchange Street bridge to the left is had, and soon on the right the First Free Baptist Church, a tasteful wooden structure is passed. A few steps above on the opposite side of the street, at junction of Broadway and Summit Street, is the handsome residence of the Hon. H. B. Metcalf. We are now at the junction of Broadway, Summit, and Cottage streets, an extensive open space. Standing here and looking down Cottage Street and Broadway, very pleasing scenes are presented. Each street is broad, lined with trees and bordered with pleasant residences, mostly wooden structures, with ample grounds. As far as the eye can see either street extends in a straight line, diverging from the common centre where the observer stands, and the trees form an inclosing arch which makes the vista one of quiet beauty with the added air of mystery often felt when looking at anything the end of which is not in view and can only be surmised. This region of the city is the place of the finest residences, as its elevated situation makes it very desirable, and Broadway, Cottage, and Walcott streets are *par excellence* the residence section.

A VIEW OF PAWTUCKET FROM BELOW DIVISION STREET BRIDGE.

Passing up Broadway, Exchange Street is soon reached. Going down this street the works of the Rhode Island Card Board Company, Perry Oil Company, and several jewelry shops are passed on the left, and then the Exchange Street bridge is reached. From this position are seen some of the chief manufacturing establishments in the city. Northward, on the eastern bank is the large factory of Greene & Daniels, while nearer on the other bank is the Dempsey Bleachery & Dye Works. But the view is not wholly of factories, for the banks of the river are in many places clothed with trees and abound in picturesque nooks. Continuing along Exchange Street, we cross North Main Street, pass on the right corner of Hamilton Street Infantry Hall, a low wooden structure used as a drill hall by local militia, and a similar building, Armory Hall, on the corner of High Street. A short distance further and we emerge on Exchange Place at the railroad station.

Starting again from the railroad, we retrace our steps to Trinity Square, but from there turn to the right along Main Street. Here at the corner of Main and Broad streets is the terminus of the horse-car line from Providence. Before the establishment of the local lines the Providence cars ran to Main Street square, connecting there with a branch to Central Falls. A short distance up, on Bailey Street, which leads out of Main at the first turn, is the establishment of Linton Brothers & Company, card board and glazed paper manufacturers. Following the horse-car track along Main Street we turn two corners, first to the left, second to the right, still keeping on Main Street, and soon are in sight of the two mills of the Slater Cotton Company, the oldest of which was erected in 1863. Across the street, on the corner of Pine, are the extensive machine shops of James Brown. Turning up Pine Street, crossing the Providence and Worcester Railroad track, and passing the works of the Union Wadding Company on the right, the new freight station of the Providence and Worcester Railroad is reached. It is a large brick building, of ample length and width, probably the best of its kind in the state, having plenty of cartage-room around it on all sides. It was built in 1882 to meet the growing necessity for better accommodations. Beyond the freight depot the large works of the E. Jenckes Manufacturing Company, makers of belt hooks, ring travelers, and manufacturers' supplies, loom up conspicuously. Next, on the right hand side of Pine Street, is a long, low, wooden building, the works of the Pawtucket Manufacturing Company, manufacturers of bolts, nuts, washers, etc. A short distance beyond on the left is a brick building which might with truth be called elegant. It looks like a beautiful mansion

THE OLD SLATER MILL.

house. This is the office of the Conant Thread Company, and their factories, great, massive buildings, cover a large extent of ground for a long distance along Pine Street, and for an equal distance back. About half way down the front of the property of the thread works, on the opposite side of Pine Street, are the works of the Fales & Jenks Machine Company, manufacturers of cotton and woolen machinery, fire pumps, and frictional gearing.

Going up Pine Street a short distance further, we turn down Cross Street. This is in Central Falls. First on the right are a row of factory tenements. Across an

PARK PLACE CONGREGATIONAL CHURCH.

open lot to the left are the low buildings of the American File Works. A walk of about half a mile along Cross Street, through a section of residences, brings us out on Broad Street again, crossing which and continuing on we emerge on Mill Street, Central Falls, a continuation of North Main Street, Pawtucket. On the northeast corner of this street and Cross Street is the large brick factory of the Pawtucket Hair Cloth Company, extending from Mill Street to the river, and built in 1864. Cross Street leads on to the Central Avenue Bridge, which crosses the river at this point. Looking north from this bridge, on the west bank are seen, just above the hair cloth factory, the brick mill and adjoining wooden buildings of the Central Falls Woolen Company, and beyond them the brick factory of the Stafford Manufacturing Company, thread manufacturers.

Crossing the bridge we are again in the corporate limits of Pawtucket, and

TRINITY CHURCH.

passing up Central Avenue, the street leading from the bridge, the large factory of Greene & Daniels is on our right. Going up the street, the elevation called Pleasant View, on the east bank of the river, is reached. On the streets nearest the mill are factory tenements, but there are also in this section many dwellings of a better class. Traversing Pleasant View through various streets we make a circuit and come out on North Main Street, a continuation of Mill Street, Central Falls; as we descend the hill toward the bridge, in sight across the river is the large factory of the United States Cotton Company alongside the Providence & Worcester railroad track, and south of it looms up " Our Lady of the Sacred Heart," the French Roman Catholic Church, in Central Falls. The Providence Division of the Old Colony, formerly the Boston & Providence Railroad, makes a junction with the Providence & Worcester opposite the factory of the United States Cotton Company. On the right-hand side of the street approaching the bridge is Collins Brothers' Machine Shop. and on the opposite side the Eagle Dye Works. Crossing the bridge, we are again in Central Falls. Proceeding up Mill Street until Central Street is reached. let us walk up this thoroughfare. On the northeast corner of Central and Mill streets is the establishment of E. L. Freeman & Son, printers to the state, and publishers of the *Weekly Visitor*. Central Street, from Mill up to the railroad track, is the chief retail business section of Central Falls. At the further side of the track is the Central Falls station of the Providence & Worcester railroad. A short distance further up is the beautiful building of the Baptist Church, on the corner of Broad and Central streets. In this neighborhood are a number of palatial residences. Turning into Broad Street we turn toward Pawtucket; the line is soon crossed, and about half way down on the right-

THE UNIVERSALIST CHURCH.

THE OLD QUAKER MEETING-HOUSE, LINCOLN.

hand side is the Broad Street Theatre, where the polo games are played. A few steps more bring us again to our starting point, the railroad station.

Woodlawn is the name applied to the southern portion of Pawtucket on the west side. The Providence & Worcester Railroad has a station here and a branch road leads from the place to Saylesville, about three miles distant. Other localities in the city are Pleasant View, on the heights east of the river opposite Central Falls; East Pleasant View, on the northeast, near the Lebanon Mills; Dunnell's, near the print works of the name, and Ingramville, both in the southern part of the city on the east side.

Notes on some of the Industries of the City.— One of the most interesting of the special manufactures in the line of appliances for use in cotton and woolen mills is that conducted at the Excelsior Loom Reed Works, 106 Broad Street, Pawtucket. Here, by means of machines so well adapted to the end in view that they almost do the whole of the work themselves, are manufactured the Adamson flexible bevel dent reeds, reinforced with solder, and especially adapted for the weaving of fine worsteds, woolens, and fancy cotton goods. This is the only patent reed in the market, and is the property of Mr. Adamson, the owner of the establishment. No matter how often or how far the wires may be separated from each by the insertion of anything between them, they are so constructed as to immediately spring back to their original position, while the bevel on each individual wire formed thereon by the automatic machinery already mentioned lessens the strain on the warp and thereby prevents the breaking of the threads. A large number of the best cotton and woolen mills in every part of the United States constantly use this reed. Mr. Adamson also deals in belting, lace leather, pickers, heddles for woolen mills, and general mill supplies.

Among the enterprising firms of Pawtucket we note especially the Pawtucket Manufacturing Company, whose plant is located at 64 Pine Street.

This Company was incorporated by act of the General Assembly, May,
1882, for the purpose of manufacturing bolts, nuts, and machinery used in the
manufacture of the same.

Mr. Stephen A. Jenks, a prominent business man, is president, and Mr.
George H. Fowler, Treasurer.

The practical management of the business is in the hands of the agent and
superintendent, Mr. George H. Webb.   The rapid growth which has attended
this business indicates the increasing demand for goods of a superior quality.
The foundation was laid December, 1881, and the first bolt headed August 12,
1882.

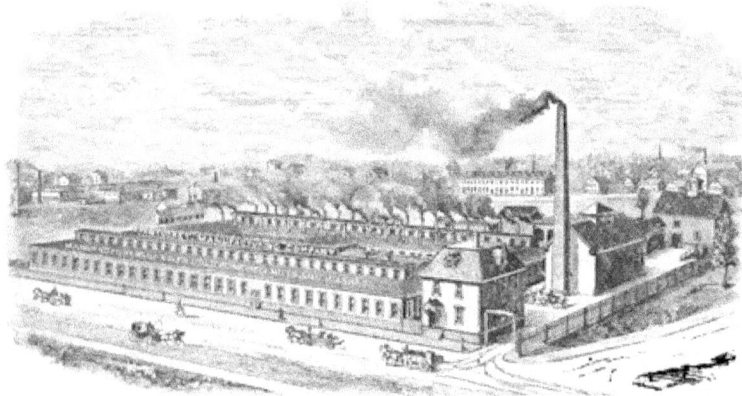

PAWTUCKET MANUFACTURING COMPANY'S WORKS.

The building, which is a model of convenience, has all departments located
on one continuous floor, originally occupying 15,400 square feet of space; but
to meet the increasing demands of the manufactures an addition of 10,000
square feet has been made during the past year, making a total of 25,400 square
feet.   It is arranged around a hollow square, in a way to secure ample light and
ventilation.

All the special machinery used was designed and built at the works, under
the direct supervision of Mr. Webb, whose extended experience and superior
ability as a mechanic enabled him to produce a class of machinery possessing
many advantages over any heretofore used.   As evidence that such is the case,
this company has furnished nearly every extensive bolt manufacturer in the
United States with some of their special machinery.   They have also made shipments to Hutchinson, Hollingsworth & Company, of Oldham, England.

This company is now engaged in the construction of a plant of ten
machines for the Amoskeag Manufacturing Company of Manchester, N. H.,
also a large press for the Knowles Loom Works of Worcester, Mass., designed
for punching sheet steel, and will weigh when completed about ten tons.   In

fact this department of their business has developed so rapidly that their present facilities are scarcely large enough to enable them to fill orders now on hand.

The bolts and nuts made by this corporation are of a superior quality and finish, and include all the regular sizes to be found in the market, besides many peculiar patterns made only to order. During the first two years after the works were established the business doubled and has since been steadily increasing.

It would repay any one to visit these works to see the various and ingenious methods employed in the process of manufacturing their regular and

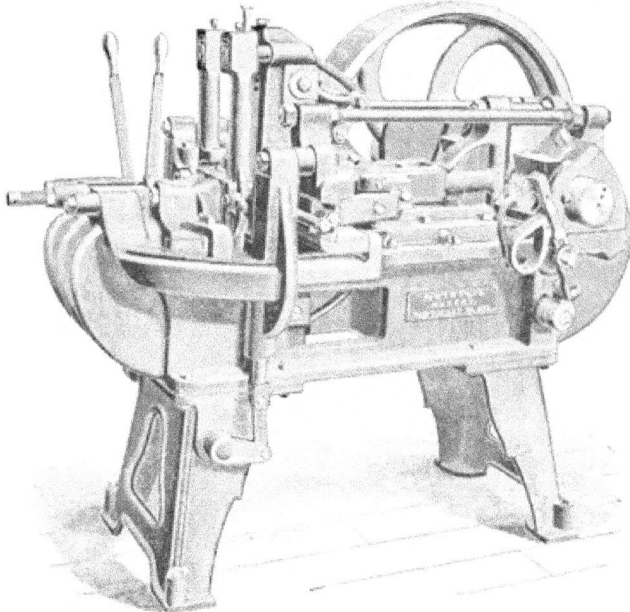

NEW SQUARE AND HEXAGON BOLT CUTTING MACHINE.

special goods, and one would be both surprised and interested to see the great variety of goods required to meet the demands of the market. Great care is exercised in selecting stock used, and every new lot of iron is tested by a hydraulic testing machine operated by power, which determines the actual tensile strength of the metal. By the same means the manufactured bolts are tested before they are put on the market. The machine originally employed for this purpose was the one in ordinary use, but it did not do the work satisfactorily, hence the requisite alterations were made to adapt it to the requirements of the business. The accompanying cut illustrates their improved machine for forging square and hexagon-headed bolts, three-fourths of an inch in diameter, and smaller. New designs are continually being turned out and already they have drawings and patterns for machines capable of heading bolts one and one-half inches in diameter. They are now working on a new illustrated chart showing the special machinery they are prepared to furnish.

Among the oldest established and best known bleacheries and dye works in
this part of the country are those of Robert D. Mason & Company, 75 East Avenue, Pawtucket. The business was first established here in 1805 by Mr. Barney
Merry, whose son, Mr. Samuel Merry, succeeded him in 1847. In 1866 Mr.
Robert D. Mason, a nephew of Samuel Merry, was admitted to partnership, and
in 1870 he assumed control as sole proprietor under the present firm name.
The business carried on is in bleaching and dyeing of spool threads, knitting
cotton, cords, braids, tapes, and all kinds of single and two-ply yarns, indigo
blues and fast blacks for milling purposes ; also, woolen and worsted yarns
and braids of every description. The works occupied for the business are
among the largest and most comprehensive of the kind in the state. The main
building is three stories in height, 100 x 70 feet in dimensions. The principal
dye-house is 150 x 70 feet, and a second dye-house is 105 x 25 feet. The capacity of the works is at present five tons per day. The machinery in use is of
the most modern and improved style that has been invented for this purpose, and
every facility is afforded for prompt, thorough, and successful work in every department. The product has always been maintained at the highest standard of
quality, and finds a ready sale and a permanent patronage wherever introduced.
A large and flourishing trade has long been enjoyed by this house in all parts
of the United States, and it has the entire confidence of its patrons to a marked
degree. Employment is given to fifty hands. The proprietor, Mr. Mason, is
a native of Pawtucket, of large and valuable experience in the business.

Among the leading manufacturers of Pawtucket is Mr. John J. Kenyon,
manufacturer of stay webbs, bindings, silk finished, plain, and fancy spool
tapes and braids for manufacturers' use. This business was first inaugurated
by Messrs. Thomas Kenyon & Son some twenty years ago, the present proprietor
succeeding to the sole control some three years later. Mr. Kenyon occupies six
floors, covering in all from eighteen to nineteen thousand feet, all fully equipped
with every modern improvement and facility in the line of machinery and
mechanical appliances for the production of first-class goods. The leading
specialties are the manufacture of silk finished, plain, and fancy spool tapes and
braids for use of manufacturers, and boot, shoe and corset lacings. In these
special branches of manufacture Mr. Kenyon has won a wide reputation for the
excellence of his product and built up a large and steadily increasing trade,
which extends throughout the New England and Western States and the Can-
adas. From 105 to 115 hands are daily employed, all skilled and experienced
in the art of manufacture, and every effort is used to produce a class of goods
which will recommend their own good qualities wherever introduced. He has
also a large trade in druggists' and other fancy twines which he manufactures.
His success in this laudable endeavor is clearly shown by the increasing demand
made for his goods throughout the country and the name and fame thereby
established for the house. Mr. Kenyon is also agent for the Pawtucket Tape
Company, a newly established firm which produces the finest line of super
tapes now on the market. Mr. Kenyon is a native of England, has resided

here for upwards of twenty-five years. and was in the Pemberton Mill at the time of its fall.

LINCOLN.

The town of Lincoln extends from Pawtucket along the western bank of the Blackstone River to Woonsocket. and contains the villages of Central Falls, Valley Falls, Lonsdale. Berkeley. Ashton, Albion, Manville, all situated on the Blackstone, and engaged in the cotton manufacture. Portions of some of these villages lie across the river in the town of Cumberland. On the Moshassuck River, a short distance west of Central Falls. is Saylesville, where are the extensive bleacheries of W. F. & F. C. Sayles. A branch railroad leads to the place from Woodlawn, the southern suburb of Pawtucket. Lincoln. according to the state census of 1885, had a population of 17,229. the largest of any town in the state. This territory was taken from Smithfield in 1871 and named in honor of Abraham Lincoln. Lime Rock, in the centre of the town, almost directly west from the village of Berkeley, has three limestone ledges, where lime-burning has been continuously carried on since the time of Roger Williams. The business is still in a flourishing condition and the supply of material is almost inexhaustible.

The Providence and Worcester Railroad runs along the Blackstone River and has stations at all the villages on its banks. The valley of the Blackstone, the chief part of which is in this town. is a beautiful region. From the train, as it follows the curves of the river, are seen a succession of pictures of wooded slopes, reaches of meadow, and glimpses of the river, with its numerous artificial waterfalls, and added to these are the villages with their factories, cottages, and churches.

THE BLACKSTONE AT LONSDALE.

Armory Hall, 79 High.
Assessor's Office, 35 High.
Benedict House, corner Main and Broad.
Broad Street Theatre, 148 Broad.
City Clerk's Office, 35 High.
City Hall, 35 High.
City Records, 35 High.
City Council Chamber, 35 High.
Court House, 73 North Main.
Cogeshall Fountain, Main Street Square.
Dexter Block, 130 to 142 Main.
Dexter Building, corner Main and East Avenue.
The Falls, at the Main Street Bridge.
High School, High street.
Infantry Hall, 74 Exchange.
Laurel Hill, east side river, off Central avenue.
Laurel Hill Park, junction Fountain and Park.
Masonic Temple, 98 North Main.
Music Hall Building, 139 to 147 Main.
Main Street Square, junction Main and North Main.
Odd Fellows Building, 235 to 231 Main.
Old Slater Mill, rear 55 North Main.
Old Town Hall, 33 School.
Pawtucket Hotel, 21 Broadway.
Police Station, 73 North Main.
Post Office, Dexter Building, corner Main and East avenue.
Probate Court, 35 High.
Steamboat Wharf, at Division Street Bridge.
Street Railway Depot, Broad, opposite Exchange.
Town Hall, Central Falls, Broad.
Trinity Square, junction Broad and Main.
Weeden Block, corner Main and Park Place.
Wilkinson Park, bounded by Park Place, Church, George Cross.
Washington Hall, School.

MANUFACTURING ESTABLISHMENTS.

American Curled Hair Co., 367 High, corner Blackstone, Central Falls.
Ætna Stopper Co., 20 River.
Bridge Mill, 64 Main.
Campbell Machine Co., 106 Broad.
Central Falls Woolen Mill, 339 Mill, Central Falls.
Conant Thread Co., Conant and Pine.
Drapery Bleachery and Dye Works, 227 North Main.
Dexter Yarn Co., 80 and 82 East avenue.
Darius Goff & Sons, 29 River.
Dunnell Print Works, 116 Prospect.
Earle Dye Works, 408 North Main.
Electric Lighting Co., The Pawtucket, 16 Wilkinson Place.
F. Jenckes Manufacturing Co., 75 and 77 Weeden.
Fales & Jenks Machine Co., 142 Dexter.
Greene Dyeing and Finishing Co., 40 and 42 Front.
Greene & Daniels Manufacturing Co., 16 Central avenue.
Hair Cloth Co., The Pawtucket, Cross, Central Falls.
James Davis Belting Co., 22, 24 and 26 Pleasant.
L. B. Darling Fertilizer Co., 290 Mineral Spring avenue.
Lebanon Mills Co., Lebanon.
Lorraine Manufacturing Co., 287 Mineral Spring ave.
New American File Co., 224 Dexter, Central Falls.
Pawtucket Gas Works.
Pawtucket Manufacturing Co., 64 Pine.
R. Bliss Manufacturing Co., 361 and 369 Main.
R. I. Card Board Co., 188 Exchange, corner Front.
Slater Cotton Co., Church and Main.
Stafford Manufacturing Co., 379 and 381 Mill, Central Falls.
United States Cotton Co., 11 Foundry, Central Falls.
Union Wadding Co., 24 Dexter, corner Weeden.
William H. Haskell Co., 277 Main.

WARD ROOMS.

First Ward — Fountain, corner Clay.
Second Ward — Old Town Hall, 33 School.
Third Ward — Police Station Building, 73 North Main.
Fourth Ward — 23 Mulberry.
Fifth Ward — 161 Pawtucket avenue.

CEMETERIES.

Mineral Spring, Mineral Spring avenue, corner Conant.
Oak Grove, North Bend.
Riverside, Pleasant, north of Swan Point.
St. Francis, Smithfield avenue, near Providence line.
Walnut Hill, opposite 47 Brook.

CHURCHES.—Pawtucket.

Broadway Christian, opposite 134 Broadway.
Calvary Baptist, 98 North Main.
Church of Our Father, High, near Miller.
Church of the Good Shepherd, Broadway, corner Woodline.
Church of the Immaculate Conception, (Roman Catholic,) Pine, corner Marion.
First Baptist, High, corner Summer.
First Methodist Episcopal, High, near Exchange.
Free Baptist, 97 Broadway.
Mission of the Advent, Pawtucket avenue, corner Trenton.
New Jerusalem, Elm.
Park Place Congregational, Park Place, near Main.
Pawtucket Congregational, junction Broadway and Walcott.
Pleasant View Baptist, Fountain, near East.
Sacred Heart of Jesus, (Roman Catholic), Park, corner Laurel.
St. Jean Baptiste, (French R. C.), Quincy avenue.
St. Joseph's, (Roman Catholic), Walcott, corner South Bend.
St. Paul's (Episcopal), Church street, corner Park Place.
Thomson M. E., Mineral Spring avenue, corner Conant.
Trinity (Episcopal), opposite 9 Main.
Woodlawn Baptist Chapel, Lonsdale avenue, corner Capital.

CHURCHES.—Central Falls.

Baptist, Broad, corner Central.
Congregational, High, corner Jenks.
Embury (Methodist Episcopal), Cross, near Hawes.
St. George's (Episcopal), Clinton, corner Central.
Our Lady of the Sacred Heart (French Roman Catholic), Fales, near Broad.

BRIDGES.

Division street.
Main street.
Exchange street.
Central avenue, from Cross street, Central Falls, to Central avenue, Pawtucket.
Mill street, from Mill street, Central Falls, to North Main street, Pawtucket.

TELEGRAPH OFFICES.

Western Union, at P. & W. R. R. Depot.
Mutual Union, 334 Main.
Pawtucket District Telegraph and Messenger Co., 9 and 11 East avenue.

NATIONAL BANKS.

First, 126 Main.
Pacific, 147 Main.
Slater, 7 East avenue.

SAVINGS BANKS.

Pawtucket Institution for Savings, 117 Main.
Providence County Savings Bank, 126 Main.
The Franklin Savings Bank, Main, corner East avenue.

FIRE STATIONS AND APPARATUS.

Washington Street, corner Brown — Steamer No. 1, Rhode Island Company.
Main Street, corner Bailey — Steamer No. 2, Rough and Ready Company; Slater Hook and Ladder Co., No. 1.
Water Street, corner Vernon — Steamer No. 3, Monitor Company.
Carnation Street — Steamer No. 4, Atlantic Company.
Pawtucket Hook and Ladder Company.

CHAPTER III.

The Town of Woonsocket.

SITUATION AND SURROUNDINGS — MANUFACTURES — EARLY HISTORY AND DEVELOPMENT — INCORPORATION — CORPORATE FACILITIES — BRIDGES — CHARACTER OF THE POPULATION — STROLLS AMONG THE FACTORIES AND ALONG THE STREETS.

MARKET SQUARE, WOONSOCKET.

SIXTEEN miles from Providence, on the Blackstone River, and one of the chief stations on the Providence and Worcester Railroad, is the town of Woonsocket, which, after Providence and Pawtucket, is the most important manufacturing centre in the state. It now has a population of nearly twenty thousand, and is the largest town in the state in point of population, — or at least, as that honor has been claimed for Lincoln, it is the largest compact community in the state or country under a town government. The Blackstone River has here a total fall of about thirty feet over three dams, and the tributary streams, the Mill and Peters, which here unite with the Blackstone, have falls respectively of sixty and fifty-two feet. These together constitute the best water-power in Rhode Island, and it is thoroughly utilized for manufacturing purposes.

The leading industry is the cotton manufacture, which is carried on in all its branches, and a larger amount of cloth is probably produced here than in any other place in the state. There are a few establishments engaged in the manufacture of yarns. The woolen manufacture is also carried on extensively. There are, besides, a variety of other manufactures, among which are those of rubber goods, knit goods, sewing machines, shuttles and bobbins.

The first settlement made at Woonsocket Falls is supposed to have been about the year 1666, when a saw mill was erected by Richard Arnold. With the beginning of the eighteenth century, the value of the water-power was seen, and various manufactures were started. Not, however, until about 1810 did the place grow to any extent. At that time the cotton manufacture was introduced, and the first mill of the Social Manufacturing Company was erected.

Since then, on account of the unrivalled water-power, the development of this and kindred manufactures has been rapid, until Woonsocket is to-day the chief place in some lines of this business in the state. In 1831, Edward Harris began the manufacture of woolen goods here, which has since grown to be the second industry in importance in the town. Mr. Harris, later in life, was instrumental in procuring a free public library for Woonsocket, and in various other ways was a public benefactor.

The name of Woonsocket was strictly applied to the compact village on the east in the neighborhood of the falls, and that side of the river was in Cumberland. In 1867, the village of Woonsocket, the neighboring village of Social, and adjoining territory, were set off from Cumberland and incorporated as the town of Woonsocket. In 1871, the west side, consisting of the villages of Globe, Bernon, and Hamlet, and neighboring regions, were set off from Smithfield and added to the town. The Blackstone River flows in a semi-circular course through the place, and the surrounding hills inclose it like an amphitheatre.

Woonsocket has a well-equipped fire department, organized in 1836, and a very efficient police force dating from 1866. The Woonsocket *Patriot*, a weekly newspaper, was started in 1833, and has been continuously published since. A daily paper, the *Evening Reporter*, has been published since 1873 and has enjoyed more than ordinary success. Horse-car lines were built in 1887, and the cars began running in August of that year. The town has seven churches of different denominations, six national and four savings banks, and a public library, and is so rapidly progressing in wealth and population, that it is but a matter of a short time before the citizens decide that it shall become the city of Woonsocket, the "spindle city" of the valley of the Blackstone.

THE HIGH SCHOOL, WOONSOCKET.

Seven highway and two railroad bridges span the Blackstone at Woonsocket, and there are besides several highway bridges over the Mill and Peters rivers. The oldest bridge is that over the river at the falls. The other bridges are the Bernon Street, the Hamlet Avenue, the Sayles Street, the River Street, and the one at Hamlet Village, besides the new one connecting Fairmount with the east side. Held back by the natural falls and by the various artificial ones, the river forms a number of ponds, the largest of which is the Bernon between the falls and the Bernon dam. On the Mill River are two large ponds called respectively the Harris and Social.

MAIN STREET AND THE PASSENGER STATION, WOONSOCKET.

WOONSOCKET FROM THE EAST.

There are said to be geological indications that the river in some far remote age flowed through the valley on the north side of the town, near the railroad. This opinion is sustained by the fact that in making excavations water worn ledges and every appearance of the ancient bed of a stream have been unearthed.

Woonsocket probably affords one of the best examples in the country of the changes that the introduction of machinery makes in the character of a population. The first settlers, and the subsequent ones for generations, were of English birth and descent. After manufacturing began to increase rapidly, from the early years of the present century onward, the general immigration brought its share to Woonsocket. About the time of the Civil War an immigration of French Canadians set in, and Woonsocket is one of the places in which they have most thickly settled. In 1880, they constituted more than one-fourth of the population; according to the state census in 1885, they still held this proportion, while there were about two hundred less of Canadian birth than in 1880, but this loss must have been by death, and would be much more than counter-balanced by the births among this class of the population, which, indeed, is clearly demonstrated by the fact that nearly five thousand of the population of native birth had both parents of foreign birth, while about eight hundred were of mixed

THE FALLS AT WOONSOCKET.

parentage.   As nearly one-half of the entire population is of foreign birth, about
five thousand more of foreign parentage, and more than eight hundred of mixed
parentage, there is only a small proportion left of the native born of Anglo-
Saxon descent.   The movement of the French Canadians to Woonsocket must
have been concluded in its large manifestations between 1875 and 1880, as
between those years they increased more than a thousand, while in 1885 persons of Canadian birth were about two hundred less than in 1880.   There is
comparatively little, consequently, of the blood of the first settlers in the community.

On account of the great number of French, their language is very generally used in the town, and the retail traders find it necessary either to speak it,
or employ French salesmen.

In order that an idea may be obtained at first hand of the character of the
place and the extent of the manufacturing, we invite the reader to take a walk
about town with us.   Of course we start from Providence, and speed up the Blackstone Valley on a Providence & Worcester railroad train, reaching Woonsocket in about three-quarters of an hour.   The train enters Woonsocket on a
high bridge over the Blackstone and an elevated way over several streets.   To
the left looking from the train we catch a glimpse of the river many feet below, and of numerous buildings and factories perched on its steep banks, and
also have a quick view of Main Street as shown in the engraving on page
93.   The station is a tasteful brick structure built in 1882, and is a story
above the street on one side.   Leaving it from the upper side we soon find our-

selves in Depot Square, formed by the junction of Main with High and Clinton streets. To the right, on the corner of High and Main streets, is the Baptist Church, and to our left Main and Clinton streets diverge, leading under the railroad tracks. The buildings around the square are three and four-story brick and wooden structures, several of which, recently erected, are tasteful and modern in design.

Proceeding up Main Street to the right. there are a number of fine brick buildings on both sides. A few steps bring us abreast of the Harris Block, a large, three-story, brick building erected in 1856, and which contains the Harris Institute Free Library, of about 10,000 volumes, the first Free Library organized in Rhode Island. The building and a library of 4,000 volumes were a gift to the town by Edward Harris, the pioneer woolen manufacturer. In this building on the ground floor is the post-office. In the next building on the left, the *Evening Reporter* and the *Weekly Patriot* are printed. Next beyond, still on the left, is the three-story brick factory occupied by the American Worsted Company. Then come the extensive factories of the Harris Woolen Company, consisting of many buildings of wood, brick, and stone, of various ages, the majority of which are on the left-hand side, but one is on the right, connected with the others by a bridge built over the street. Just beyond, and also on the left-hand side, are the connected brick and stone factories of the Lippitt Woolen Company, which extend to the corner of Bernon Street, with one factory across that street, below the corner.

Main Street here leads into Market Square, which is an open space formed by the junction of Main, South Main, Bernon, Arnold, and River streets. On the east side of this square at the foot of Arnold Street is the Woonsocket Hotel. From Depot Square to Market Square, Main Street is about a quarter of a mile long. On the opposite side from the factories are retail stores and offices, and the street runs along the brow of the high river bank. The rear of the factories reach to the edge of Clinton Pond, through which the water passes from above the falls, supplying all the factories on this side down to the Clinton

MONUMENT SQUARE.

THE BLACKSTONE AT
WOONSOCKET.

Mills. This pond and its connections make an island of the low land between it and the river, and on this territory are situated many large and small manufacturing establishments.

Leaving Market Square let us proceed down South Main Street. A few steps bring us to the extensive works of the Woonsocket Rubber Company, on the left, which consist of a number of brick and stone buildings. On the right is a large, stone cotton factory, built in 1846, and now operated by J. P. & J. G. Ray, but formerly owned by the Ballou Manufacturing Company, and known as the " White Mill." This mill stands on the river bank at the west end of the falls, and occupies the site of the saw mill and forge erected by the first settlers.

We have now arrived at the bridge. About a hundred feet above it are the falls, which are in two portions, being divided by a rocky island in the centre. At each side dams have been built, supplementing the natural advantages for the benefit of the factories, and the rocky island which divides the falls extends for about two hundred feet, the centre of the bridge resting upon it. This bridge consists of two stone arches. On the western bank, just below, are the Globe Mills, now the property of the Social Manufacturing Company. All this portion of Woonsocket across the bridge, southwest of the river, is known as the Globe, and is mainly a place of residence.

A short distance above the falls is the Sayles Street Bridge, and the houses on either side of the river above it are factory tenements. North of Globe Village, on the westerly side, is Fairmount, formerly known as Old Maid's Farm, where are the works of the Woonsocket Machine & Press Company, the Perseverance Worsted Company, and the Enterprise Mill. A new bridge, finished in 1888, connects this section with the east side of the river.

Returning to Market Square we go down Bernon Street. The wooden building at the curve of the street on the right would be taken for a church, but it is the Town Hall. Passing a number of small manufacturing establishments we soon reach the Bernon Bridge, just above which is the Bernon Dam, retaining a wide pond of the same name, extending to the falls. Crossing the bridge we are now on Bridge Street, in that part of Woonsocket known as Bernon. The river bank rises in quite a bulky hill with an easy incline, and is covered with pleasant residences and fine mansions. Turning into Front Street, the first to the left, we pass several stone factories on the bank of the river, all now the property of the Woonsocket Electric Light & Power Company, which operates its own plant in one of them, and sub-lets the others to various manufacturers. Front Street here leads along the brow of the high river bank; it is wide, and is lined on the side nearest the river with a magnificent row of elm trees.

As we emerge on Hamlet Avenue, almost in front of us is St. James Episcopal Church, a brown, wooden edifice. Looking up Hamlet Avenue from this point, two blocks above, the large brick structure of the French Roman Catholic Church looms up conspicuously. Hamlet Avenue is so named from the village of Hamlet about half a mile to the southeast at the end of the avenue, where there is a small cotton mill and a little hamlet of factory tenements.

Turning into Hamlet Avenue, we pass down the hill, and soon reach the Hamlet Avenue Bridge, crossing which we walk along beside the elevated tracks of the railroad, and soon emerge on Clinton Street, near Depot Square. From Hamlet Avenue and bridge fine views of the river and of other portions of Woonsocket are obtained.

Leaving Depot Square let us pass up Main Street to the north. We immediately pass under the railroad, and are in among the retail stores again. A short distance up the street on the left is the Methodist Episcopal Church, and almost opposite just a few steps further up, on the corner of Church Street, is the Universalist Church. A few steps further bring us out on Monument Square, a large, open space, where Main, North Main, and Social streets, and several lanes converge. In the centre of the square is the Soldiers' Monument, standing in a circular, railed plat. It consists of a square granite column, surmounted by the figure of a soldier, and appropriately inscribed. Fronting on the square is the Monument House, a large hotel, consisting of several connected buildings. From Monument Square, past Depot Square, to Market Square, Main Street extends, and contains the principal retail business of the town. This portion of the town is the original village of Woonsocket.

On North Main Street just beyond the Monument House, the new Opera House is in process of construction. It will be one of the handsomest buildings of its kind in the state. The front elevation is 58 feet, and the same in width, and will be constructed in modern style. The whole building will be 58 x 172 feet, with a large auditorium containing two galleries, the whole capable of seating 1,300 persons. The structure is expected to be completed Sept. 1, 1888. Two streets above, corner North Main and Daniels. is the St. Charles Catholic Church, a substantial, stone edifice. A few steps further North Main Street crosses the New York & New England Railroad, and on either side of the tracks are a number of establishments engaged in the manufacture of shuttles. spools. bobbins, and other mill supplies. A short distance above, near the railroad, is the Harris Woolen Mill at the Privilege. This is a large, brick factory, and is one of the largest woolen factories in the country. It is situated on Mill River, and the name is derived from the water privileges owned on the river by this company.

Leaving Monument Square by Social Street, on the right are the works of the Bailey Wringing Machine Company. About a quarter of a mile beyond we reach the Social Mill, a large brick cotton factory, built in 1874 on the site of the first cotton mill in Woonsocket. On the left, as we approach the mill, is an elegant brick building containing the offices of the Social Manufacturing Company, which owns and operates this mill, the Nourse Mill, and the Globe Mills. Fronting the Social Mill, across Social Street, are rows of brick tenement houses, extending down First, Second, and Third streets to Clinton Street, on the opposite side of which, and on the bank of the river, is the Nourse Mill, a fine brick structure, erected in 1882. The Social and Nourse mills each have two towers, on one of which is a clock, and on the other a wind indicator. These mills and their tenements are in excellent condition, and the houses are tasteful and beautiful buildings, much in contrast to the ordinary factory dwellings. Passing down Second we turn into Clinton Street, and return along the river, on the way passing the Clinton Mills on the left, and soon again emerge on Depot Square.

The question of the adoption of a city charter will be submitted to the electors at the presidential election in November. This matter, as well as the setting apart of Northern Rhode Island into a separate county with Woonsocket as the seat of justice, is exciting much local interest and discussion, and indications are not wanting that both these objects will be realized in the near future. There are movements on foot having in view the construction of a railroad from Woonsocket to Attleboro. and one from Woonsocket to a point in North Smithfield, to connect with the Providence and Springfield Railroad.

In other respects Woonsocket is showing commendable enterprise, a good example of which is the experiment with an electric motor on its street cars. With its excellent facilities, for a place of its size and the spirit of progress manifested, Woonsocket is bound to increase in business and wealth and to attract an intelligent and industrious population, so that the future will see it a growing and prosperous city.

W. of C.

THE STRANGERS' GUIDE—WOONSOCKET.

POINTS OF INTEREST.

Agricultural Fair Grounds.
American Worsted Co.'s Building, 127 to 143 Main.
Armory Hall, 62 Arnold.
Arnold Dr. Seth Medical Corporation.
Ballou Mill, South Main, near Bridge.
Bernon southern part of Woonsocket.
Base Ball Grounds, foot Canal street.
Depot Square, junction High and Main, at railroad station.
District Court, 239 Main.
Fairmount, on west side of river, north of the Globe.
Foss Memorial Building, 183 and 185 Main.
Globe Mills, west of Bernon Pond, Front street, Globe Village.
Globe Village, southwest portion of town.
G. A. R. Hall, 198 Main.
Hamlet Village, to the southeast of main town.
Hamlet Mill, at Hamlet Village.
Harris Hall, 155 Main.
Harris Institute Free Library, 155 Main.
Harris Block, 161 to 165 Main.
Harris Woolen Mill at Privilege.
Lyceum Hall, 155 Main.
L'Institute Canadien, 16 Main.
Music Hall, 42 Main.
Market Square, junction Arnold, Main, South Main and Bernon.
Monument Square, junction Main, South Main and Social.
National Globe Bank Building, 2 to 6 Main.
Jenksville, east of Social.
Privilege Village, north of Social.
Post Office, 159 Main.
Patriot Building, 171 to 181 Main.
Poor Farm, Fairmount.
Social Mill, Social street, Social village.
Social Hall, 79 Social.
Social Village, north of the river and a short distance west from the railroad station.
St. George's Hall, 185 Main.
St. Jean Baptiste Hall, 239 Main.
Street Railway Station, 294 Main.
Temple of Honor Hall, 191 Main.
Telegraph Office (Western Union), Providence & Worcester Railroad depot.
Telephone Office, 239 Main, room 12.
Woonsocket Agricultural Society.
Woonsocket Hospital, Cass road, near Cumberland st
Woonsocket Business Men's Association, 177 Main.
Woonsocket Opera House, 5 to 11 North Main.
Young Men's Christian Association, Unity Building, Main, corner Clinton.

MANUFACTURING ESTABLISH-
MENTS.

American Worsted Co., 123 Main.
Bailey Wringing Machine Co., 38 Social.
Clinton Manufacturing Co., 45 Clinton.
Dr. Seth Arnold Medical Corporation, 72 Park avenue.
Eagle Mills, 7 Clinton.
Glenark Knitting Co., 67 South Main.
Globe Mills, Globe Village.
Harris Woolen Co., mills at 73 Main, and at the Privilege.
Leicester Knitting Mills, 50 Bernon.
Lippit Woolen Co., 9 Bernon.
Nourse Mill, Clinton street.
Perseverance Worsted Co., 251 River.
Relief Washing Machine Co., 65 Arnold.
Social Mill, Social street, Social Village.
Valley Falls Co., 31 Front.
Woonsocket Electric Machine and Power Co., 33 and 35 Front.
Woonsocket Gas Co., 166 Main.
Woonsocket Machine and Press Co., 101 Second ave.
Woonsocket Rubber Co., 52 South Main.
Woonsocket Spool and Bobbin Co., 70 and 72 Pond.
Woonsocket Worsted Mill, 264 River.

BRIDGES.

Main Street, South Main, just below falls.
Bernon, from Bernon to Bridge street.
Hamlet Avenue, west of railroad bridge.
Sayles Street, north of the falls.
River Street, from Fairmount, east of railroad.
Fairmount bridge (new), between Sayles and River Street bridges.
Cumberland Road bridge, at Hamlet Village.

CHURCHES.

Baptist, Main, corner High.
Congregational, South Main, corner Pleasant.
First Presbyterian, Lyceum Hall, 155 Main.
French Baptist, Main, corner High.
French Catholic, Carrington avenue, corner Park ave.
Methodist Episcopal, Main, opposite Church.
Second Advent, Park avenue, junction Greene.
Society of Friends, near Union Village.
St. Charles Catholic, North Main, corner Daniels.
St. James Episcopal, Hamlet avenue.
Universalist.

PUBLIC SCHOOLS.

High, Boyden.
Consolidated, Boyden.
Grove Street.
Providence Street.
North Main Street.
Constitution Hill, Hope.
Jenckesville (new).
Jenckesville (old), Social Street.
Arnold Street.
Summer Street.
High Street.
Fairmount, Second avenue.
Park Avenue.
Clinton, near Clinton Mills.
Hamlet, at Hamlet Village.
Union District.

CATHOLIC.—Parochial Schools.

French Parish, Carrington avenue, corner Park ave.
Les Dames de Jesus Marie, convent and academy, 43 Hamlet avenue.
St. Bernard, convent and academy, 33 Earle.
St. Charles, Earle, corner of Daniels.
St. Michaels, 59 River.

NEWSPAPERS.

Evening Reporter (Daily), 143 Main.
Woonsocket Patriot (Weekly), 143 Main.
Newton's Textile Gazette, 226 Main.

FIRE STATIONS AND APPARATUS.

Bernon Street, Steamer No. 1, and horse hose reel, 16 men.
At Social, in Mill yard, Steamer No. 2, and horse hose reel, 16 men.
Near Monument Square, Steamer No. 3, and hose wagon, with 600 feet hose, 16 men.

STAGES.

Blackstone and Woonsocket Omnibus, 20 Main, two trips daily.
Slatersville and Woonsocket Stage, two trips daily, and extra one Saturday night.

NATIONAL BANKS.

First, 166 Main.
Citizens, 86 Main.
Globe, 8 Main.
Union, 148 Main.
Producers, 195 Main.
Woonsocket, 166 Main.

SAVINGS BANKS.

Mechanics, 6 Main.
People's, 166 Main.
Producer's, 195 Main.
Woonsocket Institution for Savings, 166 Main.

PART SECOND.

CHAPTER I.

Along Shore.

CAPTAIN WILLIAM WINSLOW
The Pioneer Proprietor of Rocky Point.

EXTENDING northward about thirty miles into the State of Rhode Island is Narragansett Bay, on the shores of which are the chief towns and cities of the state, and the history of Rhode Island may be said to have transpired on its waters and along its shores. The bay occupies nearly two hundred and fifty square miles — about one-fifth of the entire area of the state — and its shores are much indented with inlets and coves, while it is thickly studded with large and small islands. The largest is Rhode Island, at the mouth of the bay, on the southern extremity of which the city of Newport is situated. The state takes its name from this island. Providence and Pawtucket are at the head of the bay to the north, and Fall River to the northeast, while along the shores and on inlets and coves are many smaller towns, villages, and summer resorts; and on eligible situations, both on islands and mainland, are many hotels, places of entertainment or recrea-tion, and beautiful summer homes.

The fisheries of Narragansett Bay is one of the important interests of the state. In 1885 there was $688.838 invested in the business, 1,373 persons employed, and to carry on the work 14 steamers, 66 schooners, 312 sloops and sail-boats, and 908 row-boats were used. Food fish caught amounted to 6,181,-108 pounds, valued at $228.630; 65,485 bushels of clams were dug, valued at $60,807; 17,994 bushels of quahaugs, valued at $16,461; 34,608 bushels of scallops were caught, valued at $18,342; 320,059 bushels of oysters were taken up, valued at $422,863 : 449,815 pounds of lobster were caught, valued at $23,357 — thus making the total value of all shell-fish $542,296.

The oyster is a natural habitat of the bay, and those native in the upper waters have always been in great demand on account of their excellent quality. A large area of the shoals of the upper portion of the bay is devoted to the cultivation of the oyster. These beds belong to the state, and are in charge of a commissioner and two assistants, under whose direction they are leased to persons desiring to use them, and all details of the business and of the leases are strictly regulated by law. A uniform rent of $10 per acre is charged, and in the year 1887 about eight hundred acres were let at this figure; about one hundred acres are leased in water over twelve feet deep at high tide, at a dollar an acre, for the purpose of planting seed oysters. The state began leasing these beds about 1850 and the first few years the income was very small, being inside of $100 annually, but it steadily increased until in 1885 it amounted to $11,920, leaving a net income to the state of something over $10,000. Since that time a number of oyster beds have been abandoned, mainly because of the failure of the Virginia oysters which were transplanted here in the spring and taken up in the fall, and were usually placed in shoal water inside the six-foot line, where it is not safe to place the native oysters on account of the danger from ice in winter. A number of localities are reserved by law as free oyster beds, and in certain sections beds in-shore cannot be leased because of the interference with the clam and quahaug digging. Under the old charter and laws of the state the inhabitants of the state had an inalienable right to the fisheries on the bay and shores, and this made all the land between high and low water mark common property. The amendments made to the fishery laws from time to time have been mostly directed to the preservation and definition of these rights. The constitution of 1842 specially declared in the seventeenth section of the first article that the people were to continue in the enjoyment of the rights of fishery and of the shore they had enjoyed under the charter.

Clam and quahaug digging, because of the shores being thus free to the people, are carried on by a great many persons as a business on their own account. The shores of East Providence and Warwick have the largest amount of territory available for these pur-

CAPTAIN GEORGE H. KELLEY.
Of the Continental Line.

COLONEL S. S. ATWELL.
Of Field's Point

FIELD'S POINT

poses. Scallop fishing is also carried on by the same class of persons extensively, but as boats are necessary to take these shell-fish, more capital is required, and the business is being developed into one in which men are employed
instead of working for themselves.   Greenwich Bay is the principal fishing
ground for scallops, and by law no part of this bay can be leased for oyster
beds.

A great deal of work has been done by the United States Government in
deepening the channel in the upper part of the. bay.   The work was begun in
1851 and has been carried on at intervals since then, as appropriations have been
made for the purpose.   As a result, the ship-channel from Fox Point to Conimicut Point has been increased in depth from four and one-half to twenty-five
feet at mean low water.   According to the plans of the United States engineers
it is intended ultimately to form a channel 300 feet in width, 25 feet deep in
centre, and of less depth toward the sides, from Fox Point to the deep waters
of the bay.   As a consequence of work already done, vessels of the deepest
draught can now come up the bay to Providence, and everything is therefore
ready in that respect for the long-talked-of foreign commerce.

In the summer, the shores of Narragansett Bay have great attractions, not
only for the residents of the city and state, but for visitors from other states.
The great moving cause impelling people to
come here is the famous Rhode Island clam-
bake, but the character of the bay itself —
its smooth waters, beautiful inlets, coves, and
shores, with, in many cases, splendid opportunities for sailing and fishing, also draw many
visitors, and all these characteristics taken
together make the resorts on the bay popular,
and have tended to build up many places
devoted to the entertainment of the public.
During the season, which begins late in June
and continues until the middle of September,
steamers ply from Providence and Pawtucket
to all the shore places.

CAPT. J. A. PETTY,
Of Steamer " Queen City

CAPTAIN A. M. CLARK.
Of the Continental Line.

CAPTAIN G. W. CONLEY.
Of Steamer G. W. Danielson.

Across the See-
konk River from
Providence is the
town of East Prov-
idence, which ex-
tends along the east
shore of the bay to
Bullock's Point, six
miles from the city.
The compact place
formerly called
Watchemoket, but
now generally
known as East
Providence, is an important residence suburb of the city, and has largely
increased in size and population since the completion of the new Washington Bridge and the establishing of the horse-car line in 1883. It is the
largest place in the town and is connected with the city by the Washington and
Red bridges. The majority of the popular resorts on the bay are on the shores
of East Providence. From Providence Harbor the whole shore is a succession
of high bluffs, alternating with coves, headlands, and rocky islands, with sandy
beaches at the foot of the bluffs, and throughout the whole extent is occupied by
summer cottages, boarding-houses, and hotels, perched in advantageous situations
all along shore. The Providence, Warren and Bristol Railroad skirts the shore
until some distance beyond Silver Spring, and has a station there and at Riverside. The resorts on this shore are Squantum (club), Vue de L'Eau (club),
Golden Spring, Silver Spring, Pomham (club), Riverside, Camp White, Bullock's Point, and Crescent Park.

FIELD'S POINT.

The first shore resort reached from Providence is Field's Point, two miles
below the city, situated on a sandy tongue of land extending into the water from

SQUANTUM, EAST PROVIDENCE.

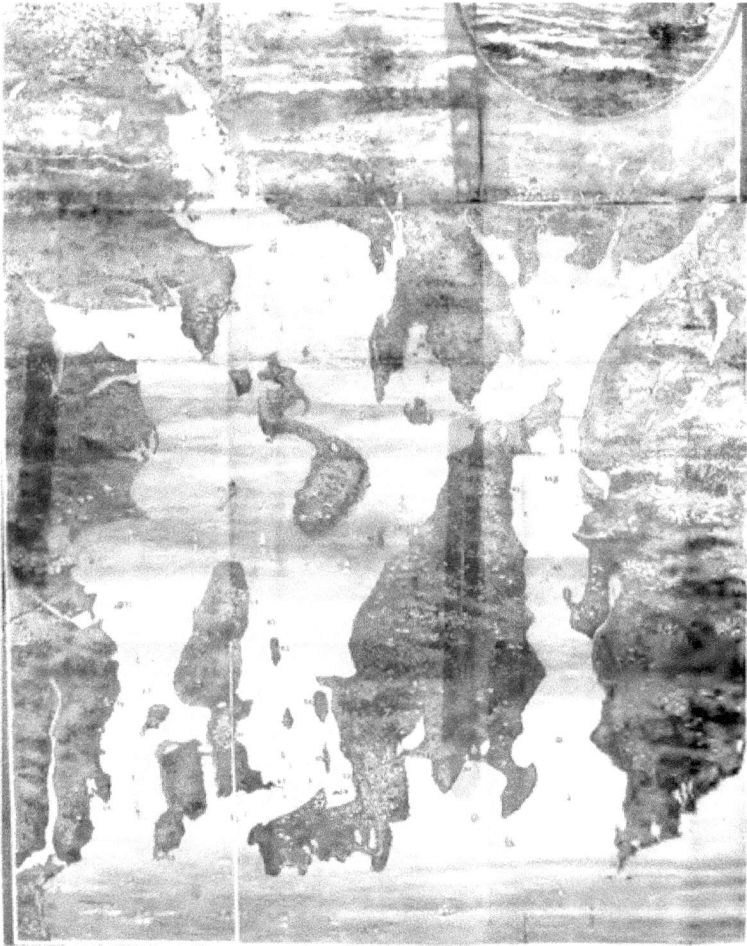

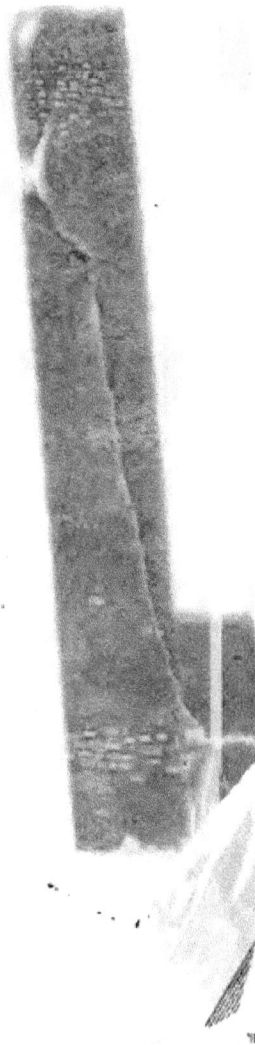

the high bluffs on the western shore, which forms a natural breakwater for Providence Harbor. The " Point " is one of the oldest resorts on the bay, and from its nearness to the city has always been a very popular place for shore dinners. On its further side, the bay widens out, and is here faced like the harbor by high bluffs, surmounted by a number of summer cottages commanding excellent views of the bay and the city. The estate of about thirty-eight acres, at the extremity of the Point, belongs to the city.

Colonel S. S. Atwell, of Providence, secured the lease of Field's Point in 1887 from the city council, for five years, and opened it to the public for his

HIRAM MAXFIELD.
A Famous Shore " King "

second season early in June. He has repainted the buildings, renovated the premises and grounds generally, erected a new telephone line to the city, and made the Point more attractive and popular with shore parties, excursionists, visitors, and patrons, than ever before.

" Starve Goat Island " with its low cottage, is located just south of Field's Point and around this island is Great Bed, the first and now one of the largest of the oyster " farms." Fuller's Rock Light-house is directly opposite the Point near the eastern shore.

SQUANTUM.

A short distance below Field's Point, on the opposite side of the river, is a rocky promontory surmounted by a number of red-roofed and picturesque buildings, and with a small wharf for a landing. This is the property of the Squantum Club, an association of Rhode Island gentlemen who monopolize the seclusion this spot affords for the especial purpose of enjoying a regular weekly clam-bake every Wednesday afternoon during the shore season. Stockholders and invited guests from abroad are alone entitled to the privileges and immunities of the club. The ladies of the proprietors and their guests are invited to monthly entertainments. The " Squantum " is the first shore club originated in this section, if not the first in the country, and has always maintained a select membership and a very high reputation. These grounds are accessible by steamer, railroad, and by carriage.

CAPT. JESSE MOTT,
Of the Providence & Stonington Line.
x

VUE DE L'EAU.

CAPT. EZRA GIFFORD.

Of the Shore Transportation Company.

Just beyond Squantum and situated on a slight elevation on the eastern shore, its pleasant undulating grounds facing the west, well-covered and ornamented by shade trees of native growth, is the Vue De L'Eau Club House. Formerly this was a popular public shore resort known as Ocean Cottage, but of late years it has been occupied by this club, a company of gentlemen similar to the Squantum, and like them it has a weekly clam-bake prepared here for members and invited guests. It can be reached from the Silver Spring station on the Providence, Warren & Bristol Railroad, by the boats to Silver Spring landing, or by carriage.

SILVER SPRING.

By this euphonious title was the next place on the eastern shore christened by Hiram Maxfield when he first set up there as a shore caterer, in 1869, and gave it a popularity as a first-class shore resort which it has ever since sustained, and under the excellent management of the present proprietor, H. P. Bliss, has been greatly improved in many respects. The spacious and conspicuous dining-hall standing on the bold rocky shore with the neat white adjoining buildings indicate the character and cleanliness of this establishment inside and out. The table service here is all performed by colored waiters, and the utmost care and attention is bestowed upon patrons, and the service approaches very near the modern hotel style. Back from the shore the diversified scenery presents hill and vale, rocks and trees in great variety, while artistic cottages with their pleasant piazzas are perched on the cliffs, the whole presenting many attractions few shore places can equal. There is a station of the Providence, Warren and Bristol Railroad here, just at the entrance to the grounds, and the steamers stop here.

MAXFIELD'S.

Just north of Silver Spring is a range of buildings of a golden canary color, where for several seasons past clam dinners have been served, and the place was known as Golden Spring, but this year has been rechristened Maxfield's. The present season the buildings have been renovated and are under the charge of Charles T. Maxfield, son of Hiram Maxfield. A landing at which the boats of the Continental Steamboat Company stops projects from the building.

POMHAM CLUB HOUSE.

Off the east shore, a short distance below Silver Spring, are Pomham Rocks, named after an Indian chief who was killed in 1676. Opposite them rises a high bluff, the highest point of land on the east side of the river, with

the exception of Fox Hill overlooking Providence Harbor. On this eminence now
stands the picturesque red-roofed Queen
Anne building of the Pomham Club, which
was built in 1887, and opened June 7th of
that year. The building is 110 feet long
by 47 wide, two stories in height, its found-
ations are 75 feet above high water-mark, its
upper balcony 90 feet, and the seats on the

H. P. BLISS, OF SILVER SPRING
Proprietor of Silver Spring.

tower 115 feet. On this account splendid views of the bay and shores can be
obtained from the house, especially
from the tower. The club is similar
to the two others further up the shore,
being an exclusive organization of men
of wealth for social purposes. Its membership is limited to 150. The Providence, Warren and Bristol Railroad
skirts the foot of the bluff, and trains
stop at a small station here when they
have on board any passengers for the
club house. Directly in front are the
two principal Pomham rocks, and on
one of them is a government light-
house, known as Pomham Rock Light.

RIVERSIDE.

Just beyond the Pomham Club
House the bluff along shore is crowned
with summer
residences ex-
tending from
the steamboat
landing for
half a mile or
more, forming
the largest resi-
dence summer
resort near Prov-
idence. The

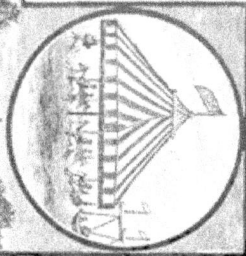

SILVER SPRING — H. P. BLISS, PROPRIETOR.

River View Park House, the large hotel on the bluff at the head of the wharf, furnishes shore dinners in excellent style. Riverside was formerly known as Cedar Grove, and was fitted up for a public resort about 1867, when a long wharf was built out to deep water as a landing for excursion steamers, and a large hotel was built which was afterwards removed bodily to Nantucket. Tents and cheap, tasteful cottages then lined the shores, but of late years these and other transient features have been replaced with a better class of houses, and the place put on a more permanent aspect, until now between two and three hundred families make this their permanent residence, and Riverside is a rapidly growing and thriving community with churches, schools, libraries, and other permanent facilities. The Warren and Bristol division of the Old Colony Railroad has a station here.

BULLOCK'S POINT.

Next below Riverside, and about two miles further south, on the eastern shore, is Bullock's Point, a fine, airy place, beautifully located on an elevated neck of land surrounded by water on all sides except the north. This place has acquired and sustained for years a great reputation for its clam-bakes and shore dinners, and is well provided with other attractions in the shape of a fine dance hall, swings, and an elevated railroad. A large and beautiful pine grove on the premises affords a fine camping place for fishing and shore parties to pitch their tents, and its beach is one of the best on the bay for bathing facilities. On the bluffs along the shore between Bullock's Point and Riverside, singly and in groups, are a large number of summer cottages and boarding-houses, including "Camp White," "Cherry Grove," "Sabin's Point," and others. The What Cheer House, a good hotel, conducted by James E. Woodward, is situated near the head of the wharf at the Point.

CRESCENT PARK.

This is the newest of the many shore places on the bay, and was opened in 1886 by George Boyden. It is very pleasantly located at the head of Crescent Cove, just east of and about three minutes' walk from the steamboat landing at Bullock's Point, over a firm and easy plank walk. The park embraces nearly one hundred acres of land, with ample room and every facility for suitably accommodating encampments, excursions, base-ball, foot-ball, cricket, or other clubs and private parties. On the grounds is a large dance hall, 30 x 100 feet, the largest on the eastern shore, entirely surrounded by a broad and airy piazza, with a large room on the second floor for the special use of musicians with excursions or with other companies.

PAWTUXET.

On the west side of the bay opposite Riverside and Bullock's Point is the ancient, quaint, bay-side village of Pawtuxet, located at the mouth of the Pawtuxet River, about four miles south of the city. It is one of the oldest places in the state, having been settled four years after Providence, and but few changes or improvements were made there for years, until recently it has become a favorite place for summer residence.

The mouth of the river forms a small harbor, separated from the bay by the peninsula of Pawtuxet Neck, which shoreward is now nearly all occupied by elegant summer residences erected within the last few years. Seen from the bay or opposite shores. Pawtuxet presents one of the most attractive and picturesque features of the entire western shore. The celebrated Gaspee Point lies a short distance south, where, on the night of June 10. 1772, the British armed schooner cruiser *Gaspee* was captured and burned by a party of dis-

CAPTAIN J. P. TAYLOR,
Superintendent Continental Line

guised Providence and Bristol men, who rowed to her in boats with muffled oars as she lay hard aground on the point. Further down the shore is Turtle Cove and "Mark Rock," formerly a very noted place for shore and picnic parties.

RHODE ISLAND YACHT CLUB.— At the elbow or northern end of Pawtuxet Neck. apparently seated right in the water, is the picturesque house of the Rhode Island Yacht Club. The house is built on Big Rock, a large, irregular mass a short distance from the shore. and is supported thereon by solid iron pillars. It is a two-story structure with deep balconies on both stories : and a graceful tower on the bay-side adds greatly to its picturesque appearance. It is reached from the shore by a foot bridge.

The club was organized in the winter of 1886, and in February. 1887. the first election of officers was held. The Pawtuxet regattas in 1885 and 1886 gave the impetus which resulted in the club's formation, as the fact was thereby shown that sufficient interest existed to sustain such an organization. The charter of the old Providence Yacht Club was obtained. amended. and used to organize

CAPTAIN S B. RHODES.
Continental Steamboat Company.

under, in order to save time. The new club is not, however, a revival of the old one, but a new organization throughout. with new constitution and by-laws. The present membership is over 500 and the number of boats owned by club members is about 80.

BARRINGTON — NAYATT.

South from the territory of East Providence. its coast line on the bay extending from Bullock's Point to Rumstick Point, at the mouth of the Warren River, is the town of Barrington. an extensive territory inhabited almost wholly by summer residents and fishermen. The Barrington River, a narrow tidal basin, unites with the Warren River at the town of that name, and makes up into the country in a northwesterly direction, setting off the larger portion of Barrington into a peninsula from two to three miles wide and about five miles long. The whole territory is level. in its limits there are no large villages, and the communities that do exist are composed of residences widely separated from each other. This circumstance, together with the beauty of the country and the general well-to-do looks of the dwellings, makes a succession of pictures of rural contentment unequaled anywhere in the state. On the bay-side are many summer residences, the majority of which are in two groups. The Warren & Bristol Division of the Old Colony Railroad runs through the centre of the town, and affords reasonably good access to the chief localities from the three stations of Drownville, Nayatt, and Barrington.

Drownville, just across Bullock's Cove from Bullock's Point, is a community composed of some dozens of residences scattered over a wide area, and is inhabited by many summer residents, although a number of Providence business men live here all the year round. On the shore are a number of oyster depots, as some of the chief oyster banks in the state are located off these shores.

Beyond Drownville, southward, is the summer seaside village of Anawomscutt, one of the prettiest little settlements of the kind to be met with anywhere. It consists of about a dozen houses, all standing in a row on a bank facing the bay, not more than twenty yards distant from high-water mark. Between the houses and the shore is a grassy lawn, and an asphalt walk runs the whole length of the settlement in the middle of this lawn, while other paths lead from the houses down to the shore. A sea wall six or eight feet in height protects this lawn and bank from the tide, and on the wall and beneath it are several isolated and artistic bathing-houses. No fences separate these dwellings from each other, so that they form a compact little community. The beach is a smooth stretch of level sand, but on account of the gentle incline there is not sufficient water for comfortable bathing unless when the tide is full.

The most important place in Barrington is Nayatt Point, where there are many fine villas, the residences of wealthy people. The Point is a headland forty or fifty feet above the sea, and by comparison with the surrounding low country is quite elevated, for this reason being also called Nayatt Hill. It faces on the bay west and south, and is the most beautiful spot in the town. The houses are perched on the bold shores, on the most picturesque sites ; they are located on fine avenues, surrounded by well-kept lawns, and embowered in trees. These fine residences are quite close together and form a pleasant little village (if it is correct to call this elegant community by such a common name). and more than any other place in the state, it seems like a detached part of Newport. Nayatt forms a complete antithesis to another seaside village ten miles distant across the bay. "Scallop Town," East Greenwich's suburb, sits like a slattern on and in the water, consists of dingy, tumble-down hovels, and is the abode of poor fishermen : Nayatt perched above the water, overlooks the bay like a queen, her houses are palaces, and her inhabitants are the wealthy, the educated, and the powerful.

Conimicut Point is opposite Nayatt, and directly south the bay expands to more than twice its previous width, measuring from Poppasquash Neck on the east opposite Bristol to the extremity of Greenwich Bay about ten miles.

Barrington Centre, a scattered looking village, a little over a mile from Warren, is the chief place in the town, and during the winter and spring of 1888, a fine new town building was erected here about a quarter of a mile from the railroad station. It is a modern looking structure, in the prevailing styles of architecture, with turrets and gables, and from the train presents a very fine appearance. It has ample accommodations for town offices, and has besides a hall for meetings or entertainments, and accommodations for a school.

GEORGE BOYDEN.
Proprietor of Crescent Park

WARREN.

Warren is a pleasant place of about four thousand inhabitants, situated on the Warren River, an inlet on the east side of Narragansett Bay. It is laid out along the east side of this inlet, which here forms a good harbor. Above the town, the river divides into two portions which run up into the country several miles, the most northerly being known as the Barrington and the other as the Palmer River, and into these tidal basins small fresh-water streams empty. The main streets of Warren run north and south parallel with the river, and are intersected by cross streets running up from the water's edge. The streets are lined with trees, mostly elms, which afford a pleasant shade and add much to the appearance of the place in summer. There are five churches in the town, the largest being the Baptist, a substantial stone edifice with a square tower and clock, which is conspicuous from the train as it approaches from Providence. On Main Street are several fine buildings, the best and latest of which is the

NAYATT POINT.

new stone structure of the George Hail Free Library. The chief industry is
the cotton manufacture, carried on by the Cutler Manufacturing Company and
the Warren Manufacturing Company, each of which has large factories. The
operatives are mostly French-Canadians, and they constitute about twenty per
cent. of the population.

Many people of small means live retired in Warren, and during the warm
weather it is patronized, to some extent, as a summer resort on account of its
fine harbor and the opportunities for sailing and fishing. Palmer River is the
only water-way in the state that runs shad. Extensive reaches of the river above
Warren are staked with traps for these fish, and in a deep pool at Shad Factory
is their favorite spawning place. Along the shore of the territory of Warren
are some of the best beds of oysters in the state. In 1885, the value of the oysters obtained off the Warren shores, mostly in the Kickemuit River, was more
than half of the entire product of the state. Two branches of the now consolidated Old Colony Railroad system make a junction at Warren, constituting
it thereby the most important way-station between Providence, Fall River, and
Newport.

The earliest settlement of the English on the shores of Narragansett Bay is
said to have been at Warren, where a trading-post was established many years
before Roger Williams settled Providence. The town met with great losses in
her commercial and ship-building interests during the Revolutionary War, and
afterward became a prominent whaling port. The name " Warren " was given
to the town early in its history, in honor of Admiral Sir Peter Warren, who
had commanded an English fleet in some important engagements.

BRISTOL.

Four miles south from Warren is the town of Bristol, one of the most beautiful places, not only in Rhode Island, but in New England. It lies on the east
shore of Narragansett Bay, fronting a capacious harbor, which is inclosed from
the bay by an arm-like peninsula known by the Indian name, Poppasquash
Neck. The town is situated on the east side of its fine harbor and extends along
the water about a mile, and back up a gentle slope half a mile. The streets are
wide, crossing each other at right angles, and are nearly all lined with rows of
large elm trees, forming in the summer magnificent arcades with leafy arches
and majestic colonnades. Many people of small means, or of inherited wealth
make Bristol their home, and it is resorted to probably more than any other
place in the upper bay as a summer residence. Many fine public buildings and
several handsome churches adorn its streets, while mansion houses and modest
private residences constitute the bulk of its dwellings. The factory tenement
hardly exists in the place, and the proportion of persons of native birth has
always been much larger here than in most of the other manufacturing towns in
the state. Bristol is the terminus of the Warren and Bristol Division of the
Old Colony Railroad and is connected thereby with both Providence and Boston, while direct communication is had by steamer with Providence and Fall
River.

In the early years of this century, Bristol had considerable foreign commerce which continued until about 1840. Manufacturing was first introduced about 1825.

Bristol's fine harbor made it a convenient place for factories, and several large establishments were founded here. For several years a line of large steamers running to New York City made Bristol their eastern port of departure, but in 1869 they were sold to the Old Colony Railroad Company and transferred to Fall River.

Thames Street, running along the water front, is lined on the side nearest the harbor with the majority of the industrial establishments in the town. The large brick factory near the railroad station is the Phenix Sugar Refinery, which has been idle for the last twelve or fifteen years. Next comes the Namquit Mill, engaged in cotton manufacture, and at the end of the street are the brick cotton mills of the Reynolds Manufacturing Company, which have been idle for a number of years. Besides these are many smaller establishments. Hope Street, next above Thames, is the chief thoroughfare of the town, and is a magnificent broad avenue lined with overarching elms. The buildings of the Roger's Free Library, the Burnside Memorial, St. Michael's Church and Chapel, are all on this street, and are excellent specimens of architecture. Next above Hope is High Street, so called from the fact that it runs along the summit of the slight acclivity on which the town is built. On this street, corner of Bradford, is the First Congregational Church, a handsome granite edifice with a square tower, built in 1857, and is the most expensive and finest finished church in the town. Adjoining is a chapel built in 1870. The Congregational Society is the oldest church organization in the town, dating back to 1687, and the present edifice is the third house of worship. The second building, erected in 1784, was given to the town in 1856, when it was moved to Bradford Street, and has since been used as a town hall.

About the central part of High Street, in a row on the east side, extending from State to Church streets, stands a brick school-house, the First Baptist Church, the Court House, and the Byfield School, and in the rear of them is an extensive common used as a park. On State Street, between Hope and High streets, is the Methodist Episcopal Church, a large, white, wooden building, with a tall, graceful spire.

Beyond High is Wood Street, on the east side of which are the works of the rubber company, the principal industrial establishment in the town. The buildings of this concern cover six acres, and when running to their full capacity 1,200 hands are employed. Near the extremity of Hope Street and abutting on the water are the works of the Herreshoff Manufacturing Company, builders of steam and sail yachts and patent coil boilers, which are under the management of the celebrated blind designer, John B. Herreshoff.

In the estimation of the inhabitants of Bristol, the finest view to be obtained on Narragansett Bay is from Ferry Hill, one and a half miles south of Bristol, and opposite the Bristol Ferry Landing on the Rhode Island shore. The hill is a rocky bluff, or a group of them. On a clear morning, the adjoining islands, the shores of Rhode Island and Tiverton, Fall River to the northeast, the whole

OAKLAND.BEACH.

expanse of Mount Hope Bay, and glimpses of the islands and shores to the west and north, are within a pleasant range of vision, so that while the outlook is not so extensive as from Mount Hope, it is much more satisfactory. When the morning sun is striking on its roofs, the city of Providence can also be seen on a clear day to rare advantage. The view of Bristol from here is the finest to be had from any point, and the whole extent of the bay down to Newport lies directly south, so that the finest long-distance view of Fort Adams to be had is obtained from this position.

Two miles eastward from Bristol, Mount Hope rises nearly three hundred feet above the level of the sea, the highest elevation in the state, and a place of historic interest in connection with King Philip, the famous Indian sachem, who was slain near here. A curious, natural-shaped rude seat in the rock on its eastern slope has long been known as "King Philip's Throne." The Rhode Island Historical Society has erected two memorials here to indicate and mark points of historical interest.

Poppasquash Neck is a long peninsula between Bristol Harbor on the west and the bay, and is a quiet farming and residence neighborhood.

One of the most charmingly situated summer hotels on Narragansett Bay is the Bristol Ferry House. It is located on a gentle rise of land directly back of and facing the steamer landing. The house is three stories in height, with a basement, has three verandas, contains thirty-five sleeping rooms, besides spacious parlors and a large dining-room, which can also be used for dancing. The house looks westward, is surrounded by large trees, mostly poplars, and is always fanned by breezes from every quarter of the bay on even the hottest days. From it are obtained views of Mount Hope Bay, part of Narragansett Bay, Hog and Prudence islands, Mount Hope, and Fall River. There are frequent trains from Newport and Fall River, and the steamers plying between Fall River and Providence stop at the landing on each trip. Fall River is seven miles distant, Boston fifty-eight miles, and the landing and station are only one minute's walk from the house. The house is open from June to October, and being under the direct care of the proprietor, Mr. Alfred Sisson, has all the advantages of a hotel with the comforts of a home.

THE WARWICK SHORE.

While the east side of the bay for a dozen miles below Providence is lined with summer residences and is a great rendezvous of the excursionists, the west side opposite has been comparatively neglected. This region, however, is not without its charms; in fact, in the opinion of residents and of disinterested visitors it has advantages in many respects superior to the east shore. The main reason for this neglect has been, not any lack of natural attractiveness, but the difficulty of access, as the east side having greater depth of water near shore, steamers have been enabled to make landings there without much inconvenience. Although the east side has thus been the most popular, it is a curious fact that one of the earliest and for a time a very noted popular resort was on the west side on the south shore of Turtle Cove, and people went there in crowds, both

BUTTONWOOD'S BEACH.

by sail-boat and carriage. It was known in its hey-day as Mark Rock from some rocks on the shore in the vicinity.

This section and the remainder of the coast line of the town of Warwick — the whole extending from the mouth of the Pawtuxet River to East Greenwich, more than twenty miles in length — has been " the shore " for the largest portion of the state and the adjoining territory to the westward. The farming and manufacturing population in the interior and in the adjoining regions of Connecticut, have for generations made annual summer pilgrimages to these shores for the purpose of enjoying on the spot the clam-bakes, the chowders, and the fish-fries that nowhere else could be had in such perfection. They came in parties, large and small, sometimes only remaining long enough to dig, cook, and eat their clams : at other times encamping on the shores for days and weeks, as inclination and means dictated. Such has always been the popularity of these summer feasts that the more remote residents looked forward to going to "the shore" as the great event of the season, while those nearer and with the means of getting there were, in general, frequent visitors.

Although the building of the railroads, the founding of the shore resorts shortly before 1860, and their development since, has done away with the necessity of driving to the shore, digging your clams, and cooking them yourself, many people prefer this old-fashioned method, and the west shore is the place where those who enjoy the individual exertion of getting a clam-dinner in the original way still resort. On holidays in summer and on Sundays, all along from Field's Point to Pawtuxet, and from there to Rocky Point, may be found little parties of city or country people down for the day, enjoying the sea breeze, and enjoying still more the old-time clambake.

The Warwick and Oakland Beach Railroad, built in 1874, running from half a mile to a mile from the shore from below Pawtuxet to Warwick Neck, and terminating at Oakland Beach, was not at first a success, and was discontinued after running two summers. But in 1880 it was reopened by the New York, Providence and Boston Railroad Company, and has been operated continuously since. By its means an impetus was given toward the erection of residences on eligible situations on the shore nearest the railroad, and as a consequence the region has developed to a considerable extent, an extensive settlement of summer homes now stretches along the shore, and the locality bids fair to become a populous district as its beauties are seen and appreciated.

About ten miles from the city, on the south shore of Turtle Cove, is River Dale, formerly Mark Rock already mentioned, and now containing the homes of a few summer and permanent residents. The shore here is a fine sandy beach, extending for about two miles to the extremity of Conimicut Point. From the bluffs at River Dale the view is excellent. A mile away to the northward is Greene's Island, connected with the mainland by a sandy bar uncovered at low tide, and this island is one of the chief clam-digging places in the state. Across the bar between this island and the mainland the famous Gaspee Point is plainly visible, while over the bay northeasterly, pleasing glimpses of the eastern shore and its numerous resorts greet the eye, Nayatt Point, directly east, standing out conspicuously.

Half a mile eastward from River Dale is Shawomet Beach, a settlement of about a score of red-roofed, tasteful cottages, a dozen of them in a line, not more than fifty feet from the beach, which here is of smooth, level sand, and the outlook is similar to that at River Dale from a different point of view. Shawomet Beach station is only a short distance from this pleasant group of cottages. A short distance beyond is a large, elegant mansion, with red out-buildings and a large, substantial red farm-house, the property of the Hon. Stephen Harris, one of the chief men of Warwick. This neighborhood is the head of Conimicut Point, a long, narrow, sandy peninsula, extending for a half mile or

CAPTAIN P. W. WIGHTMAN,
Of Steamer "Eolus."

more into the bay, on the extremity of which are a number of dingy buildings.

Extending along the shore south from the point is River View, and the railroad station and a hotel here located are all called by the same name. The houses are more scattered than at Shawomet Beach, but they are as numerous and not more than a quarter of a mile from the latter place. During the past spring many improvements have been made here, and River View is, for convenience of access, location, wide and good roads, one of the best resorts on the bay. A wide avenue leads down to the shore from the station.

A quarter of a mile further is Bay Side, where there is also a station and a hotel of the same name. The hotel was formerly known as the Long Meadow House. A new Methodist Episcopal Church was built here this season. Beyond, and near Grant's Station on the railroad, are the house and grounds of the Warwick Club, a private association of Providence business men. A mile further along the river road is Rocky Point, the noted shore resort.

All the way from Shawomet Beach through River View, Bay Side, and beyond, the region is dotted with cottages, not very thickly, it is true, but still so

A SHORE VIEW OF WICKFORD.

close together that they may be said to be in a continuous line, and the majority of them are so located as to afford excellent views of the bay and the neighboring and opposite shores.

OLD WARWICK.

The country westward from these groups of summer houses, as far as the water-shed of the Pawtuxet River, is very level, and has accordingly been known as the Warwick Plains. In this region, near the head of the neck, is Old Warwick, a centre for the original settlers, where they came to church and to trade, and a little hamlet still exists at the cross-roads. There are several ancient dwellings here of which the most noticeable is the Lippitt House, said to be two hundred years old.

WARWICK NECK.

Extending southward from Rocky Point is a narrow peninsula, surrounded by water on all sides except the north, and with the Warwick Neck Lighthouse, a conspicuous object, on its extreme southern point. The Neck is an elevated ridge sloping gradually each way from the centre towards the shores, and is crowned with many fine villas and cottages owned and occupied in the summer season by prominent citizens of Providence. The locality bears a strong resemblance to portions of Newport in the beauty of the houses and grounds, the elegance of the surroundings, and the fine and well-kept avenues. A good hotel, the Warwick Neck House, is situated on the main avenue in a commanding location.

An avenue leads over the highest portion of the Neck to the lighthouse, and from it really magnificent views are had of the bay and shores on either side. To the east, Bristol, Warren, the adjoining shores and waters, and from some points Fall River, are visible, while the reaches of the bay and the islands to the southward complete the picture. To the west, Oakland Beach, the Buttonwoods, and the shores of Greenwich Bay lie spread out at the observer's feet. Beyond is East Greenwich on the high western shore, and through the natural defiles, we catch glimpses of the villages back in Warwick, the whole landscape spread out before the eye like an immense profile map, and constituting, for variety and beauty, pictures of natural scenery unsurpassed in the state.

ROCKY POINT.

The largest, most famous and popular resort on the bay is Rocky Point. It is located on the west shore about twelve miles below Providence, on the northeast shoulder of Warwick Neck, in the township of Warwick. The Point is noted for the great diversity of its natural beauties, its broken surface, combining hill and dale, rocks and glens, its bold, rocky bluffs, high enough above the water to give a commanding view of the bay and shore for miles around, with most of the grounds pleasantly shaded by a handsome grove of native growth. In the rocky hillsides of broken ledges and huge boulders are numerous caves and cavities, and these covered with shrubbery and luxuriant clusters of trailing vines, give a unique effect, a peculiar fascination, and a wildness of beauty to the scene.

There are fountains, parterres of flowers, winding concrete walks and groups of buildings devoted to every variety of amusement, with other artistic attractions which greatly increase the interest of the crowds of visitors to this favorite summer resort. So many and varied are its scenes and attractions that all classes of excursionists patronize and greatly enjoy this popular place. After the burning of the hotel and the adjoining buildings, in March, 1883, handsome new buildings were erected for the accommodation of the public, and the Warwick Arms Hotel, retired a little from the busy front, and overlooking the bay southward, has been the only hotel on the premises since then. The buildings, consisting of a pavilion and a dining-hall directly on the shore near the landing, are the largest on the bay devoted to the business of catering to the multitude in the matter of shore dinners.

The bracing air, the fine southern view of the bay and islands, and the good bathing, choice table and quietude, make this a charming seaside home for a short or a long tarry. Rhode Island's great sea-shore celebrity, the "clam," is also a central attraction at Rocky Point, and at the proper season and hour it is served here in excellent style.

The Point has also other allurements to suit the various tastes of the multitudes that every summer seek its shores for recreation; among them are the fine bathing beach, houses, and appurtenances, just north of the landing. Here is a large hall for music

A HARBOR VIEW OF WARREN

9

and dancing for all who wish, and swings and flying horses to please the children and keep them good natured; bowling alleys and shooting galleries for all who seek such sport as that. Here, too, is the monkey cage, containing twenty or more of these interesting creatures, always busy cutting up their "monkey shines," to the great delectation of the crowd of admiring youngsters, and affording merriment to all who visit them. A special attraction at Rocky Point is the strong well-built circular observatory standing on the highest spot on the place, and all the eastern shore from Providence on the north to Nayatt Point almost opposite can be plainly seen, while Warren, Bristol, Fall River, and Newport can be partially seen over the islands and intervening land. At our feet lies the main portion of the bay, with its many beautiful islands plainly in sight, and landward to the south is the high ridge of Warwick Neck, shutting out the view to the southwest; while to the north and west, is the beautiful Warwick country and shore.

Here the observer may feast his eye, and enjoy the landscape and sea-view in blended beauty as from few other points of view. Here he can see the entire length of the island of Rhode Island, from Bristol Ferry to Newport, with its handsome farm-houses and farms and the marked lines of stone wall fences, and the busy steamers passing to and fro on the bosom of the bay add much beauty and animation to the charming scene which is well worth the labor of climbing the tower to see. Among the many beautiful and attractive places on Narragansett Bay, none afford a greater variety of entertainment or more extensive facilities than Rocky Point.

A new attraction at the Point this season is the water slide situated in front of the pavilion by the side of the wharf. Above water it is about 200 feet long, and the boat, or car, will proceed 150 feet farther into the water, making a slide of about 350 feet. The boat is about fifteen feet in length, and slides on a hard-pine track, which it descends at a very rapid rate. There is just enough salt spray thrown when the water is reached to make the trip exhilarating.

OAKLAND BEACH.

One of the most noted and popular of the prominent shore resorts of Narragansett Bay is Oakland Beach, located between one and two miles west from Rocky Point on the southern extremity of the peninsula of Horse Neck, fronting on Greenwich Bay. It was first opened to the public by the Oakland Beach Association in 1873. The Oakland Beach Hotel, located on the western borders of the grounds, and surrounded with numerous shore attractions, has established an excellent reputation and popularity. The large dining-hall at the beach is very spacious, roomy, and cool, with seating capacity for 1,200 persons, which can be readily extended to accommodate 5,000, if required, and gives ample scope to cater comfortably for the largest parties that can congregate there.

The Pavilion, the large building near the beach, 80 x 150 feet, is made a delightfully cool and comfortable place for visitors by opening its sides outward, thus forming a shady awning, giving free admission to the refreshing sea breezes. The pleasant, airy dance hall, with excellent music and ample room for all, will

VIEW ON MAIN STREET, WARREN.

be made more attractive to the dancers than ever. The English Coach Café, the unique ice-cream and refreshment saloon, is continued as one of the peculiar features. Oakland Beach is now owned by the Oakland Beach Association, composed of a number of prominent citizens of Providence, and during the season of 1888 will be under the management of Mr. R. A. Harrington.

The twenty-five safe and handsome row boats for excursions on the creek, the flying-horses, swings, and other amusements for the children and juvenile excursionists, the bowling saloon, base ball, foot ball, and cricket grounds for the older pleasure seekers, all easily accessible at the Beach, furnish ample and varied amusements for visitors. Now-a-days all Providence people go to the Beach by railroad, but it is one of the most popular resorts for excursion parties by water on steamers or sailing craft, and entertains large companies from Pawtucket, Fall River, Newport, and other places, who come by water. The Rhode Island militia for several years past has held its annual encampment at the Beach, on each occasion passing a week doing camp duty. This year the troops will go into camp here on Monday, August 6th, and remain until the following Saturday morning.

One of the attractions added this season is an aquatic toboggan, an amphibious creation invented and patented by Mr. Harrington, which is both interesting to behold, and affords much sport to the younger excursionists. A light boat slides down an incline 165 feet long, into the lake. The voyager sails far over the surface of the lake, and the boat is drawn back and up the incline by an endless cable. The boats are double-enders, carry four persons, make the distance in three seconds, and the slide and sail are both perfectly safe and very pleasant.

THE BUTTONWOODS.

About half a mile west of Oakland Beach is a long stretch of sandy shore known usually as the "Buttonwoods," and famous in local annals as a great clam-digging and clam-eating resort.

The "The Buttonwoods Beach Association," in 1871, purchased a large tract of land at the east end of the beach. erected a large hotel, and platted their land for cottage lots. and since then a large number of tasteful cottages have been erected, forming one of the most beautiful residence resorts on the bay. The fine beach is over a mile in length, and affords facilities for bathing, boating, and fishing equal to any other place on the bay. East Greenwich lies in view to the west and can be reached in thirty minutes by water; Rocky Point lies about the same distance away to the eastward.

Directly south of the Buttonwoods, on the opposite shore of Greenwich Bay, lies Potowomut Neck, occupied by farmers and summer residents. This is a favorite summer resort for many prominent city families, who wish for a quiet retreat and love the real Rhode Island country style of living which they secure here.

"Old Buttonwoods," the western end of the beach, is probably the oldest resort on the bay. Here the farming population have been in the habit of coming to get their shore dinners for generations. During the celebrated presidential campaign of 1840, a great political clambake was held here. Buttonwoods is the terminus of the Warwick and Oakland Beach Railroad.

APPONAUG.

Apponaug is a little village at the head of a short inlet which makes in from the northeast corner of Greenwich Bay, and is one of the quaintest and most ancient looking places in the state. It consists of two streets crossing each other at right angles, lined with comfortable houses, some of them of a very antiquated appearance. The Warwick town-house is on the principal street and here the whole town always came to vote until a few years back when election districts were formed in the more populous villages westward. An extensive print-work is located here, but has been idle for the past five years, and the only other manufactory is a small woolen concern. Many of the inhabitants make a living "along shore." The Hon. Charles R. Brayton, one of the most conspicuous leaders in Rhode Island politics at present, is a native of this village. A small stream flows into the inlet on which Apponaug is located. and is the outlet of a large pond lying back of the village. This body of water is named Gorton Pond, from Samuel Gorton, the founder of the colony of Warwick. which was one of the four original towns in the state, and Gorton was a very unique character, to whom justice, as compared with the laudations bestowed on his contemporaries, has hardly been done.

EAST GREENWICH.

On a steep hill-side, facing eastward along the shores of the southwest corner of Greenwich Bay. and on Greenwich Cove which runs south from the bay for a mile or more, is the village of East Greenwich, the chief place in the township of that name, and the county seat of Kent County. The New York, Providence and Boston Railroad runs along between the base of the hill and the shore, and the traveler in a passing train has thereby a panoramic view of the entire surroundings. The chief streets run parallel with the shore, as far as the conformation of the land will admit, and are intersected by most of the hillside streets at right angles. These latter, running from the railroad on the shore to the top of the hill, are, with few exceptions, very steep.

Main Street, the business thoroughfare, is half way up the slope, and on it are the old Court House and the new Town Hall, a beautiful Queen Anne structure. Above, on the brow of the hill, are the large buildings of the East Greenwich Academy, the Episcopal Church, a fine stone structure, and the Baptist Church, a new and tasteful wooden edifice. The dwellings upon the slope of the hill are attractive residences, many of them the homes of people doing business in the city, which can be readily reached on account of the excellent service of the New York, Providence & Boston Railroad. The academy is an educational institution under the auspices of the Methodist Episcopal denomination, and dates back to the beginning of the century. It is in a flourishing condition and has an excellent reputation.

VEIW OF BRISTOL FROM THE HARBOR.

The town of East Greenwich was incorporated in 1677, and is therefore one of the oldest in the state. In its early history, because of its excellent harbor, great commercial prosperity was anticipated, which was not realized, although at one time it had considerable commerce. Manufacturing was early introduced. At present the place has a woolen mill, a yarn mill, a bleachery, saw mills, and some minor industries. The Union Mill, corner of Union and Main streets, formerly engaged in the cotton manufacture, has been idle for a number of years.

Greenwich Bay is the best fishing ground for scallops on Narragansett Bay; clams and quahaugs are plentiful on its shores, and the oyster is also found in its waters. The bay, sometimes called Cowesett, is about two miles wide by four in length. Because of the abundance of shell fish many of the inhabitants make a living by the fisheries, and the "rights of the shore" were the means by which many a family, when the factories were closed some years ago, during the business depression, were enabled to keep the wolf from the door. Greenwich Bay is reserved by law for free fisheries, no portion of it can be leased for oyster beds, and this gives the people on its shores opportunities greater than enjoyed elsewhere in the state.

A peculiar feature of the place is a locality known either as "Shanty Town" or "Scallop Town," at the foot of a projecting bluff between the railroad and the shores of the cove, and opposite the southern part of the compact town. It consists of a hundred or more small houses, all close to the water's edge — some even standing on piles below high water mark, — and all unpainted, crooked, patched up, and dilapidated in general appearance. The dwellers here get a living by fishing; but as scallops are the most plentiful, the settlement has been named after them "Scallop Town," and judging from the number of shells of that species to be seen on its one street, this suburb of East Greenwich deserves its name. Many of its inhabitants are colored people.

Across the cove from East Greenwich is the peninsula of Potowomut Neck, said to have been a favorite camping-ground for the Indians, and where they indulged in clambakes. It is now occupied by the summer homes of affluent Providence families.

On account of its elevated situation, splendid views of the adjoining lands and waters are had from many points on the upper streets. The tower of the Academy building is, however, the best place for a comprehensive outlook. The entire expanse of Greenwich Bay and the whole of Potowomut peninsula lie beneath the eye, spread out so near at hand that every variation of the coast line can be clearly seen. The Buttonwoods, Oakland Beach Hotel, the dwellings and light-house on Warwick Neck, are within easy range of vision. Eastward the spires of Bristol, and beyond on the horizon, the huge factories, with their tall chimneys out of which the smoke curls up, in the southern part of Fall River, can be quite clearly discerned with the aid of a glass, although eighteen miles away. The islands of the bay are also readily picked out: nearest and directly opposite us, is Patience, then Prudence, Hog Island, and as we sweep the bay with our field glass, the whole western coast line of Rhode Island and Conanicut passes before us. Northward in the foreground is Hill's Grove, the

VIEW OF HIGH STREET, BRISTOL.

tall chimneys of the Pumping Station, and on the horizon the towers and spires of Providence. To the west and south are plains, and miles away, low hills, the backbone of the state.

WICKFORD.

On the western shore of the bay, ten miles south of East Greenwich and twenty from Providence, is located the pleasant village of Wickford, on a bay of the same name, one of the oldest settlements in the state. A small amount of manufacturing is carried on. Wickford is the largest and most important village in the town of North Kingstown and is the seat of the town government. In the village are two banks, two churches, a town hall, and a goodly number of handsome dwelling-houses. Many Providence people and others have summer residences here, and several hotels in the village and vicinity do a good business.

The residents find good bathing at Cold Spring Beach, near by, and " The Cedars," an attractive woodland grove two or three miles south of the village, is a favorite resort of Wickford folks and their guests for picnic parties and rural reunions. From here it is a very pleasant country drive of ten miles south to Narragansett Pier. The Wickford Branch Railroad connects with the New York, Providence and Boston line at Wickford Junction, and with Newport by steamer from Wickford.

CONANICUT ISLAND.—JAMESTOWN.

Conanicut Island, the second largest island in the bay, is nine miles in length by two in breadth, and is divided into two unequal parts by Mackerel Cove. It lies southwest of Prudence, and its southern extremity is midway between Narragansett Pier and Newport. The southern portion of the island resembles a beaver in shape, the northern section of which is known as Beaver Head and the southern point as Beaver Tail, upon which is located the noted Beaver Tail Light-house. At the southern extremity of the north or larger section of the island is a rocky promontory, upon which are the remains of the old redoubt known as Fort Dumpling. The island was incorporated as a town and named Jamestown, November 4. 1768, and has the smallest population of any town in the state. For the past few years it has attracted many summer residents, whose dwellings are now scattered over the island. At the north end of the island is Conanicut Park, where are a number of cottages and a hotel. The steamers plying between Providence and Newport, and between Wickford and Newport stop here.

Opposite Newport is the village of Jamestown, consisting of less than a hundred houses and several hotels situated on a slope facing the water. A steam ferry connects Newport with this place which is near the central portion of the island.

The Newport and Jamestown Steam Ferry and Navigation Company the first week in July, began running a steam ferry boat from the west side of Conanicut Island to South Ferry on the shores of the town of South Kingstown, connecting across Conanicut Island with the Jamestown Ferry, the distance overland being only about a mile. This is the route of the old South Ferry, the chief highway between the South County and Newport before the era of railroads and steam navigation, and the new facilities afford opportunity to drive from Newport to Narragansett Pier. the route including five miles of travel by water and six by land, and it would be difficult to find a more enjoyable journey.

At the extreme north end of the island stands a light-house recently established by the government, and a new shore drive of five miles, alone the line of which the scenery is of surpassing beauty, connects the east ferry landing at Jamestown with Conanicut Park.

Mr. Daniel Watson's plan, to cut a canal through the island, as a means of shortening the time, by about one hour, between Newport and New York, is attracting much attention, and the charter for the Newport and New York Rapid Transit Company, was recently accepted by the company which he has formed. This company proposes to have a steamboat landing almost exactly in the middle of the island (in the canal midway of the east and west shores of the island). The line has the right, under its charter, to contract for making connection with the Narragansett Pier Railroad. The plan is for the new company to construct a railroad to run from Eaton's Ferry, on the Narragansett shore, to the Pier road. or to some point on the Shore Line, the canal steamer from Newport to make railroad connection at Eaton's Ferry. The great progress made by Conanicut Island as a watering place within a few years is largely due to the public spirit and enterprise of Mr. Watson.

Among the cottage owners on this island are Admiral David D. Porter, Captain Thomas O. Selfridge : Medical Director, David Kidleberger, United States Navy ; Joseph Wharton. Wistar Morris, Charles W. Wharton, General

BURNSIDE MEMORIAL BUILDING, BRISTOL.

Robert E. Patterson, Philadelphia; Professor C. W. Larned, West Point, N. Y.; Charles Fletcher, Richard J. Arnold, Providence; Mrs. Harriet L. Stevens, H. Audley Clarke, Daniel L. Hazard, Newport; George B. Emmons, Boston; Mrs. A. E. Tilden, New York City; Mr. C. A. Mann, Washington, D. C., Mrs. E. P. Rhett, Baltimore. The artist Richards, too, has his summer residence here, and when he bought the site upon which he has built he remarked that he expected to do the best artistic work of his life on Conanicut. Among those who have recently bought land on this island are the Hon. Wayne McVeigh, of Philadelphia; D. Bethune Duffield, of Detroit, Mich.; Dr. William Argyle Watson, of New York; Judge Russell Houston, of Louisville, Ky., and Robert B. King, of St. Louis.

THE ISLANDS.

The state of Rhode Island is very appropriately named, as the islands of Narragansett Bay comprise a large portion of its area. The full name of the state, "Rhode Island and Providence Plantations," comes from the fact that the separate colonies of Rhode Island and of Providence Plantations were consolidated by the terms of the royal charter, and when they declared their independence, they retained the old name. Rhode Island, however, being the first part of the title is all that is used except in legal or official documents, and thus the name which properly and originally belonged to the island, is now, by common usage, the name of the state. But Rhode Island or Aquidneck, as originally known, is the proper name of the largest and most beautiful of the islands in Narragansett Bay, and contains the towns of Portsmouth and Middletown and the city of Newport.

Nearly midway in the bay is Prudence Island, once owned by Roger

Williams, the founder of the state, who was the first man to till its soil. It is the third largest island in the bay, being six miles long by three wide, and is very irregular in shape. The Newport steamers make a landing several times a week. From a comparative desert with a dozen houses inhabited by tillers of the soil, the island has, within a few years, blossomed out as a family summer resort, the main portion of which is near the centre of the island and is known as Prudence Park. Here there is now a casino, a summer pavilion, and several new residences have been erected this season. Prudence divides the commerce of the bay, the New York and southern steamers passing out to the westward of it, while the Fall River and sometimes the Providence and Newport steamers pass it to the eastward.

Patience and Hope Islands lie to the west of Prudence, Patience being the largest and situated near the north end of Prudence. Hope Island, nearly as large as Patience, is situated off the south end of Prudence, midway between that island and the Kingston shore. Despair Island, sometimes associated in name with the others, is a mere speck of an islet lying near the north end of Hope.

Dutch Island is situated in the "West Passage," midway between Conanicut Island and the main land, and comprises about three hundred acres. It was very early used as a trading station by the Dutch, which gave it the name, and in 1658 was purchased from the Indians by the colony of Rhode Island. In 1864 it came into possession of the United States Government, and upon it were erected extensive earth-work batteries, designed to command the "West Passage" entrance to the bay. During the War of the Rebellion it was the rendezvous of the Fourteenth Regiment, Rhode Island Heavy Artillery. Dutch Island Harbor is deemed by coastwise navigators one of the best "havens" of the entire Atlantic coast.

"Whale Rock," located near the entrance to the West Passage is a noted and dangerous rocky ledge of only half an acre in extent, but though a very small island it has been the scene of many a shipwreck, and has long been the dread of mariners. The iron light-house erected a few years ago upon this ledge furnishes the long-needed protection of voyagers from its dangers.

Dyer's Island is a small island lying off the west shore of Portsmouth.

Gould Island, lying east of Conanicut, contains only about one hundred acres of land, and is the property of Mr. Homans, of New York. The steamers plying between Providence and Newport pass close to it, and it is within five miles of the latter place. A small island of the same name lies in the Seaconnet River between Rhode Island and the mainland.

Hog Island, at the mouth of Bristol Harbor, is about the same size as Prudence.

In and around Newport Harbor are a number of islands, all of which belong to the United States Government. The largest of these. Coaster's Harbor Island, separated from Newport by a narrow strait and formerly a part of the city, was presented several years ago to the United States Government for a naval station, to which purpose it is now entirely devoted. Rose Island,

THE B. M. C. DURFEE HIGH SCHOOL, FALL RIVER

in Newport Harbor, north from Fort Adams, has on it an important light-house. Goat Island is directly opposite Newport, and has a light-house and the United States Torpedo Station located upon it. Lime Rock, a small islet between Fort Adams and Newport, has a light-house, the home of the celebrated Ida Lewis.

Besides these important islands, there are numerous small ones scattered all along the shores, many of which are the rendezvous of fishermen.

FALL RIVER.

Fall River is the principal seat of the cotton manufacture in the United States, nearly one-seventh of the entire amount being carried on in its borders. It lies on the eastern border of Mount Hope Bay, at the mouth of the Taunton River, and the greater portion is built on hillsides rising quite abruptly from the water's edge to a height of more than one hundred and fifty feet. From the summits of these hills the country extends back in a comparatively level table-land, on which a large section of the city now stands, and two miles eastward from the shore lies a chain of deep and narrow ponds, eight miles long, of an average width of three-quarters of a mile, covering an area of 3,500 acres. These ponds are supplied by springs and brooks, draining a water-shed of 20,000 acres, and are connected with the sea by a stream which, originally flowing unconfined over an almost level course for more than a mile, in the last half mile of its progress rushes down the hillside in a narrow, precipitous, rocky chan-nel. In this distance the total fall is about 132 feet, and the volume of water 122 cubic feet per second.

Massive factories, each several hundred feet in length, five and six stories in height, the majority of them built of granite, loom up in every section of the city and suburbs, and in their neighborhoods are the houses inhabited by the operatives, consisting in many instances of long buildings, or large detached blocks in rows similar to the factory villages throughout New England, although in Fall River they are on a much larger scale, and some of the tene-ment blocks are as large as small fac-tories elsewhere. These houses are mostly built of wood, although in a few instances they are of brick, and belong to the mill corporations. The number of corporations engaged in the cotton manufacture is thirty-eight, owning fifty-seven mills, con-taining 1,823,472 spindles, and 41,219 looms, and employing 19,195 per-sons. The production of print cloths is the leading specialty, but in the past few years the making of wide goods, sheetings, twills, lawns, and various fancy patterns has been intro-duced. These goods have met with ready sale because the development of taste has created a demand for a greater variety of style than had for-merly been manufactured. Besides

FALL RIVER FROM THE WATER

the cotton corporations there are twenty others not including railroad, steamboat, and telephone companies, engaged in various industries, namely, calico
printing, bleaching and dyeing of cotton goods, manufacture of cotton and
other machinery, cotton thread, woolen goods, comforters, felt hats, boots,
shoes, etc.

SEACONNET POINT.

The " Land's End " of the mainland of the state on the east side of Narragansett Bay is Seaconnet Point, the southern extremity of the township of
Little Compton. It is one of the most picturesque bits of land on the Rhode
Island coast, but on account of the difficulty of getting there, it remained in
rural seclusion until recently. Many years ago there was a hotel here which
had to be discontinued for lack of business, but this season a new one, "The
Sakonnet" has been opened by Mr. J. L. Slocum. The only means of reaching the point has been by the mail stage from Fall River, or by private conveyance, until, in 1886, a small steamer began running from Providence, and in
1887 two steamers were on the route all summer.

A number of summer " cottages," in reality, fine residences, have, within
the past few years, been built, and the locality has attracted many artists, fishermen, and other lovers of nature. Several prominent Providence gentlemen
have their summer houses here, among them being Dr. C. T. Gardner, the
Rev. Thomas R. Slicer, and W. H. Low, Jr.

Just off the Point, perched on the rocks, are the white houses with their red
roofs, of the West Island Fishing Club, an association of men prominent in
social and business circles. The coast in the neighborhood of the Point is a
wild jumble of ragged rocks, but the country back of it is mostly broad meadow
land. From the Point toward the east can be seen Gay Head, Martha's Vineyard, and the island of Cuttyhunk, while westward Point Judith is sometimes
seen, but the ocean edge of Newport generally forms the horizon line. Between these widely separated points, the ocean lies before the observer unobstructed in all its grandeur.

Seaconnet River is that part of Narragansett Bay between the island of
Rhode Island and the townships of Tiverton and Little Compton. It is about
ten miles in length by one and a half in average breadth, and is sometimes
called the East Passage. At the north it is connected with Mount Hope Bay by
a strait, which is spanned by the " Stone Bridge " so called, joining Rhode
Island to the mainland. A mile above this bridge, the Old Colony Railroad
also crosses on a fine bridge.

PART THIRD.

CHAPTER I.

Newport, the City by the Sea,

A SOUND BOAT.

SEATED on the southern extremity of Rhode Island at the main entrance to Narragansett Bay, Newport, with its halls and towers is a veritable queen of the waters, and its fame as the summer metropolis of wealth and fashion is world-wide. Other places have a fame and standing and attractions of their own, but they do not rival Newport nor compete with her, for the devotees of all the other centres of summer fashion gravitate to "the city by the sea" as naturally as flowers turn to the sun.

Nowhere on our Atlantic coast can be found a better harbor. Its deep waters, its perfect security — being sheltered from the storms of the ocean on all sides — and its ample size, render it a favorite haven of refuge for vessels

FORT DUMPLINGS

in distress. During the summer its placid bosom is
always dotted with graceful
yachts, and it is frequently
visited by the war vessels of
our own country and of foreign powers, whose officers
are attracted by the cultured
and cosmopolitan society
here assembled. In the winter the coasting schooners
and coal barges often anchor
in the inner harbor when
wind bound, and large fleets
of fishing vessels come in
during their season.

The territory of Newport
comprises the southern portion of the island of Rhode Island, forming an elbow-
shaped peninsula, of an average width of about two miles, the harbor being
on the inside. The townships of Middletown and Portsmouth occupy the
central and northern portions of the island, and contain some of the finest and
most productive farms in the state.

The city is really divided into two parts. All that section near the wharves
and for some distance back is the old and historic Newport, and is the seat
of the business of the city. Here are still to be seen many old houses with
gambrel roofs or pro-
jecting eaves, built
previous to the Revo-
lution, and most of
them have interesting
histories of old colon-
ial days, famous fam-
ilies, or revolutionary
events. The appear-
ance of antiquity is
further heightened in
this quarter by the nar-
rowness of the side
streets, lined in places
with the ancient
houses. Thames, the
chief street of the city,
runs the entire length
of this older section,
and on it is transacted
most of the business
of the permanent

THAMES STREET.

NEWPORT VIEWS.

The Old Mill.   The Cliff Walk.   Washington Square.

FORT ADAMS.

residents. It is a narrow thoroughfare, and between it and the harbor on the west
are all the wharves, on many of which are work-a-day, unpainted, and tumble-
down looking buildings. On this account the first view of the queen of watering places is somewhat of a disappointment to strangers, but to those familiar
with the city it is rather an added charm, indicating the glories of the past in a
graphic and interesting manner.

Lying to the east and south of the older portion, on the ridge of the peninsula, on all the intersecting avenues, and all along the bold and picturesque
coast, are palatial mansions, known by the unpretentious name of "cottages,"
but in reality many of them palaces, rich in treasures of wealth and taste,
and fitted up with all imaginable luxury. They are embowered in trees, surrounded with pleasant lawns, some perched on the edge of cliffs overlooking
the sea, and nearly all within sight and hearing of the ever-restless ocean.

The climate of Newport is peculiarly equable and soft, and is adapted
to invalids at all seasons of the year. While the icy current from Labrador and
Newfoundland pours into Massachusetts Bay, the south shore is struck by the
warm current from the tropics, which is thence deflected by Cape Cod toward
Ireland. This gives to Newport its mild atmosphere and the comfortable
waters, adapted for bathing during the three summer months.

Newport was first settled in 1639, by a portion of the exiled company
of Puritans from the Massachusetts Bay Colony. By reason of its excellent
harbor, in colonial days it became the most important commercial port on the
Atlantic coast, even surpassing New York. It was then, as now, noted for its
charming climate and beautiful scenery, and was the centre of the best, the
most learned and cultured society in America. During the Revolutionary War

the commerce was destroyed, and at its close Newport recovered but slowly from the devastating effects, and never regained its commercial position.

In 1830 the prospects of the town began to brighten, about which time the present "order of the town" was really inaugurated, and boarding-house keepers were taxed to their utmost to accommodate the summer visitors who flocked hither from all parts of our country. Soon after this large hotels and cottages began to be erected, and the town gradually gained the coveted reputation of *the* watering-place of America. It became a city in 1783; in 1787

THE LIME ROCK LIGHT.

surrendered its charter, and remained under a town government until 1853, when a second city charter was obtained.

The best place to start from for a brief view of the chief points of interest is Washington Square, a wide, open space an eighth of a mile in length, with a

STATUE OF COM. O. H. PERRY.

park-like inclosure called the Mall on the south side. On Thames Street at the foot of the square is the City Hall, built in 1763; in the Common Council Chamber, in the second story, can now be seen the escutcheon and portrait of William Coddington, the first governor of the island. At the head of the square is the State House, erected in 1741, where the May sessions of the Rhode Island Legislature are held and the state officers installed in office, the result of the election being proclaimed from the balcony. At the foot of the small inclosed park is a statue of Commodore Oliver Hazard Perry, commemorating his great victory on Lake Erie in the War of 1812, and on the pedestal is inscribed the celebrated report made by him on that occasion: "We have met the enemy and they are ours." On the south side of the square, just above the opera house and directly opposite the statue, is the mansion where the great naval commander lived both before and after his famous victory.

On Clarke Street, leading out of the square to the south, is the armory of the Newport Artillery, which contains an interesting and valuable collection of relics. On the opposite side, corner of Mary Street, is the Vernon house, where Washington was entertained on his visit to Count Rochambeau at Newport, in 1781.

Returning to the square and proceeding up Touro Street we soon reach Spring Street. A short distance northward on this latter street on the right-hand side opposite Stone Street, is the oldest house in Newport, built of stone in 1639, by Henry Bull. It has been renovated and restored, and bears a somewhat modern air. Returning and continuing our journey up Touro Street, we immediately come upon the Jewish Synagogue on the left, a small stone structure erected in 1763, and used as a place of worship until the Revolution. Services are now regularly held therein every Friday and Saturday. Abraham Touro, a Jewish merchant, left the sum of $20,000 in charge of the town, the interest to be expended for the care of the ancient edifice and its surroundings.

JOHN G. WEAVER.
Senior Proprietor of the Ocean House.

VIEW OF NEWPORT FROM THE HARBOR.

On the lot adjoining the synagogue is the Newport Historical Society's building, originally the church of the Seventh-day Baptist Society, which was erected in 1729, and from whose pulpit the Rev. Mr. Callendar preached his famous centennial discourse in 1738. It stood on Barney Street until 1887, when it was removed to its present location. The edifice was purchased by the Historical Society in 1884, and was dedicated November 10th of that year, having been renovated and restored so as to preserve its historic features. It stands a short distance back from the street, and is a rather plain-looking, wooden structure, and its dimensions are thirty-seven feet front by twenty-seven deep. A wide gallery runs around three sides of the interior, an old-fashioned pulpit overshadowed by a sounding board faces the entrance, and on the gallery fronting the pulpit is an old clock made by William Claggett in 1731. On the wall back of the pulpit are two tablets containing the Ten Commandments. The entire edifice is filled with books and relics, among the latter being pictures of many of the old houses and land-marks of the city, with numerous other interesting historical mementoes. The Newport Historical Society was organized in 1853 and incorporated the following year. From 1877 until the purchase of its present building it had its home in the Redwood Library building. For the study of the antiquities of Newport the rooms of the society afford the best, and it may be truly said, the only facilities in the city, and they are open to the public every day, except Sundays and holidays, from 10 A. M. to 2 P. M., and also on Tuesday evenings.

Leaving the Historical Society's building and proceeding up Touro Street, the next object of interest is the Jewish Cemetery, corner Kay Street. The fence and gateway were erected in 1843, by Judah Touro, and are maintained and kept in repair from the proceeds of a fund left by him for that purpose. From this point the street takes the name of Bellevue Avenue. On the south corner of Church, the next street to the right, is the Newport Reading Room Club House, a large, square, wooden building, the headquarters of an incorporated society of wealthy residents for literary and social purposes.

A short distance beyond on the left, south corner of Redwood Street, is the Redwood Library, which was incorporated in 1747, and the original building completed in 1750, is still standing, although an important addition to the rear was built a few years ago. The library is a private institution, but is open to the public at certain hours each day (from 12 to 2 P. M.). The paintings and statuary in the rooms are well worth a visit.

A few steps further bring us to Touro Park, a large open space in the centre of which is the Old Stone Mill, one of Newport's chief attractions. So far no absolutely authentic evidence has been produced as to the date of its erection, and the theory at one time was widely prevalent that the Northmen, who are supposed to have visited these shores about the year 1,000, built it. Longfellow in his poem "The Skeleton in Armor," adopts this tradition. Recent investigation, however, has led local antiquarians to the belief that it was built by the early settlers, and it is said that very conclusive evidence in this direction is now at hand.

Between the avenue and the old mill stands the handsome bronze statue

THE CASINO, BELLEVUE AVENUE.

of Commodore M. C. Perry, the younger brother of Commodore Oliver Hazard Perry. The younger Perry was instrumental in effecting the treaty with Japan in 1854, and this monument was erected by his daughter, Mrs. August Belmont, of New York.

On Pelham Street, almost opposite the Old Stone Mill, is the Channing Memorial Church, erected in 1880 in honor of William Ellery Channing, the great apostle of Unitarianism, who was a native of Newport. The church is an elegant stone structure, in early English gothic style, and has a beautiful tower with a spire 125 feet in height.

From Touro Park for a distance of about an eighth of a mile, the avenue on both sides is lined with summer stores, and a few hotels and restaurants. Many of the shops are branches of New York houses, and they all cater to the wants of the summer visitors. During the winter this region is a "deserted village," and the gay windows are covered with shutters. Bath road, the main thoroughfare to the beach, runs out of the avenue in this section. At the south corner of Bath road, on the left, is Travers block, the most ornate of the buildings devoted to summer shops. Just beyond it is the Casino, the chief of Newport summer institutions. The building has a frontage of 186 feet, and is in imitation of the old colonial style of architecture, the first floor being occupied by stores and the upper part by the stockholders. In the grounds to the rear are a theatre, a tennis court building, and an extensive bowling alley. The question will be asked, "What is the Casino"? and the answer, as near as can be given without entering into tedious details, is that it is an association of gentlemen who, in connection with an elegant private club, have introduced means for the entertainment of the fashionable society around them. The Casino was erected by James Gordon Bennett, but in 1880 it became the property of a joint stock company, incorporated under Rhode Island laws.

THE GRAND DRIVE — BELLEVUE AVENUE.

Across the avenue from the Casino is James Gordon Bennett's " stone villa,'' a square granite mansion, situated on a terrace a short distance back from the roadway. On the right, down Jones Avenue, is the residence of Mrs. Paran Stevens, where the Duke of Marlboro was entertained in 1887 and fêted by Newport society. Next south on the left, on the corner of Bellevue Avenue and Bowery Street, is the Ocean House, the property of John G. Weaver & Son. It is the largest wooden building and the largest hotel in Newport.

Bellevue Avenue is a continuation of Touro Street, and was originally known as South Touro Street. It was opened after Newport began to develop as a summer resort, and runs from Kay Street to Bailey's Beach in an almost straight line for two and a quarter miles along the summit of the ridge of the peninsula. For the whole distance it is lined on both sides with the most elegant residences in the city. It is the principal promenade and drive of the fashionable society in the season, and on it at the regulation hour may be seen such a display of style and fashion, of wealth, elegance, and beauty as no watering-place in all the country can out-rival. The most brilliant equipages, in styles the most unique, from a jaunty dog-cart, or pony phaeton, to a spanking four-in-hand, with here and there a dashing cavalier, all whirling along this famous " drive," bearing their precious freight,— men of wealth, of rank, of learning ; women of beauty, culture, and refinement ; and merry children, with bright, laughing faces. All are in happiest mood, exchanging salutations as they pass ; noting a strange or beautiful face ; commenting on the last new turnout ; observing the landscape ; indulging in pleasant banter, or in more serious converse. The scene is not a dull one nor uninteresting. It gives us a glimpse, a passing outside glance, at society life in Newport, which we would not have missed, and which we can take away with us and study at our leisure.

Having strolled through that portion of Newport from Washington Square to the Ocean House, and seen all the objects of historic interest, the best manner of continuing the sight-seeing is to take a drive. If you wish to " do the town" in grand style and with the most comfort, you will hire a carriage and driver. If, on the other hand, either necessity compels economy, or taste inclines you to be democratic, you had better take a drag or barge, as the commodious stage coaches plying to all points of interest, are called. They are of various sizes and will accommodate from fifteen to thirty persons. They start from the steamboat landing, from Washington Sq., and from Touro Park, but by waiting a little on the avenue one will be certain to pass. For a short journey, to visit the beaches or for a view of the avenue, these conveyances have many recommendations, as they afford facilities for reaching every locality of interest and leave you free to embark or disembark at will. For the longer drives a more expensive turnout is a necessity.

Let us go down Bellevue Avenue

THE POST-OFFICE AND CUSTOM HOUSE.

SCENES ON BELLEVUE AVENUE.—THE OCEAN HOUSE.

THE SPOUTING ROCK.

in one of these coaches. Already in our
pedestrian stroll we have passed a number of elegant residences, but our attention has been distracted by other objects
of interest. In the region we are now
entering, however, there is nothing to
divert attention from the summer palaces.
Without attempting to give a complete
inventory we will only notice the most
striking, or those rendered interesting
from the renown of their occupants.
Entering the stage in front of the Ocean
House on the south corner of Bowery
Street, almost opposite is the large brick
mansion, the property of the Duchess
de Dino, formerly Mrs. F. A. Stevens,
of New York, who after her divorce,
which created much sensation at the
time, married the Marquis de Tallerand-
Perigord, February, 1887, from whose
father she received her present title. On
the left north corner of Berkeley Avenue is the residence of John G. Weaver,
proprietor of the Ocean House. The
house burned several years ago by Kate Judd, now serving a sentence in the
State Prison for that offense, stood on this site.

On the right north corner of Perry Street, is the handsome Queen Anne
villa of the Hon. Isaac Bell, Jr., late minister to the Netherlands. Directly opposite is " Snug Harbor," formerly the residence of Rear Admiral C. H.
Baldwin, U. S. N.

After passing down the avenue for the next half mile between many very fine residences, we see on the left, a con-
siderable distance from the roadway, the residence of ex-Governor
George Peabody Wetmore, a
colossal stone villa, one of the
most expensive places in Newport. Half way up the drive-
way leading to the house is a free-
stone archway, with a cottage on
the left embowered in English
ivy. The next estate on the left
south corner of Shepard Avenue,
formerly belonged to James R.
Keene, of New York, the well-
known stock broker, and the

HAPPY VALLEY.

foundation walls of his villa, which was burned Dec. 31. 1880, are yet visible.

Two streets beyond south, corner of Ruggles Avenue on the left, is the estate of the Hon. Levi P. Morton, the present nominee of the Republican Party for the vice-presidency. Still on the left, south corner of next street, Marine Avenue, is " By the Sea," the villa of August Belmont, the well-known New York banker. Just beyond on the right, north corner of Bancroft Avenue is a mammoth wooden house, the residence of Theodore A. Havemeyer, the Austrian Consul General in New York. Opposite the Havemeyer villa is a short court leading down to the house of the Hon. George Bancroft, the historian.

Just beyond the Havemeyer place, but on the opposite side of the street, is the estate of William Astor, of New York. The house is in spacious grounds, which run to the cliffs. The next residence but one on the left is that of W. W. Astor, son of John Jacob Astor. The house was formerly known as the " Barreda Place," being built by the Spanish minister of that name.

A quarter of a mile further and Bellevue Avenue turns a right angle to the west. At the outside of the angle on the left is the magnificent new house of Frederick W. Vanderbilt, situated almost directly on the cliffs, and commanding a wide outlook over the sea. It occupies the estate formerly owned by Jacob Dunnell, of Pawtucket.

About a quarter of a mile from the turn Bellevue Avenue terminates at Bailey's Beach, and on this short stretch there are some very elegant residences. Bailey's Beach is a smooth little beach about a quarter of a mile wide, with a few bathing houses near

LAND'S END.

the end of the avenue. From here also the graded cliff walk starts, and a walk
of a short distance along the cliffs will bring you to a wooden observatory,
somewhat shaky, it is true, but from which you will have an excellent view of
the cliffs to the southwest. On the further side of the beach perched on
the rocks is the residence of Henry Clews, the New York banker, and in the
mass of rocks to the southward of this house is Spouting Rock, through
which the water is forced in a jet during powerful southeast storms.

When returning from the end of the avenue if you form a party you can get
the driver to take another route back. Returning along Bellevue, turn down
Marine Avenue, then into Wetmore Avenue on the left, passing a number of
very beautiful houses on either side. Then turn to the right into Ruggles
Avenue and take Ochre Point Avenue, the second street to the left. The first
house on the right as we turn into Ochre Point Avenue is the residence of Cornelius Vanderbilt, formerly the property of Pierre Lorillard. On the side toward the cliffs, north corner of the next street, Shepard, is the beautiful residence

LIME ROCKS AND LIGHTHOUSE, THE HOME OF IDA LEWIS.

built by Miss Catherine Wolfe, and now belonging to Louis Lorillard. On the
right is the estate of J. J. Van Alien, whose house of cream colored stone fronts
on Lawrence Avenue. A short distance further, on the right, are the "cottages" of Ogden Goelet and Robert Goelet, both estates fronting on the cliffs, the
latter being at the foot of Narragansett Avenue. Across the street from Robert
Goelet is the estate of the late W. R. Travers, of New York. A short drive up
Narragansett Avenue brings us to Bellevue Avenue and we return to our starting point. This drive takes us past the most stylish and expensive group

of Newport's summer residences. If the
visitor wishes to continue the pleasure of
inspecting these beautiful abodes a drive
from the union of Touro Street and Bellevue Avenue, through Kay Street, Rhode
Island Avenue, Buena Vista Street, and
Gibbs Avenue to Bath Road, will afford
all requisite opportunity.

The grand drive in Newport is around
Ocean Avenue, sometimes called the ten
mile drive from the fact that the circuit
from Washington Square and return is between ten and eleven miles. The first
portion of this drive is up Touro Street
and along Bellevue Avenue already described. Starting from Bailey's Beach the
road follows the indentations of the shore,
affording magnificent views of the rocky
coast. In arranging for this drive it is an
easy matter to get a driver who can point

PURGATORY.

out the different residences and the places of interest, but the chief attraction is
the scenery. On the return half of the circuit very fine views of the city and
harbor are obtained.

Other drives to the northward, along either shore of the island, through
beautiful scenery, and past historic places, will amply repay the cost of time and
money which you can justifiably spend upon them.

Two miles across the city from the landing of the Providence and Wickford boats is Easton's Beach, one of the chief attractions of Newport. During
the season the coaches already mentioned ply regularly from the boats and trains
to the beach, and for ten cents any of them will carry you there. The route is
directly east over the neck of the peninsula, first up some of the narrow, hillside
streets, then through the business portion
of Bellevue Avenue and down the Bath
Road to the beach. The first portion of
the latter avenue is not at all a handsome
neighborhood, but at the eastern end are
the outposts of the summer residences, and
in fact this highway is the dividing line between the two chief groups. Approaching
the beach the road leads down a steep incline and an excellent view is obtained of
the long stretch of level sand with the surf
dashing in upon it. The beach is at the
head of an inlet open to the ocean from the
south, on which account there is always a
good surf. It is smooth, wide, and level.

THE FORTY STEPS

formed of fine, hard sand, and is nearly a mile in extent in a straight line. Formerly the bathing houses and the buildings for the accommodation of visitors were very dilapidated in appearance, but in 1887, extensive new structures were erected, the sea wall bounding the roadway was extended and repaired, the roadway rebuilt, the locality generally improved in appearance and made to correspond with modern Newport. These changes have rendered the beach more popular with the residents, among whom for years it had evidently fallen into disfavor.

On the west side of Easton's Beach the shore is faced with cliffs of broken, jagged rocks, twenty or more feet in height, which extend all the way around to Bailey's Beach, and the residences on Ochre Point and on the east side of the lower part of Bellevue Avenue are nearly all so situated as to overlook the cliffs. For all this distance, about three miles, a graded path leads along the edge affording magnificent views of the ocean on the one hand, and on the other the finest views of the gardens and homes of the summer residents to be had in Newport. Various spots in the rocks have been given names and are connected with story and legend. At the foot of Narragansett Avenue are the Forty Steps, so called, where there was originally a number of natural steps in the rocks leading down to the water, but these having crumbled away are now replaced by a wooden stairway. Many of the residents along the cliffs have private stairways, locked and barred, leading down the face of the rock to the water, and the jutting headlands are dotted with little summer houses.

But although this pathway just described is justly called the "cliff walk," it is not the only pathway by the sea. In *Oldport Days*, by Thomas Wentworth Higginson, is a very comprehensive description of the walk by the sea: " All round the shores of the island there runs a winding path. It is probably as old as the settlement of the country, and has been kept open with pertinacious fidelity by the fishermen, whose right of way it represents. In some places, as between Fort Adams and Castle Hill, it exists in its primitive form, an irregular track above rough cliffs, where you look down upon the entrance to the harbor and watch the white sailed schooners that glide beneath.   Elsewhere the high road has usurped its place and you have the privilege of the path without its charm.   Along the eastern cliff it runs for some miles in the rear of beautiful estates, whose owners have seized on it and graded it and gravelled it and made stiles for it, and done for it everything that landscape gardening could do, while leaving it a footpath still. In remoter places the path grows wilder and has ramifications striking boldly across the peninsula through rough moorland and among great ledges of rock."

Beyond Easton's Beach and separated from it by the peninsula of Easton's Point is Sachuest Beach, which is much larger than Easton's, but not so safe, which fact, together with its distance, two miles beyond Easton's, causes it to be almost wholly neglected. On the east side of the peninsula and fronting on Sachuest Beach is a deep yawning crevice in the face of the cliff, 160 feet long, 8 to 14 feet wide, and 50 feet in depth. The sea flows into it at the bottom of the cliffs. It is known as Purgatory, and there are various legends connected with it.

BIRD'S EYE VIEW OF NEWPORT.

From the summit of the precipitous cliffs in the neighborhood of Purgatory, the scenery within range of vision is probably the most picturesque in the vicinity of Newport. Sachuest Beach, in its whole extent, is seen at once, while a few hundred rods to the northward are a series of rugged, rocky ridges, broken up into crags and peaks, rising to a height of fifty feet or more, and separated from each other by deep valleys or gullies. At the southern extremity of the most eastern ridge are the Hanging Rocks, where the famous Dean, afterwards Bishop Berkeley, is said to have penned his most celebrated writings. The Happy Valley of Paradise is a small, level vale, inclosed on all but one side by the high cliffs, and is in close proximity to the Hanging Rocks. None of the localities just mentioned are in Newport, but in the adjoining town of Middletown.

In the past Newport has been careless about perfect sanitary arrangements, but the matter was agitated for years, and as a result a good system of sewerage is in operation, and although the entire city has not yet been furnished with the means of utilizing it, the work is being pushed rapidly forward. In 1885 a plan was agreed upon providing for the discharge of the sewerage into Narragansett Bay, west of the Goat Island Breakwater, by means of a submerged iron pipe across the bottom of the harbor. During 1887 the pipe was laid and the outlet constructed 300 feet beyond the breakwater, and sewerage began to flow through August 1st, 1887. About one-third of the city is provided for by new sewers, and as others are now in process of construction, before the end of the present season the major part of the city will probably be provided for. November 9, 1887, the City Council voted $88,000 for the further carrying out of the system in the lower part of the city, and for diverting into the new system the sewers which now flow into the inner harbor.

An excellent system of water works was built some years ago by George H. Norman. The water was at first wholly obtained just north of the beach from Easton's Pond, on the west side of which the pumping station is located, but this supply not proving as satisfactory in quality as desirable, a further supply has been obtained from the pond near the Hanging Rocks. The city was given the option of purchasing the works after they were put in operation, but the electors voted not to do so, and they are now operated by a joint stock company.

Not the least of the attractions of Newport are the short excursions that can be made to points in and about the harbor. You can go to Fort Adams, to the United States Training Ship, to Jamestown, and if you have audacity and influence, to the Torpedo station. Fort Adams, one of the strongest fortifications in the country, guards the entrance to the harbor between Newport and Conanicut Island. You can drive there, a distance of between three and four miles, or if you have friends or acquaintances in the fort you will be allowed to go over in the government tug boat, the distance across the harbor being less than a mile. On the way Lime Rock Light is passed in the upper part of the harbor near the shore, on the rock of the same name, and the keeper of the light is Ida (Wilson) Lewis, a brave woman who has acquired a national reputation for the daring manner in which, at various times, she has rescued persons from drowning. The tug starts from Ferry Wharf at foot of Market Square.

The fort is an immense structure, the parade-ground in the interior covering no less than eleven
acres, and there is an extensive redoubt to the south. Half a mile
beyond along the Inner shore is
Brenton's Cove, the head of the
harbor. On the south side are
frowning cliffs, and the place would
look well in a picture under the
title of "Pirates' Haven." A number of old hulks line the shore, in
all stages of dismemberment; this
locality, on account of being out of
the way, has been used as the place
to beach old wrecks and let them
break up. Captain Cook's ship
Endeavor was here left to rot
many years ago. To carry out the

THE GLEN.

idea of its being a pirate's harbor, the story has gained credence in some quarters that Captain Kidd's ship was left here, and some of the soldiers will point
out to you the ribs of the old vessel to this day.

The United States Training ship *New Hampshire* is moored off the southern end of Coaster's Harbor Island, which lies along the shore at the north of the
harbor and city. The island formerly belonged to the city, but was ceded
to the government several years ago on condition that it would be used
for a training school. The large white building on the slope of the hill is the
War College, formerly the Almshouse of Newport. Visitors can drive to the
island and inspect the college and the ship, but if you exercise a little diplomacy
you may be allowed to go in the launch which starts from Commercial Wharf
about every hour.

The Torpedo Station is on Goat Island which separates the inner harbor
from the main passage into the
bay, and lies about half a mile
from Newport's wharves. Strangers are not allowed on the island,
as the work of the station is the
construction of and experimenting
with sub-marine projectiles, and
visitors might be exposed to danger
or would be in the way. If you
are acquainted with one of the officers you may, however, get an
opportunity to go over in the steam
launch which makes frequent trips
from Ferry Wharf. The view of

THE REDWOOD LIBRARY.

11

the island from the wharves or from the deck of a steamer is usually quite sufficient, and it presents the appearance of a place of residence or of trade with hardly any warlike character.

But the finest harbor excursion is over to Jamestown on Conanicut Island by the steam ferry boat, a distance of about two miles. Leaving the wharf we move across the harbor and out of it to the north passing Goat Island on the left with its long breakwater at the north end, terminating in a light-house. On our right while skirting the breakwater, are Long Wharf and the Old Colony Railroad wharves and docks, with some of the mam-

CAPT. THOS. CROSBY.

moth vessels of the Fall River line lying alongside.   Northward about three-quarters of a mile along the shore is Coaster's Harbor Island, with the training ship in the fore-ground.   Circling around the end of the breakwater the boat heads due west, and we soon pass close to the south side of Rose Island, mid-way between Jamestown and Newport.   Perched on the top of what appears to be an old fortification is Rose Island light, while beyond are evident remains of old earthworks.   Directly south we have an excellent view of Fort Adams about a mile distant, while across the entrance of the bay from it is the historic Fort Dumplings perched on the rocky cliffs at the southeastern extremity of Co-nanicut Island.   After passing beyond range of Rose Island to the northward about two miles away, in midchannel, standing up out of the water clear and distinct, is Gould Island, the property of Edward C. Homans, of New York, who has a summer residence on the island, which is also used as a rendezvous for the New York Yacht Club.   By this time we are in plain sight of Jamestown, which is a collection of less than a hundred houses, mostly summer resi-dences, of a good size and two or three hotels, situated on a gentle slope.   A highway leads from the landing across the island, here only a mile wide, and at the other side, if you care to go, you can have a view of Dutch Island Harbor, a roadstead between the island of that name and Conanicut.   The Kingston shore is also in full view, and to the south the southern portion of Conanicut Island with the narrow isthmus connecting it with the main island. This excursion probably affords the most varied illustration of physical geogra-phy in the neighborhood of Newport.

Several of the existing church edifices are historic structures dating back to colonial times.   Of these the Sabbatarian Church, now used by the Historical Society, and the Jewish Synagogue have already been mentioned.   The most noteworthy, however, of all these edifices is Trinity Church, corner of Spring and Church streets, erected in 1725, and enlarged in 1762, which is worth a visit on account of the old-fashioned character of the interior.   The meeting-house of the Society of Friends on Marlboro Street was built in 1700 but has since been reconstructed.   It is a large plain edifice and in June of each alter-nate year, here are held the yearly meetings for New England.   The oldest

THE MARQUAND COTTAGE.

church organization is that of the First Baptist Society, which is said to date from the first settlement of the island. The present fine edifice, corner of Spring and Sherman streets, was erected in 1841. Of existing churches the finest structures are the Channing Memorial, Pelham Street, opposite Touro Park ; St. Mary's, Roman Catholic, corner Spring and Levin streets, and the United Congregational, corner Pelham and Spring streets. The colored people have three churches, a Baptist, a Methodist, and a Congregational, all in a flourishing condition.

The streets of Newport while open to objection during rainy weather or in the winter months on account of not being as generally paved as in cities of its size, are yet, during the summer, probably better adapted to its own peculiar life than otherwise they would be. In the older portion the paving both in the roadways and on the sidewalks needs repairing, but a great deal has been done to remedy this recently. The avenues, however, are many of them macadamized and make almost perfect roadways.

Although possessing such splendid facilities for business afforded by her fine harbor and excellent railroad and steamboat connections, Newport has never been successful in manufacturing like other places in the state. At one time there were three cotton mills in operation, but they all met with misfortune in some shape or other, and to-day not a spindle revolves in the city. The Perry Mill still standing on Thames Street, near the steamboat landing, was erected in 1835, but has been idle for years. A short distance further down on the same street is the Aquidneck Mill of which the stone part was built in 1831 and the brick addition on the front in 1863 by the Richmond Manufacturing Company, when they purchased the concern. The mill is now idle, as are also the works of the Newport Shot and Lead Company adjoining. In 1837 the Coddington Mill was erected near the end of Thames Street, but was burned December 31, 1859, and was never rebuilt.

In view of this dearth of manufacturing the question arises how the permanent population of 20,000 people earn a living. This is not, however, such a difficult question as at first appears. The government stations in and around the harbor give employment to many people who reside in the city, the Old Colony Railroad and the Fall River Line of steamers bring considerable work and business, there are a number of minor manufactures, such as fine furniture, rubber specialties, etc., many fishermen have their homes here, and a great deal of business is done in catering to the summer visitors, so that, take it all in all, there is much more work than would be thought at first sight. But there seems to be some evidence that a revival of business is at hand as two electric light companies, a building association, a lath company, and a land company were formed the past spring.

There are three routes to reach Newport from Providence and two from New York. From Providence you can go by the Providence, Warren & Bristol Railroad, via Warren and Fall River, the railroad skirting the shores of the bay for a large portion of the whole distance and affording many pleasant and some grand views; the most popular way, and in fact almost the only route from Providence patronized in the summer, is by the bay steamers from whose decks the shores and islands of the beautiful Narragansett please the senses with their ever-varying panorama; the third route is by the New York, Providence & Boston Railroad, via Wickford, connecting at Wickford Landing with a steamer which, after an hour's sail across the bay, lands the traveler in Newport.

The chief route from New York is by the Old Colony Steamboat line, but the Wickford line is also patronized by many on account of being nearly an all rail route. From Boston the main line of the Old Colony, running through Fall River, terminates at Newport.

With a climate for mildness and equableness unsurpassed on the Atlantic coast, a purity of atmosphere resulting from the nearness of old ocean, a good water supply, a fine system of sewerage, broad avenues, beautiful homes, unequaled in the country, an old, historic town, a magnificent harbor, the city ought to continue to be a summer emporium of fashion, and with all these advantages should develop in other lines as well.

The old Engs building, 203 Thames Street, corner of Lopez wharf, is said to have been, during the years when the slave trade flourished, the largest slave station in New England; and some of the adjacent buildings still standing were used as slave pens. To-day, however, these premises are used for much different purposes, and Mr. J. H. Martin occupies the old slave mart with his fine stock of china, crockery, glass, fancy goods, and one of the largest assortments of Japanese ware in the country. Mementoes of Newport are here in abundance, so that a visit to the store will repay the trouble any time, for the opportunities of inspecting the historical souvenirs, as well as the large selection of general novelties.

With the improvements in sewerage that have been introduced in Newport the present and past years, increased attention is required to all forms of sanitary plumbing. For all such work Joseph Haire, practical plumber, is well prepared, and has on hand all the latest improvements in closets, traps, wash bowls, and other appliances. At his place of business, 132 Spring Street, four doors north of Church Street, prompt attention is given to all orders.

THE STRANGERS' GUIDE–NEWPORT.

RESIDENCES OF SOME NOTED PEOPLE.

Agassiz, Prof. Alexander, Castle Hill.

Astor, William, Bellevue ave. and the Cliffs, south end.

Astor, W. Waldorf, Bellevue Ave. and the Cliffs, south end.

Bennett, James Gordon, Bellevue Ave. opp. Casino.

Belmont, August, southeast corner of Marine and Bellevue aves.

Bancroft, George, Bancroft Ave. and Cliffs.

Brewer, Mrs. Gardner, Ledge Road, Bellevue Ave. and the Cliffs.

Blatchford, Justice Samuel, Greenough Place.

Bell, Isaac, Jr., northwest corner Bellevue Ave. and Perry.

Bonaparte, Col. Jerome N., Harrison Ave.

Baldwin, C. C., northeast corner of Narragansett and Bellevue aves.

Carroll, Ex-Gov. John Lee, of Maryland, Clay.

Cullum, Gen. George W., Sea View Ave. and the Cliffs.

Chews, Henry, Ocean Ave. near Spouting Rock and Bailey's Beach.

D'Hauteville, F. S. G., southwest corner Gordon and Bellevue Ave.

Goelet, Ogden, northeast corner Ochre Point Ave. and Webster, to the Cliffs.

Goelet, Robert, foot of Narragansett Ave., on Ochre Point Ave. and the Cliffs.

Gammell, William, Narragansett Ave. and the Cliffs.

Gammell, R. H. I., Narragansett Ave. and the Cliffs.

Howe, Mrs. Julia Ward, Lawton's Valley.

Havemeyer, Theodore A., northwest corner of Bancroft and Bellevue Aves.

Hunt, Richard M., northwest corner of Church and Bellevue Ave.

Kernochan, James P., Marine Ave.

Low, A. A., near Castle Hill.

Luce, Rear Admiral S. B., Francis and Rhode Island Ave.

Lorillard, Louis L., Shepard and Ochre Point aves. and the Cliffs.

Marquand, Henry Q., northeast corner Rhode Island Ave. and Buena Vista.

Stevens, Mrs. Paran, Bellevue Ave. and Jones, near Casino.

Van Alen, J. J., Ochre Point and Lawrence Aves.

Vanderbilt, Cornelius, south side Ruggles Ave., Ochre Point Ave. and the Cliffs.

Vanderbilt, Frederick W., new house at the turn of Bellevue Ave., on Cliffs at Rough Point.

Winans, Ross R., Ocean Ave.

Weld, William G., northeast corner of Bellevue and Parker Aves.

Wetmore, Ex-Gov. George Peabody, Bellevue and Shepard Aves.

POINTS OF INTEREST.

Almy's Pond, near Bailey's Beach, north.

Bailey's Beach, end of Bellevue ave.

Black Rock, near Brenton's Point.

Brenton's Point, the most southerly extremity of the Island, off Ocean ave.

Brenton's Cove, head of harbor to southwest, near Fort Adams.

Bull House (oldest in Newport), Spring Street, short distance from Washington square.

City Hall, foot Washington Square, Thames street.

Channing Memorial Church, Pelham, opposite Touro Park.

Channing House (old), Thames Street.

Children's Home, 24 School.

Casino, 194 Bellevue ave.

Coddington School.

Castle Hill, Western extremity of peninsula, overlooking main entrance to Narragansett Bay.

Conanicut Lodge, at end of Ledge Road.

Castle Hill Point, northern point of Castle Hill.

County Jail, 13 Marlborough.

Cherry Neck, ocean road, just beyond Lily Pond.

Cliff Walk, from Easton's to Bailey's Beach.

Easton Beach, and Bath road.

Easton Pond, north of Easton Beach.

Fort Adams, entrance harbor.

Fort Greene, on harbor, and Washington.

Fort Walcott, near Fort Greene.

Forty Steps, end Narragansett ave.

Friend's Meeting House, Farewell and Marlboro.

Gooseberry Island, off Cherry Neck.

Goat Island, in harbor.

Halidon Hill, overlooking harbor from south.

High School, Church.

Industrial School for Girls, Broadway.

Jewish Synagogue, Touro, near Washington Square.

Jewish Cemetery, eastern corner of Kay Street and Bellevue ave.

Liberty Tree, Liberty Square, junction of Warner, Farewell and Thames.

Land's End, near end Ledge road, overlooking Bailey's Beach.

Lily Pond, west of Almy's Pond and Bailey's Beach.

Lime Rock (and lighthouse), in south part of harbor.

Mason's Hall, corner Church and School.

Music Hall, Bellevue ave., between Casino and Ocean House.

Miantonomi Hill, an elevation 160 feet in height, a mile and a half north of Washington Square.

Newport Gas Co., 181 Thames.

Newport Artillery Armory, Clark.

Newport Historical Society building, next above Jewish synagogue on Touro.

Newport Reading Room, corner Church street and Bellevue ave.

Newport Hospital, 16 Howard ave. and Friendship street.

Opera House, Washington Square.

Old Stone Mill, Touro Park.

Ochre Point, off Marine and Ruggles aves.

Ocean House, Bellevue ave., corner Bowery.

Perry House, Washington Square.

Perry Statues; Com. Oliver Hazard Perry, Washington Square; Com. M. C. Perry, Touro Park.

Parade, Washington Square.

People's Free Library, 296 Thames.

Polo Grounds, north end Thames.

Price's Neck, Ocean Road, beyond Cherry Neck, U. S. Life Saving Station at its extremity.

Rough Point, off F. W. Vanderbilt's house, Bellevue ave.

Rocky Farm Gully, off Ocean road, south from Lily Pond.

Ragged Point, the southern point of Castle Hill.

Ramshead, Castle Hill.

Redwood Library, Bellevue ave., near Touro Park.

St. Mary's Church (R. C.), corner Levina and Spring.

State House, head Washington Square.

Sheep Point, Cliffs off Ynmas ave.

Sporting Rock, west of Bailey's Beach.

Telegraph Hill, Beacon Road, about five miles south of Washington Square.

Touro Park, Bellevue ave., Pelham and Mill.

Trinity Church, Spring, corner Church.

United Congregational Church, corner Pelham and Spring.

United States Custom House and Post-office, corner Thames and Franklin.

U. S. Engineer's office.

U. S. Torpedo Station, Goat Island.

U. S. Naval Training Station, including Training Ship "New Hampshire," and the War College, on Coaster's Harbor Island.

Vernon House (old), corner Clark and Mary.

Water Works, Pumping Station, north shore Easton's Pond.

Washington Square, Thames and Touro.

POINTS OF INTEREST OUTSIDE CITY LIMITS.*

Lawton's Valley about six miles north on west shore of Island.
The Glen, about six miles north, on east shore of Island.
Sachuest Beach, beyond Easton's Beach.
Hanging Rocks, back of Sachuest beach.
Happy Valley of Paradise, near Happy Rocks.
Purgatory, on Cliffs west of Sachuest Beach.
Whitehall, back of Happy Valley, ancient residence of Bishop Berkley.

WHARVES.

Aquidneck Mill, 447 Thames.
Bull's 197 Thames.
Bowen's, 269 Thames.
Bannister's.
Brown & Howard's, from 411 Thames.
Champlin Wharf, 185 Thames.
City Wharf, adjoining Long Wharf.
Coddington, 513 Thames.
Commercial, 303 Thames.
Perry, 241 Thames.
Hammett's, 345 Thames.
Kinsley's, 271 Thames
Langley's, 305 Thames.
Lawton's.
Lee's, 431 Thames.
Long, 125 Thames.
Lopez, 203 Thames.
Old Colony, R. R. station.
Perry Mill, 339 Thames.
Peckham's, 215 Thames.
Sherman's 169 Thames.
Swinburne's, 173 and 213 Thames.
Sayer's, 283 Thames.
Scott's, 283 Thames.
Swan's, 151 Thames.
Spring, 469 Thames.
Sisson's, 479 Thames.
William's.
Wait's, 495 Thames.

HOTELS.

Aquidneck House, Pelham, corner Corne.
Brayton's, 38 & 44 Pelham.
Cliff Avenue Hotel and Cottage, 20 Cliff Ave.
Cliffton House, 113 Bellevue Ave.
Germania Hotel, 22 State Street.
Hartman House, 10 Bellevue Ave.
Ocean House, Bellevue Ave. corner East Bowery.
Park Hotel, Washington Sq. opp. State House.
Perry House, Washington Sq.

DEPOTS.

Old Colony R. R., West Marlboro, near Thames.
Old Colony Line, end of Long Wharf.
Continental Steamboat Co., Commercial Wharf.
Jamestown Ferry, Ferry Wharf.
Newport & Wickford R. R. and Steamboat Co., Commercial Wharf.

CEMETERIES.

Friend's Cemetery, Tilden Ave. corner Kay.
St. Mary's Catholic Cemetery, Warner and Spruce.
North City Cemetery, Farewell.
Island Cemetery, Warner.
Old City Cemetery, Warner, adjoining Island Cemetery.
Jewish Cemetery, corner Kay and Bellevue Ave.

CHURCHES.

All Saints' Memorial (Episcopal), Beach, corner Cottage.
Central Baptist, Clarke.
Channing Memorial, Pelham, opposite Touro Park.
Emanuel, (Episcopal), Spring, corner Dearborn.
Friends' Meeting House, West Broadway and Marlborough.
First Baptist, Spring, corner Sherman.
First Methodist, Marlboro, near Charles.

*The first two places are in Portsmouth, the remainder in Middletown.

Grace Chapel, Thames, corner Wellington ave.
Mt. Zion A. M. E., Bellevue ave., next to Jewish Cemetery.
Second Baptist, corner North Baptist and Farewell.
Shiloh Baptist (colored), Mary, corner School.
St. John, The Evangelist (Episcopal), Poplar.
St. Marys R. C. Church, Convent and School, Spring, corner Levin.
St. George Chapel (Episcopal), Rhode Island ave., near Broadway.
St. Joseph Church (R. C.), Touro, corner Clarke.
Swedish M. E. Church, 173 Spring.
Thames St. M. E., Thames, corner Brewer.
Touro Synagogue, Touro St.
Trinity Episcopal, Spring, corner Church.
Union Congregational, Division, bet. Church and Mary.
United Congregational, corner Spring and Pelham.

PARKS.

Touro Park, Bellevue Avenue, Mill and Belham, area 18,350 sq. ft.
The Mall, Washington Square, Thames and Touro, area 17,750 sq. ft.
Liberty Park, Marlboro, Meeting and Farewell, area 2,500 sq. ft.
Equality Park, Broadway and West Broadway, area 13,200 sq. ft.
Congdon Park, Broadway and Cranston, area 8,650 sq. ft.
Morton Park, Coggeshall Avenue and Brenton, area 534,800 sq. ft.

FIRE DEPARTMENT.

The apparatus consists of four steam fire engines, four hose reels, and one hook and ladder truck.

FIRE STATIONS.

Hose Tower and Battery Station, West Marlboro St., near O. C. R. R. Depot.
Hook and Ladder No. 1, Long Wharf, near City Hall.
Steam Fire Engine No. 1, Mill St., near Thames.
Steam Fire Engine No. 2, Bridge St., near Third.
Hose Reel No. 4, Equality Park Place.
Steam Fire Engine No. 5, Touro, Junction of Mary.
Hose Rena No. 6, Court, rear of old Gas Works, near Thames.
Steam Fire Engine No. 7, Young, near Thames.
Hose Reel No. 8, Prospect Hill Street, near Bellevue Avenue.

PUBLIC SCHOOL BUILDINGS.

Willow Street School, (Fee in Long Wharf Trustees), corner Willow and Third.
Potter School, (Fee in Long Wharf Trustees), Elm.
Farewell Street, Farewell, op. North Baptist.
Edward Street, Edward, near Covell.
Cranston Street, Cranston.
Cranston Avenue, Cranston Avenue, near Broadway.
Coddington School, Mill.
Clarke Street, Clarke, rear of Artillery Armory.
Rogers High School, Church, op. High.
Lethal School, corner Spring and Perry.
Parrish School, (fee in private persons), South Spring, near Wheatland ave.

PRIVATE SCHOOLS.

St. Mary's Parochial, (Roman Catholic), Levin.
The Newport Industrial School for Girls, W. Broadway.
Industrial School for Boys, Perry Mill Wharf.

BANKS.

Aquidneck National, 284 Thames.
First National, 231 Thames.
Merchants', 223 Thames.
National Exchange, 38 Washington Sq.
National Bank of Rhode Island, 343 Thames.
New England Commercial, 263 Thames.
Newport National, 8 Washington Sq.
Union National, 250 Thames.

SAVINGS BANKS.

Coddington, 231 Thames.
Island, 38 Washington Square.
Savings Bank of Newport, 282 Thames.

LIST OF NEWPORT COTTAGERS, 1888.

Astor William, New York, Bellevue Ave. & the Cliffs.
Astor W. Waldorf, New York, Bellevue Ave. and the Cliffs.
Agassiz Prof. Alexander, Cambridge, Castle Hill.
Almon A. P., Salem, Mass., Red Cross Ave.
Andrews Frank W., Boston, Maple Ave.
Arnold Mrs. Samuel G., Providence, East Shore.
Auchincloss Henry B., New York, Washington.
Arnold Dr. F. S. E., Yonkers, N.Y., Carroll ave.
Austin John C., Providence, Paradise ave. [Beach.
Ashhurst Mrs. W. H., Philadelphia, Bellevue ave. and
Appleton W. W., New York, (Whitehouse's) Rhode Island ave.
Auchincloss John W., New York, (Russell's) Narragansett ave.
Auchincloss Mrs. Elizabeth, New York, Washington.
Backus Mrs. Dr., Baltimore, (Hazard's), Kay
Bell Isaac, New York, (Kine's) Narragansett ave.
Brewster Mrs. Oliver, New York, (Townsend's) Kay & Brinley. [Island ave.
Bacon Dr. Gorham, New York, (Yardley's) Rhode
Boynton Jesse V., Providence, (Channing's) Tucker-man ave. [ington.
Bigelow Mrs. J. W., New York (Sanford's), Wash-
Harger Samuel F., New York (Traver's), Narragansett ave. [Beach.
Brownell Seth H., Providence, (Smith's) near Easton's
Beckwith N. M., New York, (Weaver's) Bellevue ave.
Belmont Mrs O. H. P., New York, Webster.
Bennett James Gordon, New York, Bellevue ave.
Bancroft George, Washington, Bancroft ave. and the Cliffs.
Blatchford Mrs. R. M., New York, beach and Green-ough Place. [Place.
Blatchford Justice Samuel, Washington, Greenough
Blatchford Miss S. E., New York, Catherine.
Brewer Mrs. Gardner, Boston, Bellevue ave and the Cliffs. [the Cliffs
Bancroft John C., Melrose, Mass., Bancroft ave. and
Bowen Stephen, Boston, Spring
Bruen Mrs. Mary L., Boston, Bellevue ave.
Belmont August, New York, Bellevue and Marine ave, and the Cliffs.
Bell Dr. C. M., New York, Bellevue ave. and the Cliffs.
Bull Charles M., Brooklyn, One Mile Corner.
Baker Mrs. Richard Jr., Boston, Bellevue ave. and Ledge Road.
Barstow Captain, U. S. A., East Shore.
Barstow D. H., Boston, East Shore.
Bryer Benjamin, New York, near Miantonomi Hill.
Black Mrs. Francis L., New York, Honeyman Hill.
Bonaparte Col. J. N., Baltimore, Harrison ave.
Borden J. C., Fall River, Ocean ave.
Borden T. W., Fall River, Ocean ave. [ave.
Baldwin C. C., New York, Narragansett and Bellevue
Barret Mrs. Alexander, New York, Catherine.
Bell Isaac Jr., New York, Bellevue ave. and Perry.
Blight Atherton, Philadelphia, Bellevue ave. [ave.
Bryce J. Smith, New York, Narragansett and Bellevue
Berryman Mrs., New York, Rhode Island ave.
Beeckman Mrs. J. L., New York, Ochre Point.
Carroll Charles, Baltimore, (Phelp's) Clev.
Carroll John Lee, Baltimore, (Phelp's) Clay.
Clift Smith, New York, (Stitt's) Bellevue ave. and Pelham. [Island.
Carlisle Mrs. M. E., Washington, (Douglass') Conanicut
Cram Henry A., New York, (Hunnewell's) Yznaga ave.
Caldwell Misses, New York, Kay and Ayrault.
Cushing Thomas F., Boston, Bellevue ave. and the Cliffs.
Coit Rev. Dr., Concord, N. H., Indian ave. [Corner.
Cooke Mrs. Joseph J., Providence, near One Mile
Chickering Charles F., New York, Bellevue ave. [ave.
Cullum Gen. G. W., U. S. Engineer Corps, Sea View
Conkling F. A., Jr., New York, Pelham, Mill and George Streets.
Coleman Samuel, New York, Red Cross ave.
Coles Mrs. Elizabeth G., New York, Bellevue ave.
Churchill Capt. C. C., U. S. Army, Ayrault St.
Caswell John R., New York, Bull St.
Cleveland Dr. Clement, New York, Merton ave.

Cook Henry H., New York, Bellevue ave and the Cliffs.
Cadwalader John, Philadelphia, Bellevue ave. and Lodge Road.
Cope M. C., Cincinnati, Washington St.
Carley Francis D., Louisville, Ky., Bellevue ave.
Clews Henry, New York, Ocean ave. near Spouting Rock. [Streets.
Cunningham Dr. E. L., Boston, Catherine and Cottage
Cushing R. M., Boston, Ocean ave.
Cassels Col. Washington, (Wells') Conanicut Island.
De Barrios, Madame Francisca, New York, not decided.
Dutton E. P., New York, (Cooke's), Gibbs ave.
Dunston H. R., New York, (Fearing's) Bath Road.
Denison Mrs. H. A., New York, (Wildes') Kay st.
Dore Mrs. John, New York, (Burrows') Gibbs ave
Davis Theodore M., New York, Ocean ave. [vue ave.
DeForest George B., New York, (Chickering's) Belle-
Davies Julian T., New York, Purgatory Road.
D'Hauteville F. S. G., New York, Bellevue ave.
Dale Thomas N., Patterson, N.J., Gibbs ave. and Bue-na Vista St.
Erving Mrs. Shirley, Boston, (Griswold's), Kay St
Evans Jonathan, New York, (Dean'), Easton's Point
Eustis F. A., Cambridge, Mass., Conanicut Island
Ellis John W., New York, Bellevue ave. and the Cliffs.
Edgar Mrs. William, New York, Beach St.
Emmons Mrs. J. W. Boston, Gibbs ave.
Emmons A. B., Boston, Gibbs ave
Emmons G. R., Boston, Conanicut Island.
Easton F. W., Pawtucket, R.I., Paradise ave
Fearing Daniel B., New York, Annandale Road.
Fearing George R., New York, Narragansett ave.
Ferrill Joseph L., Philadelphia, Conanicut Island.
Francis Rev. Lewis, Brooklyn, Honeyman Hill.
French Abel, New York, Bellevue ave. and the Cliffs.
French Francis O., New York, Halidon Hill.
Freeman Francis F., New York, Bellevue ave.
Foster John, Boston, Le Roy ave.
Fiske Josiah M., New York, Ochre Point.
Fellows F. W., New York, Washington St.
Filley Mrs. G. B., St. Louis, Conanicut Island.
Fry Gen. James B., U. S. A., (Brenon's), Francis Street and Everett Place.
French Seth Barton, New York, (Whipple's), Cliff ave.
French Hugo, O., New York, Bellevue ave. [Cliffs.
Goelet Robert, New York, Narragansett ave. and the
Goelet Ogden, New York, (Sherman's) Victoria and Ruggles ave.
Gibbs Miss Sarah B., New York, Gibbs ave.
Gibbs Miss Emily O., New York, Rhode Island ave. and Beach St.
Gibbs Major T. S., New York, Gibbs ave.
Gibbs Prof. Wolcott, Cambridge, Mass., Gibbs ave.
Gilbert Mrs. J. T., New York, Bellevue ave.
Gammell William, Providence, Narragansett ave. and the Cliffs.
Gammell R. H. I., Providence, Narragansett ave. and the Cliffs. [ave.
Gammell William, Jr., Providence, (Carey's), Channing
Greene C., Providence, Conanicut Island.
Greene William R., New York, Mallone ave. and Brookway.
Gray Mrs. M. E., New York, Narragansett ave.
Griffith Dr. R. E., Philadelphia, Conanicut Island
Geraghty J. M., New York, (Brown's) Summer St.
Grosvenor William, Jr., Providence, (Stout's), Bellevue ave. and the Cliffs. [Island.
Green John J., Philadelphia, (Peckham's), Conanicut
Green Mrs. J. C., New York, No. 2 Linard Cottage, Narragansett ave. [ave.
Goddard E. Fay, New York, (Munchinger's), Bellevue
Gregory Charles E., New York, (Clark's), Kay St.
Haryou R. L., New York, (not decided)
Harriman James, Boston, (Thayer's), Bellevue ave.
Haydon Mrs. D. H., Boston, (Jay's), Buena Vista St.
Howe Walter, New York, Beacon Hill
Hopkins Mrs. J. B., Philadelphia, Conanicut Island.
Hutton G. M., Baltimore, Castle Hill.
Honatas E. C., New York, Goold Island. [don aves.
Hamilton Schuyler, Jr., New York, Harrison and Hali-

Howe Mrs. Julia Ward, Boston, Lawton's Valley.
Hazard Rowland N., New York, One Mile Corner.
Hoyt Henry S., New York, Beach at and Sunnyside pl.
Hartshorn Mrs. E. G., Providence, Halidon Hill.
Hoffman Miss Susan O., New York, Bellevue ave.
Huntington Prof. John T., Hartford, Indian ave.
Havemeyer Theodore A., New York, Bellevue ave.
Hunt Richard M., New York, Bellevue ave. and Church.
Herrick Elias J., New York, Clay st.
Hamilton Dr. Allan McLane, New York, Price's Neck.
Hodgson J. M., New York, LeRoy ave.
Howe Judge, New Orleans, (Fairchild's), Washington.
Hills George H. B., New York, (Swift's), Bellevue ave.
Hobbs Paymaster I. G., U. S. N., (Hunter's), DeBlois ave.
Hitchcock Mrs. Thomas, New York, (Hone's) Spring at.
Harris R. Duncan, New York, Bellevue ave.   [ave.
Heckscher Mrs. John G., New York, (Burrows'), Gibbs
Hill Mrs. J. M., New York, Bellevue ave.   [Cliffs.
Ingersoll Mrs. H., Philadelphia, Yznaca ave. and the
Josephs Lyman C., New York, Purgatory Road.
Jones Mrs. George F., New York, Harrison ave.
Jones Harry E., New York Harrison ave.
Jones the Misses, New York (Acosta's), Ochre Point.
Jones Miss C. Ogden, New York, Ochre Point.
Johnson Joseph G., Philadelphia, Bellevue Court.
Jones Miss Emily, New York, Wellington ave.
Johnson Levi, New Haven, Everett.   [casicut Is.
Jenks Mrs. Hannah M., Philadelphia, (Howland's) Con-
Kane Mrs. DeLancey, New York, (Langdon's), Sunnyside Place.
King Ronald, Boston, Kay.
Knowlton E. J., New York (Warren's). Gibbs ave.
Kingsland William M., Scarboro-on-Hudson (Pendleton's), Ochre Point.
Kendall Mrs. S. A., New York, Washington.
Kerr William G., Brooklyn, Washington.
Ketaltas Mrs. Eugene, New York, Webster.
Knower John, New York, Bellevue ave. and the Cliffs.
King Mrs. Edward, New York, Bowery ave. and Spring.
King LeRoy, New York, Bellevue and Berkeley aves.
King G. G., New York, Beacon Hill.   [Point.
Kernochan J. F., New York, Marine ave. and Ochre
Kindleberger Dr. D., U. S. Navy, Conanicut Island.
King Mrs A. M., Hartford, Ayrault.   [ave.
Leith Alexander J., New York (Griswold's), Bellevue
Leary Arthur, New York, (Paul's), Mill.
Lyon T., New York, (Groffe's), Bull.
Livermore C. F., New York, (O'Brien's), Bellevue ave.
Livingston Edward, New York, Ayrault.
Logan Lieut. L. C., U. S. N., Conanicut Island.
LeRoy Mrs. Daniel, New York, Bellevue ave.
LeRoy Stuyvesant, New York, Mann ave.
Livingston Herman T., New York, Sea View ave. and the Cliffs.
Livingston Maturin, New York, Bellevue Court.
Low A. A., Brooklyn, Castle Hill.
Low Josiah O., Brooklyn, Castle Hill.
Lyman Miss Florence, Boston, Webster.
Ledyard Mrs. Henry, New York, Catherine.
Lorillard Louis L., New York, Ochre Point.
Lyman the Misses, New York, Webster.
Lafarge John, New York, Sunnyside Place.
Langdon Walter, New York, Sunnyside Place.
Lusk Dr. W. T., New York (Bruen's), Bellevue ave.
Livingston Mrs. Edward Louis, New York (Bush's), Ayrault.   [the Cliffs.
Lawrence John, New York (Chanler's), Bath Road and
Miller George M., New York, Bellevue ave.
Mason the Misses, Boston, Bath Road and Rhode Island ave.
Miller W. Starr, New York, Bellevue ave.
Maxten J. Griffith, Albany, Everett Place.
Morris Wistar, Philadelphia, Conanicut Island.
Morris Miss Jane, Philadelphia, Washington.
McElhenen H. J., Boston, (Burkinshaw's) Howard ave.
Moffat Miss Myra, New York (Hartshorn's), Halidon Hill.
Mason A. Livingston, Providence, Halidon Hill.
Matthews Mrs. Mary, New York, Bellevue ave.
Maynard Lieut. Com. W., U. S. N., (Weeden's), Conanicut Island.
Merritt George, New York, Bellevue ave. and Spring.
McClellan Dr. George, Philadelphia, Conanicut Island.
Morrison W. H., New York, Honeyman Hill.
Mahoney John H, New York, Bellevue ave.
Marquand, Henry G., New York, Rhode Island ave. and Bonus Vista.
McKay Gordon, Boston, Marine ave.
Morehous C. P., Chicago, Howard ave.
Marin Capt. M. C., U. S. N., Kay.
Mann Henry A., Washington, Conanicut Island.
Mills, Charles E. Boston, (Barker's) Paradise ave.
McKim Dr. W. D., New York (King's) Bellevue ave.
Mitchell, Mrs. Alexander, Milwaukee (Ferguson's) Halidon Hill.   [Rhode Island ave.
McClure C. D., St. Louis, (Cushman's) Catherine and
Mendelssohn, H. E. London (Gray's) Bellevue ave.
Mendes Rev. A. P., New York, (Finn') Brinley
Mitchell Dr. S. Weir, Philadelphia, (King & Wetmore) Parker ave.   [ave.
Mott Thomas, Philadelphia, (Rutherford's) Harrison
Mills Ogden, New York, (Anthony's) Bellevue ave. and the Cliffs.

Neilson Miss Mary N., New York, Cottage.   [ave.
Nugent Mrs. George Germantown, Penn., Coggeshall
Norman Hugh E., Boston, Lawton'svalley
Nelson Mrs. Belle, New York, (Swinburne's) Greenough Place.   [Beach.
Norman, George H., Boston, Greenough Place and
Newcombe H. victor, New York, (Morton's) Bellevue ave.
Newlin Professor, Philadelphia, Conanicut Island.
Osgood William H., New York, (Delham's), Bellevue ave.
O'Brien John, New York, Bellevue ave.
Ogden the Misses, New York, Red Cross ave.
O'Donnell Mrs., Baltimore, Ochre Point.
Ogden Mrs. J. D., New York, Red Cross ave.
Oothout William, New York, (Burns') Hazard ave.
Oelrichs Charles M., New York, (Havemeyer's), Kay st.
Osgood Mrs George A., New York, No. 1 Pinard Cottage, Narragansett ave.   [Island.
Patterson Gen. Robert E., Philadelphia, Conanicut
Powell Dr. S. C., New Haven, Beach st.
Pinard Mrs. J. B., New York, Annandale Road.
Post Mrs. L. F., New York, Bellevue ave.
Pierson J. Fred, New York, (Hall's), Bellevue ave.
Paul J. W., Philadelphia, (Maitland's), Third st.
Post Mrs. N. A. V., New York, (Hall's), Bellevue ave.
Pond Anson P., New York, Rhode Island ave.
Pryor S. Morris, New York, (Goodridge's), Pelham at
Pearson Frederick, New York, (Sands'), Ocean ave. and Ledge Road.
Parrish Edward, New York, (Robinson's), Catherine st.
Potter Frank E., New York, (Willett's), Catherine st.
Perry Mrs. C. G., Philadelphia, Greenough Place.
Philbrick Edward S., Boston, Coddington Point.
Pabaney Theo. W., Chicago, Carroll ave.
Pratt Samuel F., Boston, Bellevue ave.
Pell John B., Brooklyn, Purgatory Road.   [ave.
Porter Frank B., New York, (Leiber's), Rhode Island
Pratt H. Ruthven, New York, Bellevue ave.
Potter Edward T., New York, Catherine st.
Potter Bishop H. C., New York, Rhode Island ave.
Parkman George F., Boston, Bellevue ave.
Pond Mrs. Harriet N., New York, (Lieber's), Rhode Island ave.
Porter Admiral D. D., U. S. Navy, Conanicut Island.
Perkins Capt. C. H., U. S. Navy, Bellevue ave.
Prince Col. W. E., U. S. Army, Beach View ave.
Pratt Albert J., Boston, Greenough Place.   [ave.
Patterson Miss Laura, Baltimore, (Best's), Bellevue
Peckham W. M., New York, (Honey's), Gibbs ave.
Powel Samuel, Philadelphia, (Enstis'), Gibbs ave.
Pattison E. J., New York, (Malcom's) Kay st.
Post Miss Laura, of New York, (Baker's) Cranston ave.
Rogers Fairman, Philadelphia, Ochre Point.
Rice Henry A., Boston, Washington st.
Rives William J., Boston, Red Cross ave.
Rhinelander Frederick W., New York, Redwood st.
Richards W. T., Germantown, Penn., Conanicut Island.
Riggs Mrs. Elisha, New York (King Wetmore's) Parker ave.
Rosengarten G. D., Philadelphia, (Mason's), Rhode Island ave.   [Point.
Rhinelander Miss Julia, New York, (Lewis'), Ochre
Rives Karrick, New York, (Burns'), Hazard ave.
Reed J. Van D., New York, (Howard's), Kay st.
Rosengarten J. G., Philadelphia, (Mason's), Rhode Island ave.
Robinson Dr. Beverly, New York, (Carey's), Bath road.
Schroeder Lieut. Seaton, U. S. Navy (Greene's), Conanicut Island.
Swan J. A., Columbus, O., (DeBlois'), Gibbs ave.
Spencer J. Thompson, Philadelphia (O'Donnell's), Ochre Point.
Stanickson Charles F., Philadelphia (Terry's), Gibb's ave.
Strowbridge Mrs. J. C., Philadelphia (Anthony's), Conanicut Island.
Schermerhorn W. C., New York, No. 2 Pinard Cottage, Narragansett ave.
Stetson George W., New York (Woolsey's), Rhode Island ave.
Stone Mrs. Joseph F., New York, Bellevue ave.
Smith Henry J., Providence, Bellevue court.
Stevens Mrs. Paran, New York, Bellevue ave. and Jones Court.
Smith Benjamin B., Philadelphia, Washington.
Schermerhorn Edward H., New York, Narragansett ave.
Smyth Frank, Philadelphia, One Mile Corner.
Steele Theodore, New York, The Point.
Shoemaker Benjamin H., Philadelphia, Conanicut Island.
Sheldon Frederic, New York, Narragansett ave. and Annandale Road.
Schott Mrs. Ellen L., New York, Cranston ave.
Stimard Mrs. Martha, Virginia, Bull Street.
Skinner Francis L., Red Cross ave.
Sands Mrs. A. L., New York, Catherine St. and Greenough Place.
Sands F. P., New York, Catherine Street.
Snydam Henry, New York, Clay Street.
Satterlee Dr. F. Le Roy, New York, Clay.
Selfridge Capt. T. O., U. S. Navy, Conanicut Island.
Sturgis Frank, New York (Holmes'), Bellevue ave.

Steele Charles, New York, Cliff ave.
Shaw Mrs. E. M., Boston, Harrison ave.
Steward Mrs. Lispenard, New York, (King's), Bellevue ave.
Sigourney Henry, New York (DeBlois'), Cranston ave.
Stockton Mrs. Bayard, Princeton, N. J., (Rutherford's) Harrison ave. [and Bellevue Court.
Swan Donnell, Baltimore (Stockton's), Bellevue ave.
Spencer Lorillard, New York (Sargent's), Rhode Island ave. [cut Island.
Strowbridge C. C., Philadelphia (Hammett's), Conanicut Slater Mrs. J. W., Providence (Rhus Cottage), Bellevue ave.
Tailer Edward N., New York (Geo. VanAlen's), Ochre Point.
Tooker G. Mead, New York, Kay and Touro.
Thorn Mrs. W. K., New York, Narragansett ave.
Tuckerman Joseph, New York, Mill.
Turnbull Mrs. Grace, New York, Kay. [Island.
Turnbull Dr. Lawrence, Philadelphia, Conanicut
Taylor Henry A. C., New York, Annandale Road
Terry Rev. Roderick, New York, (Ford's), Halidon Hill.
Tyler George F., Philadelphia Bellevue Court.
Taggart Philip S., New York, Broadway
Tennant Mrs. D. B., Petersburg, Va., Bellevue ave.
Thomas Rev. Dr. Jesse B., Brooklyn, Conanicut Island.
Tysen Robert F., New York (Tiffany's), Narragansett ave. [wood.
Tuckerman Dr. Samuel P., Boston (Tompkins'), Red-
Tuckerman Dr. Alfred, New York (Crate's), Ayrault.
Thomas Addison, New York (Honey's), Francis st. and Everett Place.
Thomas Kebald, New York, (Derby's), Kay.
Townsend James B., New York, Bellevue ave.
Thorn W. K., New York, Narragansett ave.
VanAlen James J., New York Ochre Point.
Vanderbilt Cornelius, New York, Ochre Point.
Vanderbilt Fred W., New York, Bellevue ave. and the Cliffs. [ave.
Van Rensselaer Mrs. Alex., New York, Beach View
Vernon Mrs. J. P., Providence, Everett Place. [ave.
Vanderbilt William K., New York (Norton's) Bellevue
Waterbury James M., New York, (Stevens'), Bellevue ave.

Woodworth Mrs. A. P., New York, Merton Road.
White John N., New York (Wheeler's), Channing ave. and Bath Road. [ston Cottage, on the Cliffs.
Whitney Mrs. Charles L., New Orleans, No. 2 Living-
Whitney George O., New Orleans, (Livingston's), Sea View ave. [ave.
Whitney Charles, Boston, (Traver's), Rhode Island
Wheeler Miss E. B., Philadelphia, (Kendall's), Washington.
Wright Mrs. H. A., New York, Rhode Island ave.
Whitridge John C., Baltimore, Sandy Point.
Winans Ross R., Baltimore, Ocean ave.
Wales George W., Boston, Yznaga ave. and the Cliffs.
Wilson Richard T., New York, Narragansett ave.
Wharton Job, Philadelphia, Conanicut Island.
Wharton Mrs. Charles W., Philadelphia, Conanicut Island.
Wharton Joseph, Philadelphia, Conanicut Island.
Wheeler J. C., Philadelphia, Washington.
Witherbee Silas H., New York, Honeyman Hill.
Whitwell Miss, Boston, Berkeley ave.
Whitwell S. Horatio, Boston, Berkeley ave.
Warren Mrs. Geo. G. K. (Griswold's), Channing ave.
Wheeler C. G., Philadelphia, Washington.
Weld Mrs. William F., Philadelphia, Narragansett ave.
Weld William G., Boston, Bellevue ave.
Weld George W., Boston, Narragansett ave.
Warren O. Henry, New York, Narragansett ave.
Wheeler Mrs. Charles, Philadelphia, Channing ave.
Winthrop E. L., New York, Bellevue ave.
Whiting Mrs. Sarah S., New York, Bellevue ave.
Whiting Augustus L., New York, Bellevue ave. and Webster.
Willoughby Hugh L., Saratoga Springs, Halidon ave.
Watson Dr. W. A., New York, Spring and John.
Wilson Fred Jas. Hazard, New York, Coddington Point.
Walles W. N., New York, Bellevue and Ruggles ave.
Wharton Mrs. Edward, New York, Harrison ave.
Willard E. W., Chicago, Miantonomah ave.
Wetmore Samuel, New York, Bellevue ave.
Wysong John J., New York, Ochre Point
Wilson M. Orme, New York (Carey's), Narragansett ave.
Zabriskie Andrew C., New York, (Arnold's), Rhode Island ave.

HIGH TIDE AT NEWPORT.—Eastern Standard Time.

☞This table will also show the time of the tide at other places on Narragansett Bay and adjacent points, by means of the following easy calculations:

For Providence,	add 30 minutes.	For Wickford,	add 12 minutes.
" Bristol and Warren,	" 30 "	" Beaver Tail,	" 00 "
" Fall River,	" 25 "	" Narragansett Pier,	subtract 10 "
" East Greenwich,	" 18 "	" Point Judith,	" 12 "
" Nayatt Point,	" 05 "	" Block Island,	" 11 "
" Bullock's Point,	" 10 "		

Day of Month	JULY		AUGUST		SEPTEMBER		Day of Month	JULY		AUGUST		SEPTEMBER	
	A. M.	P. M.	A. M.	P. M.	A. M.	P. M.		A. M.	P. M.	A. M.	P. M.	A. M.	P. M.
1	2.00	2.28	3.22	3.43	4.18	4.42	17	2.34	2.52	4.36	4.29	5.37	5.50
2	3.00	3.12	4.10	3.56	4.52	4.55	18	3.35	3.44	5.09	5.12	6.21	6.39
3	3.55	3.52	4.50	4.36	5.34	5.42	19	4.32	4.35	5.58	6.02	7.02	7.24
4	4.42	4.29	5.28	5.15	6.12	6.26	20	5.36	5.36	6.44	9.50	7.40	8.07
5	5.22	5.05	6.03	5.54	6.50	7.09	21	8.16	6.14	7.30	7.38	8.08	8.49
6	6.00	5.40	6.40	6.38	7.32	7.56	22	7.05	7.02	8.12	8.24	8.54	9.32
7	6.34	6.17	7.17	7.20	8.16	8.44	23	7.52	7.50	8.55	9.10	9.31	10.16
8	7.09	7.00	7.58	8.08	9.03	9.35	24	8.40	8.49	9.38	9.58	10.10	11.08
9	7.45	7.33	8.43	8.45	9.54	10.34	25	9.28	9.38	10.22	10.56	10.56	11.45
10	8.26	8.18	9.32	9.49	10.52	11.38	26	10.18	10.22	11.07	11.44	0.04	11.48
11	9.11	9.08	10.26	10.50	11.52	11.45	27	11.08	11.20	11.56	11.45	1.07	12.49
12	10.02	10.04	11.24	11.45	0.47	12.57	28	Noon	11.45	0.44	12.40	2.08	1.58
13	11.01	11.08	mdn	12.24	1.36	2.03	29	0.20	12.51	1.48	1.40	2.59	2.54
14	Noon	11.45	1.04	1.26	3.00	3.06	30	1.24	1.40	2.46	2.34	3.44	3.49
15	0.17	12.56	2.14	2.27	4.00	4.04	31	2.36	2.28	3.36	3.26		
16	1.27	1.55	3.18	3.24	4.50	5.00							

FOR MARTHA'S VINEYARD, NANTUCKET AND NEW BEDFORD.

☞ Add to the time of the above table as follows for the places named:

	H. M.		H. M.
New Bedford, Clark's Point,	0 31	Brant Point, Nantucket,	4 42
Edgartown and Cottage City, M. V.,	4 30	Siasconset, Nantucket,	3 47
Vineyard Haven and West Chop, M. V.,	4 00	Muskeget Channel, west end Nantucket,	0 00

NOTE.—For all places given, the nearest tidal station is Newport, R. I.

EXAMPLE.—Suppose you wanted to find the time of high tide September 13, at Cottage City, Martha's Vineyard. Looking in the table you learn the tide is full at Newport on that date at 47 minutes after midnight and again at 57 minutes after noon, or 12.57 P. M. Add to either the ratio given for Cottage City, and the result will be, for the first, 5.17 A. M., and for the other, 5.27 P. M.

PART FOURTH.

CHAPTER I.

The South County.

WESTERLY.

THE township of Westerly forms the southwest corner to the State of Rhode Island, but the name is also applied more particularly to the busy manufacturing village on the east bank of the Paw-catuck River, five miles from its mouth and navigable to this point. The river forms here the boundary between Rhode Island and Connecticut, and directly across on the west bank is the village of Pawcatuck in the township of Stonington, Conn., but which in common parlance is included in Westerly. From the river the land rises on either side to quite high elevations between one and two hundred feet in height, but the slopes are gradual, and the villages are situated along the river banks and extend back up the hillsides. Westerly, as thus constituted, is the largest and most populous place in southern Rhode Island. In

BROAD STREET, WESTERLY, DIXON HOUSE ON THE RIGHT.

its borders much manufacturing is carried on, and it is the centre for the surrounding regions, in which there are a number of small manufacturing villages. The business in the compact portion extends for half a mile along the river on both banks, and on the streets running up and along the hillsides are the churches, schools, and residences, the whole forming a pleasant town, which, from its situation, has a good drainage, and being near the sea, while it is protected by high land to the north and east, has a salubrious climate.

On the Rhode Island side, leading from the railroad station, the principal streets follow the east bank of the river. A walk down High, across Dixon House Square, down Main, up Cross, and back through Elm and Broad to the Square will afford an excellent idea of the town. The Square and its neighborhood is the central place for business; it is about a quarter of a mile from the station and fronting on it is the Dixon House, a mammoth four-story brick hotel, while next east is the First Baptist Church. Immediately westward the Broad Street bridge spans the river, connecting Pawcatuck with Westerly, and to the south Main Street runs out of it. On the river bank, corner of Broad and Main, are the woolen

VIEW OF WESTERLY AND THE PAWCATUCK RIVER.

mills of the Stillman Manufacturing Company, which have been idle during the past winter. The third mill from the corner has recently been purchased by the Atwood Manufacturing Company, of Stonington, and will be started as a silk mill. Further down the street, on the river side, are lumber yards, coal depots, etc., with coasting vessels lying along side, while on the landward side of the street in succession are the Opera House, Armory Hall, and the fine Seventh Day Baptist Church. Across the river a little above here are the cotton mills of the Moss Manufacturing Company, and the extensive printing-press works of C. B. Cottrell & Sons, adjoining each other on the west bank, and from here can also be seen the main portion of Pawcatuck.

Turning to the left up Cross Street, Elm Street is soon reached, which runs parallel with Main but further up the slope of the hill. It is bordered in its whole extent with substantial and some elegant mansion houses, lined with fine rows of trees, and constitutes a very beautiful neighborhood. At the corner of Elm and School streets is the High School, and just beyond on the west side is the Calvary Baptist Church. Proceeding northward we soon reach the junction of Elm, Broad, and Granite streets. Facing Broad Street is the Christian Church. A few steps down Broad, running through to Main, is Union Street, on which is the Town Hall, a fine brick building with a tower and clock, and near it is the engine station of the Westerly fire district, containing two good steamers, while further down, near Main, is the Episcopal Church.

Westerly is famous for its granite. Half a mile up the hill, by way of Granite Street, the summit of the ridge is reached, and here are the extensive quarries and yards of the Smith Granite and Rhode Island Granite Companies. The quarries are immense, wide, and deep holes in the ground out of which already many thousand tons of stone have been taken, and the work still goes on. Here there are three quarries. Extending in rows around them on all sides but the east are the sheds in which the stone is dressed, or cut into figures, statuary, and all sorts of monuments, and it is a sight worth seeing to go through these buildings, especially the ones where life-like figures are being cut from the dead blocks of granite, as an inspection of the models will afford more pleasure than can be had in visiting most art museums. To the northward, along Granite road about a mile further, are other extensive quarries operated by the Chapman Granite Company and other firms, and at Niantic, five miles from the village but within the limits of the town, are other quarries.

Half a mile north from the railroad depot, but in a component part of the village of Westerly is the locality known as Stillmanville, where are the factories and tenements of the Westerly Woolen Company. Two of the mills of this concern are on the Rhode Island side and one on the Connecticut side, and they are all built on the river bank. A highway bridge crosses the river just above the mills.

There are a number of factory villages within the limits of the town. Two miles north of Westerly is the cotton mill and village known as White Rock, belonging to B. B. & R. Knight. Three and a half miles from the station is Potter Hill, where are situated the woolen mills of J. P. Campbell & Company. At Niantic, five miles distant, the Carmichael Manufacturing Company have a mill, and the same company also have a small establishment just across the Broad Street bridge in Pawcatuck.

Although there are more separate factories engaged in the woolen manufacture according to the last census, the number of persons engaged in the cotton and woolen

THE CONGREGATIONAL CHURCH, WESTERLY.

business was in each a little over three hundred. The most important industry in the town is the granite business, employing over four hundred men, a large majority of them skilled workmen. During the winter of 1887-8, the woolen business has been very dull; the factories in Westerly and Niantic were stopped all winter, those at Stillmanville, the Westerly Woolen Company, were idle several months, but started in spring. During the same time the cotton mills at White Rock, the Moss Manufacturing Company's Mill across the river, and

SEVENTH-DAY BAPTIST CHURCH, WESTERLY.

Cottrell & Sons' press works have been running full. During the winter the granite works are usually quite slack.

Westerly is the stronghold of the Seven-day Baptists, and their presence brings about the curious condition of affairs that a portion of the people hold their day of worship and rest on Saturday. Some of the stores are closed on Saturday, and services are held in the churches of the denomination, while on Sunday these stores are opened, and the Seven-day people go about their usual occupations. They were formerly much more numerous than at present, and several of the factories conformed to the system, but now the only concern that does so is the works of C. B. Cottrell & Sons.

On February 11, 1871, the Westerly Fire District was organized under a charter from the General Assembly, practically forming the inhabitants of the village of Westerly into a separate town for the purpose of providing and maintaining means to put out fires, and all taxable voters were made members thereof. The district now has two fire engines.

A system of water-works was started by a private corporation, November, 1886, and is now in successful working order. On the hill near the quarries is a large boiler iron stand pipe about seventy feet in height, which gives a head of water sufficient for any portion of the place.

From Granite Hill on the Rhode Island side, or from Hinckley Hill across the river in Connecticut, the whole village can be viewed to rare advantage. To the south, Block Island, Long Island, Fisher's Island, Watch Hill and its hotels, Stonington, Little Narragansett Bay and the narrow strip of land inclosing it, can all be very clearly distinguished, while glimpses of the Pawcatuck at various points for eight or ten miles of its course can be had.

In the limits of the town and of Pawcatuck there are fourteen churches : three Seven Day Baptists, one Seven Day Advent, two each of Roman Catholic and Baptist, and one each of Methodist, Congregational, Christian, Friends, Episcopal, and Advent. Of these nine are in the village of Westerly.

The main line of the New York, Providence and Boston Railroad runs through Westerly, the station being on the Rhode Island side, forty-four miles from Providence. Stages run daily to Hopkinton City, Ashaway, Potter's Hill Clark's Falls, and White Rock, affording good opportunity to see the country ; trips are also made to Voluntown and Wakefield, the route to the latter place through a sparsely settled country, on a mail stage. During the summer steamers run from Westerly to Watch Hill, six miles distant down the river.

The population of the entire town of Westerly by the census of 1885, was 6,333. It is quite safe to say that Westerly proper with Pawcatuck has a population of at least five thousand.

NARRAGANSETT PIER.

Imagine, if you can, a rugged, rocky sea coast, on which the waves are constantly beating with a force that cannot be appreciated unless seen, and cannot then be estimated ; imagine further a less wild adjoining portion, formed, not of rock, but of sand, which the waves approach with a force similar and equal to their assaults on the rocky ramparts, but finding less resistance melt and merge away in long graceful rollers, chasing each other up and down the smooth and level sands ; between these picture a region of chaos, neither wholly rock nor sand, but a confused jumble of both, the connecting link between the rock and sand shore. When you have succeeded in forming such a picture in your mind you will then have an idea of the physical features of Narraganset Pier, but unless you are familiar with the ocean in its varying moods, your imagination will but faintly picture the ever-changing form of the crested waves as they

NARRAGANSETT — THE PIER AND THE OCEAN FRONT.

roll in on the sands, the dashing and breaking, and thundering of the surf on the rocks, and the manifold forms of the ever-troubled waters, always different in appearance with every successive changing aspect of the sky, the atmosphere, or the sunlight, reflecting on its broad but fretful surface glints and rays of all the changes in the wonderful and beautiful firmament above.

That such a locality should attract the lovers of the beautiful in nature is not to be wondered at: that it should become a summer resort of wealth and fashion was inevitable; for, while the coast has all these charms, the country is beautiful, with broad meadows, hills, ponds, streams of water, villages and farms, and it has many pleasing historical associations, in fact, surpassing any other part of the state in this regard. Here in colonial times, resided great landed proprietors, who kept up, with their numerous slaves, a sort of feudal magnificence and princely hospitality; here the celebrated breed of horses, the Narragansett pacers, had their home; here in the kindly and primitive fashion of the age, the slaves imitated their masters in holding elections, as narrated in some of the old books, which so garrulously set forth all these particulars. And the aroma of this kindly olden life still clings to the hills and valleys of the country, and can be enjoyed by the visitor either on the spot by association or through the literature which deals with the South County, both directly and indirectly.

Narragansett Pier is on the eastern coast of the town of North Kingstown, R. I., near the western entrance to Narragansett Bay, about ten miles southwest from Newport, and four or five miles north of that dread of mariners, Point Judith. It is thus exposed to the full, uninterrupted sweep of the ocean on the east from the Pier to the Point. While there are indentations in the shore, no harbor is possible, as on the calmest day the long ocean swell is on the water and the waves dash strongly against every rock and beach, and enter into every bay with undiminished force. In fact, it is from this circumstance that the Pier takes its name. As the inhabitants found it desirable to have water communication with the outside world, in the least exposed portion of the coast, about the year 1780, a pier was built by John Robinson, and as all back of it was the Narragansett County, of course the pier soon came to be known as the Narragansett Pier. The sea has battered down many of the piers that were built since that time, and their ruins can be seen on the shore between the beach and the South Pier, the only one remaining, where are two wharves inclosing a dock, which serves the purpose of a harbor, and will accommodate several vessels. On the largest and most southerly of these wharves, is a large coal and grain elevator, where nearly all the coal and building material used in the town is received and handled.

The fashionable resort may be said now to consist of two portions. Several years ago the statement was true that it was a settlement of great hotels. To-day, while the hotels are still here, and have increased in number, "cottages" similar to those at Newport have become proportionately more numerous, and to the south of the original section, within the past few years, on situations overlooking the rocks, is a group of elegant and expensive residences.

The main portion of Narragansett Pier extends along the shore from the bathing beach on the north to the South Pier, a distance perhaps of an eighth of a mile, and consists of about a score of large hotels, and perhaps a little more than double that number of cottages, two churches, a chapel, the post-office, a few stores, and last, but not least, the Casino.

A few cottages and eight of the hotels, with wide lawns in front, face the

BATHING SCENE.

ocean, from which they are separated by a fine macadamized street. At the northward end of this row is the Casino, an elegant stone structure, a portion of which is thrown across the ocean avenue, in a fine arch ; extensive grounds and buildings run from the avenue westward along Beach Place, and the whole affords opportunity for entertainments and for social intercourse for the wealthy sojourners. From Beach or Exchange Place, a short street on which the Casino borders, all roads diverge : here are all the summer stores and offices ; here you start for any one of the beautiful drives to be had in the vicinity. Across Exchange Place from the Casino is the Rockingham, until this season known as the McSparran House, to which a large addition was built the past spring. The beach begins just beyond this hotel to the north, and a lane leads down to it past the house. Leading out of Beach Place southward and passing through Mathewson, Central, and back through Caswell streets to the starting point, a circuit of not more than half a mile, we pass the rest of the hotels and cottages in the main portion of the Pier. On Boon Street, leading out of Central, and the street that runs from the railroad station, is the Presbyterian Church, and a little further on Central Street is the Episcopal Church, both tasteful edifices.

METATOXET HOUSE, JOHN M. CASWELL, PROPRIETOR.

On a side street is a small Roman Catholic Chapel.

The chief attraction at the Pier is the bathing beach, which is situated just north of the hotels and extends about a mile in a crescent-shaped curve until it reaches the mouth of the Pettaquamscutt River. It is gently inclined, is as level as a floor, and so packed down by the beating of the waves as to be extremely smooth and hard. No

12

life-lines are necessary, as there is no undertow, and in comparison to the strength of the surf the beach is very safe. Only a small section of it is used — the southern end of the curve, — and opposite this space are commodious bathing-houses, belonging to the various hotels and to private parties, all forming a continuous range of buildings along which in front runs a broad covered promenade connecting them together, and at the same time affording opportunity for spectators. On the second story of many of these houses are balconies from which spectators may view the scene below without being troubled by the passing of the dripping bathers. Between the promenade and the edge of the water, rows of tents are pitched, and these shelters from the sun are favorite places for the on-lookers. The fashionable hours are at midday, when the scene here presented surpasses in the multitude and character of the bathers that at any other resort in New England. Sometimes as many as a thousand persons are tumbling in the surf, the waves come in rapidly, the bathers are dashed and buffeted about, and when an extra strong breaker overwhelms the throng the scene is a gay one, the sudden and forcible concussions that follow are taken as a matter of course, so that here in the water democracy prevails; and a plebeian may not only rub elbows with a prince, but he may perforce be obliged to embrace a princess.

Just north of the bathing-beach a United States Life-Saving Station has been located for years, but the past spring a picturesque stone building was erected on the shore just south of the Casino, and at the head of one of the ruined piers.

At the other end of the seaward row of hotels are the two wharves, and in the neighborhood is a lumber yard, the terminal buildings of the Narragansett Pier Railroad, a kiln for steam-drying lumber, and a large grocery store. The railroad station was formerly located here, but it has been moved a short distance up the track the better to accommodate the whole place. The magnificent rocky shore already mentioned begins a short distance south of the landing, and continues all the way to Point Judith, five miles distant. A path leads along the upper edge of these rocks which, in general, shelve down into the water; but there are many that project boldly into the sea, and not a few rise in steep cliffs bidding defiance to the waves.

Leading out of Ocean Avenue at the landing is the road to Point Judith, built in 1882, which follows the coast all the way. Since its opening many cottages, similar to the Newport villas, have been built between it and the cliffs. To the west of the road on the first rise of land after leaving the landing, is Earlscourt, on which are four elegant residences. In the foreground at the head of a straight avenue leading from the highway and in front of these residences, is a water-tower of very unique appearance. On its front is the figure of a griffin, with large, outspread wings laid back against the wooden superstructure, and its immense tail coiled around the supporting pillar, looking as one might imagine some of the fabled monsters of antiquity appeared, or a semblance like the frequently seen sea-serpent. The tower, however, is eminently practical in its purpose. In the upper part is a tank into which water is pumped from a well just outside the tower by a small engine in the bottom of the structure, and the cottages are supplied from the tank. Visitors can ascend by a spiral staircase to the top of the tower from where a fine view can be obtained of the surrounding country.

Beyond Earlscourt the road leads past what is now *par ex-*

THE MATHEWSON— S. W. MATHEWSON, PROPRIETOR.

cellence the cottage region of the Pier. For half or three-quarters of a mile are a score or more of villas, all but one or two between the highway and the sea. The finest of the group is " Dunmere," the property of R. G. Dun, Esq., of New York. It is the most southerly but one of this group, and is a magnificent residence with surroundings almost fairly-like in their beauty. Overlooking this group of residences on the western side of the road is the Hazard estate, a well wooded tract, the highest land along the shore in the neighborhood. About the centre of the grounds is Hazard Castle, a feudal looking stone tower, visible from all the country round as it looms above the trees. At its base is a low, rambling stone house built in many sections. The tower was for many years an element of mystery, but the riddle was solved in 1883, when the property was sold by its original owner, Joseph Peace Hazard, to his nephew Rowland N. Hazard, of New York, for a small sum on condition that the original plan be carried out. The tower is 105 feet high, 160 feet above the level of the sea, 25 feet square at the base, and 20 feet at the top, with walls from 3 to 4 feet thick, and is divided into seven stories. In the third story is a tablet inserted in the east wall with the following inscription :

THIS TOWER, ERECTED TO MEMORY OF HIS
ANCESTORS, WAS FOUNDED A. D. 1846,
COMPLETED 1884.
BY JOSEPH PEACE HAZARD,
SON OF ROWLAND AND MARY HAZARD
BORN 1807 — DIED 18

If you are fortunate enough to gain access to it the view from the top of the tower is the most magnificent in the state. The south shores of Newport and Conanicut Island, Beaver Tail and Whale Rock Light-houses, the main passage and the western entrance to Narragansett Bay all lie to the northeast. Before you to the east and south is the wide ocean, from Seaconnet Point to Block Island, the horizon describing an arc of ninety degrees. To the south is Point

THE GLADSTONE — W. A. NYE, PROPRIETOR.

Judith, clearly defined, and running out into the water like a finger, while further away across the intervening water, the bulk of Block Island rises out of the sea in clear, sharp outline.   At your feet is the entire rocky coast with the group of cottages along the Ocean road, and north, half a mile away, is the main portion of the Pier, so distinct that you can pick out nearly every building.   To the south, beyond Point Judith, is a large extent of the southern coast of the state, flanked by numerous ponds glistening in the sun ; to the northwest the villages of Wakefield and Peacedale are clearly discerned, while all around on the west and north are ranges of low hills shutting out the view.

A drive along the River road northward leads through a charming and picturesque country.   Just after leaving the Pier you pass Canonchet, the splendid mansion of the Spragues, now the property of Mrs. William Sprague, and the residence of the ex-governor and his family.   At Hammond Mills, seven miles up this road, is the birthplace of Gilbert Stuart, the celebrated artist.

The hotels at the Pier are : On Ocean Avenue — Narragansett, Mathewson, Atwood, Revere, Continental, Mount Hope, Greene's Inn ; Mathewson Street — Delavan, Massasoit : Central Street — Columbus ; Ocean Street — Ocean House ; Caswell Street — Metatoxet, Sea View, Gladstone ; Beach Place — Rockingham : Tower Hill — Tower Hill House.

THE CASINO.

In May, 1887, the Rhode Island General Assembly constituted Narragansett Pier and vicinity into a district, by the name of Narragansett, with all the powers of a town in regard to its local self government, but gave it no representation in the legislature.   The district has also been empowered by act of the legislature to borrow $150,000 to be expended for highways, sewerage and the erection of public buildings, and, as provided, this act received the confirmation of the taxpayers in June, 1888. The members of the District Council are: Ex-Governor and Senator William Sprague, the owner of Canonchet and over 400 acres of land: Mr. S. W. Mathewson, of the Mathewson House: Mr. F. P. W. Tefft, of the Revere House: Mr. Geo. G. Pearce, a farmer on Point Judith, and Mr. Joseph G. Johnston, formerly of Providence, and now a large farm owner at Boston Neck.

ATWOOD HOUSE—J. A. TUCKER PROPRIETOR.

An electric light plant has been erected, and already more than 1,200 lights are in use. A project is on foot for the construction of water works to supply not only Narragansett Pier, but also the neighboring villages of Wakefield and Peace Dale. The company has been already organized, is known as the Wakefield Water Company, and has a capital of $150,000. Thirteen miles of pipe will be required, and a standpipe on an adjoining high hill will secure a fall of two hundred feet. This will insure a plentiful supply of water and ample provision in case of fire, and will also be of great value as an auxiliary in any future system of sewerage adopted.

The Pier is reached by the Narragansett Pier Railroad, which connects with the main line of the New York, Providence & Boston Railroad at Kingston. During the summer a small but staunch propeller plies between the Pier and Newport, but unless you are a good sailor you had better not attempt the passage, as the tossing you will experience in coming or going through the long ocean swell breaking on the coast will be sure to make you seasick.

The new ferry running between the Kingston shore and the west side of

REVERE HOUSE.
F. W. P. Tefft, Lessee.

Conanicut Island which was started this season and runs in connection with the Jamestown Ferry, affords splendid opportunity for a drive from Narragansett to Newport and return, through charming scenery both on shore and afloat. The ferry boats, of course, are so arranged that carriages can very conveniently be driven onto them. The distance is about five miles by water and six or seven miles by land. Seven or eight connecting trips are made each week-day both ways, and on Sunday there are three such trips.

ATLANTIC HOUSE — S. T. BROWNING PROPRIETOR

Centrally located on Ocean Avenue, easy of access from both railroad station and the steamboat landing is the Atlantic House, one of the largest and finest hotels at the Pier. It is in within two minutes' walk of the Casino, and but little farther from the beach. The house is located far enough back from the street to avoid all dust, while there is nothing between to prevent the full sweep of the ocean breezes, and the intervening space is taken up by a large open lawn which affords a fine playground for the children, as well as ample facilities for tennis courts. Swings and tents for the younger guests are provided, and from the broad piazzas, which extend the entire length of the house, an excellent ocean view can be gained. The hotel has eighty-seven sleeping rooms, giving a capacity for one hundred and fifty guests. It is four stories high, and the rooms are large and well arranged for comfort. The dining hall is one of the cosiest and coolest at the Pier. Electric bells are in every room, and the house is supplied with hot or cold sea water baths. Since last year the house has been refurnished in part and put in complete order. The house has always held the reputation of being a well kept family resort, and under its present proprietor, S. T. Browning, is adding largely to its former excellent reputation.

On Ocean Avenue, commanding a fine view of the ocean, is the Continental Hotel, one of the finest houses at the Pier. It is equipped with all modern appliances for safety, convenience and comfort, such as fire escapes, electric bells, electric lights, gas, and has the most perfect drainage and sanitary arrangements: it is also furnished with fresh and sea water baths, and supplied with

CONTINENTAL HOTEL — A. F. SAUNDERS. PROPRIETOR

pure spring water. Broad piazzas encircle the front and back of the house, which is four stories in height and has accommodations for 200 guests. The rooms are large and airy, and all command magnificent views of land or water. The lawns are wide and spacious, suitable for summer games of lawn tennis, etc., while facing directly on the sea a delightful air always prevails.

MASSASOIT HOUSE—JOHN BABCOCK, SUPERINTENDENT.

The Massasoit House is one of the most desirably located hotels at Narragansett Pier, as it stands on high ground, in the midst of a pleasant, grassy lawn, and is within three minutes' walk of the bathing beach, to which a concrete walk leads the entire distance. From its rooms and piazzas excellent views of the ocean are obtained, some of its rooms overlook the Casino, while from the upper windows, wide stretches of the beautiful Narragansett country lie in sight. The house in four stories in height, will accommodate one hundred and forty guests, has about three hundred feet of piazzas, and is provided with wrought iron fire escape, electric bells, and other necessary conveniences. The sleeping rooms are large and airy, and the table is provided with the best the market affords. Mr. John Babcock, the manager, is president of the Wakefield Institution for Savings, which concern owns the house. The guests in the past have included notable people, authors, diplomats, military and naval officers, legislators, and distinguished foreigners.

———

For a quiet, first-class retreat during the summer months, the Ocean House has rare advantages. It is within five minutes' walk of the beach, is under the management of its proprietor, Mr. George N. Kenyon, who has looked after the comfort of his guests for the past seventeen years. The house is large and airy, and has every convenience, including electric lights, pure water and the best of sanitary facilities, with good drainage. It is not a transient hostelry, but is a summer home, and only those accepted as guests whose reputations are known. Around the house is a large shady lawn. The table is supplied with the best the market affords.

PEACE DALE.

On the Narragansett Pier Railroad, in the town of South Kingstown, is the pleasant village of Peace Dale. It has a population of about twelve hundred inhabitants, and is distant from the city of Providence thirty miles southwest, while it is within sight of the noted shore resort, Narragansett Pier. A stream known by the Indian name, Saugatucket (Dead-Man's Brook), flows through the village and affords water-power for the factories. The place is best known as the location of the Peace Dale Manufacturing Company, and the seat of the great woolen manufacturing business of the well-known Hazard family. This manufacture was started here by Rowland Hazard about the beginning of the present century, and it is claimed that the first power loom successfully operated in the world was in his factory in the year 1814 or 1815, at least two years before a similar machine was first started in Judge Lyman's mill in North Providence. From 1820 to 1864 Isaac P. and Rowland G., the sons of Rowland Hazard, carried on and enlarged the business, the manufacture of kerseys being their specialty. In 1847 they organized the Peace Dale Manufacturing Company, and began the manufacture of shawls. Isaac P. Hazard retired in 1864, and Rowland G. Hazard in 1866, leaving the business to the management of his sons, Rowland and John N. The present officers are: John N. Hazard, president; Rowland Hazard, treasurer; Rowland G. Hazard, 2d, assistant-treasurer; William Drysdale, superintendent; John A. Brown, clerk. In 1856 the works were greatly enlarged, and in 1872 a new mill was added for the manufacture of worsted goods. The Hazards have thus for four generations, extending over a period of about ninety years, been successful manufacturers in the place where the business was first started.

WATCH HILL.

Six miles from Westerly at the extreme southwestern point of the state, is Watch Hill and Point. The hill is a considerable elevation, composed of abrupt sand hills with small valleys between, the whole forming a series of rounded eminences, rising quite abruptly from the water, and a point juts out from it in a short promontory directly to the south. Beginning from the base of the highest hill, a long and narrow strip of land extends directly west for more than a mile, and then runs north for about a mile, terminating in Sandy Po'nt, and at the elbow the outer point is known as Nappatree, the whole being nothing more than a low sand bar, shaped as has been often said like a sickle. This natural breakwater incloses Little Narragansett Bay, which is an almost circular body of water nine miles in circumference, into which the Pawcatuck River empties. Three miles distant, near the mouth of the bay, is Stonington.

On the eastern side of Watch Hill Point the surf comes in with such force and there is so much undertow that it is not safe for swimmers, and here there are always to be seen a number of wrecks strewn along the sands. On the other side of the point, however, and on the south shore of the sandy breakwater, is a fine beach, where the water is usually calm and the bathing safe. The fashionable hours are from 11 A. M. to 1 P. M.

The hill is literally covered with hotels, there being eight on its sides and summit, and in the neighborhood are about two dozen fine cottages. The development of the place as a summer resort began about 1840, when the first Watch Hill House was built. In 1856, the Atlantic was erected; in 1869 the Larkin House was opened; then followed the Plimpton and the Ocean House, and these five are now the largest of the hotels. In 1870 began an era of cottage building, and since 1886 new cottages have been erected every year, the indications being that the future will witness the construction of many additional residences.

From the hill or any of the hotels, a splendid seaward prospect lies in view, eleven light-houses and one light-ship being in sight. The temperature ranges from sixty-six to seventy-five degrees in the season, the ocean breezes continually sweep over it, the inclosed bay affords splendid opportunities for sailing or fishing, and the resort is easily reached, being but a short distance from the great highway of travel between New York and Boston—the Shore Line route. During the summer a small steamer runs from Stonington connecting with Shore Line trains, and the run is only three miles across the bay. From Westerly a steamer also comes down the Pawcatuck River, a distance of about six miles but affording very charming views of the scenery. The steamer from New London to and from Block Island stops at Watch Hill both going and returning, and a smaller steamer also makes regular trips from the same place. On the extremity of the point is a light-house, and on its southern side is a United States Life Saving Station.

The names of the hotels at Watch Hill are the Ocean, Plimpton, Larkin, Atlantic, Watch Hill, Narragansett, Bay View, and Dickens.

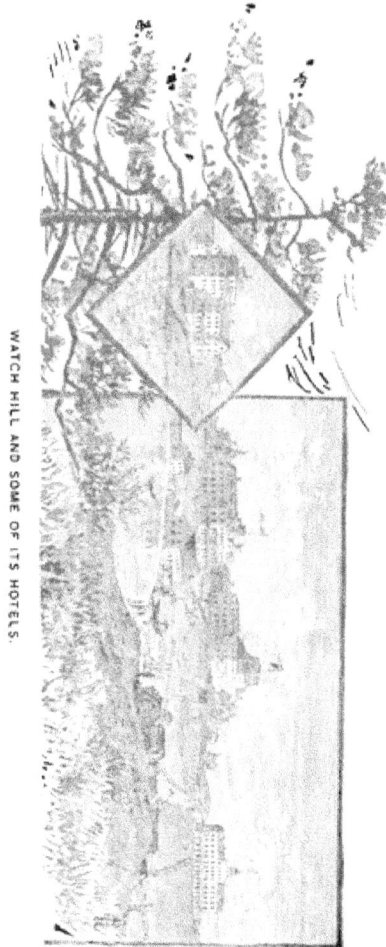

The Plimpton House and its two annexes, the Bay View and the Dickens houses, constitute the largest establishment under one management at Watch Hill. In the three fine structures there are two hundred and fifty rooms, affording accommodation, of course, if necessary, for a much larger number of persons. They are all adorned with fine verandas from which the ocean views are unequaled, all have elegant parlors, and at the central house, the Plimpton, is a magnificent music room, forty by fifty feet. The rooms are provided with gas and electric bells, and the houses throughout have all the modern conveniences. The sanitary condition of the premises, under the personal attention of the proprietor, Mr. William Hill, has been most carefully attended to, and the sewerage is lead out into the sea by pipes which extend fifty feet below low water mark. In the vicinity are pleasant drives, and good teams are furnished on short notice. A telegraph station and the post-office are near, there being two mails in and out daily. The houses are all supplied from a spring of pure water. A short distance away is the bathing beach, to which a plank walk leads all the way. Porters from the houses will be on the wharf on arrival of boats, and take charge of all baggage. For families who desire to remain by the week, month or season, special arrangements will be made and liberal inducements offered, and nothing left undone to promote the comfort and enjoyment of guests. For enjoyment and comfort these houses and the resort are unequaled. The bathing and fishing in the adjoining waters are unsurpassed, and there is an entire absence of mosquitoes, caused by the continual breeze and the encircling sea which nearly surrounds the Hill. In addition to the other attractions, a first-class orchestra furnishes music for the season.

NOYES' BEACH.

Six miles east of Watch Hill, but yet in the limits of the town of Westerly, is Noyes' Beach, a small shore resort, where are about a dozen cottages on a bluff overlooking a beach. These dwellings are mostly occupied by Westerly people, and in one or two of them guests are entertained. The difficulty of getting to this place, it being six miles away over a dusty road from Niantic, the nearest station on the railroad, renders it not so popular as its natural advantages warrant. Near the beach, on either side, are extensive shore ponds.

Three miles further east is Quonocontaug, another small resort, situated directly on the beach, and consisting of a few houses inhabited mostly by Washington County people.

SOUTH FERRY AND SAUNDERSTOWN.

South Ferry, in South Kingstown, is pleasantly located on the shore, facing Conanicut and Dutch islands. There is here a church, a post-office, a telephone and telegraph station, and splendid fishing, as well as good shooting can be had in the vicinity.

Saunderstown, about a mile above South Ferry, is a cluster of cottages on the shore picturesquely situated.

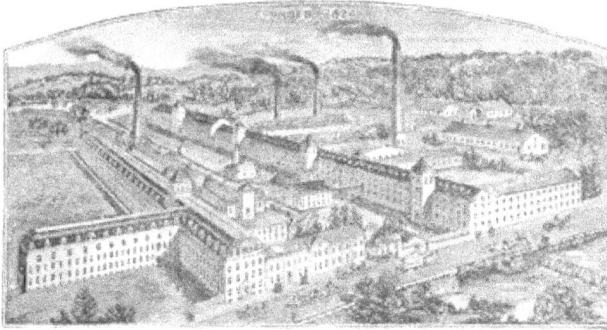

WORKS OF REED & BARTON, TAUNTON, MASS.

The largest electro-plating works in the United States are those of Reed & Barton at Taunton, about a mile from City Square. The group of large brick buildings cover four acres along both banks of the Mill River. The silver plated goods here manufactured are considered the best in the market, and this is undoubtedly owing to the fact that this special business was first made a success, and the methods of manufacture were originally developed in these works. The specialties at present are the manufacture of the finest electro-plated white metal hollow ware, nickel silver spoons, forks, ladles, and all kinds of nickel silver ware. The entire works are supplied with the best machinery and devices so far designed for the manufacture of these goods, and the ample rooms and splendid facilities in general give great opportunity for the production not only of the best work, but for its rapid execution. Eight hundred operatives are constantly employed and the machinery is operated both by steam and water-power. Artists of talent and long experience are employed to design the new patterns constantly being put forth. The firm are thereby enabled to produce articles of a high degree of artistic excellence.

These works were first established in 1824, on a small scale, and as new methods have been discovered and put in practice, the business has developed from the very insignificant beginning to its present splendid proportions. The goods are not only in demand in the United States but large orders are being constantly received from foreign countries. The elegant silver plated articles cannot be distinguished from real silver, and in beauty, finish, durability and excellence of design compare favorably with genuine silver plate. In competition with domestic and foreign manufacturers at expositions and industrial exhibitions the electro-plated goods of the firm have come out triumphant from every trial, and a long list of medals were awarded them on these occasions.

The salesrooms are situated at the factories at Taunton, and at 37 Union Square, New York. At these emporiums, are all descriptions of useful and ornamental articles in almost endless variety, and they are likewise for sale by all the principal dealers in silver and plated ware in America, Europe, South America, the West Indies, and Australia. The members of the firm are Messrs. H. G. Reed, George Brabrook, F. L. Fish and George H. Fish, all of whom have had great practical experience in the business.

PART FIFTH.

Block Island.

OUT at sea, unprotected by any intervening land, lies Block Island, exposed to the full fury of the winds and waves. Standing out in a bold, clear-cut mass, the island is a conspicuous object from any elevated point on the southern coast of Rhode Island, or from the decks of vessels traversing the upper part of Long Island Sound. It is triangular in shape, from seven to eight miles long by about three and a half in its widest part, lies out at sea twelve miles from the nearest point on the southern coast of Rhode Island, fifteen miles southwest from Point Judith, thirty miles from Newport, and eighteen miles northeast from Montaup Point, the eastern extremity of Long Island. Geologists say that it was originally a continuation of Long Island, but that the waves, through a long succession of ages, broke down the intervening land and left the island, a lonely sentinel, the outpost of the continent.

In approaching the island from Newport the first portion that comes into view is the northeast coasts formed of high, bold, sand-faced bluff, less than fifty feet in height, with rock-strewn beaches at their bases, while perched on their summits some distance back from the edge many houses are scattered. Coasting along these bluffs for nearly two miles we soon come in sight of Block Island Bay, so called, an indentation in the coast hardly deserving the name of a bay, because it affords little shelter, for although it lies for two miles along shore its extent as a bay measured from the centre of a straight line drawn from the breakwater to the northerly headland is not more than half a mile, and the waves continually beat on its shores in a moderate surf. The sole reason it is entitled to that name is the fact that it is the only approach to a natural harbor on the island, the remainder of the coast line being exposed to the full force of the waves. The shore of the bay forms a long sweeping curve, is known by the name of Crescent Beach, and at its southern part is the principal bathing place. At the extreme southern end the shore makes a deeper sweep, and here an artificial harbor has been formed by the construction of a government breakwater.

As we steam across the bay, the harbor, the hotels and dwellings on shore in its neighborhood gradually become more distinct. Soon we pass the end of the breakwater, consisting of a huge rough wall of immense blocks of granite piled upon each other, and enter a small inclosed basin formed by two "L" shaped wharves, the "Ls" coming together so closely as to form gateway into the dock. Here there are accommodations for several vessels. The southerly wharf is backed up directly by the breakwater and is the landing place for all steamers. The northerly one is of the nature of a breakwater, and at its inner-side are usually tied up, head on, as many of the medium sized fishing crafts of the islanders as can be accommodated. Outside of this basin, in the space pro-tected by the breakwater, is good anchorage ground, much utilized by fishing vessels at certain seasons of the year. As many as a hundred and fifty sail some-times are counted here waiting for one of the frequent fogs to lift so that they can pursue their avocation again. This harbor, if it can be called such, is only available in comparatively mild weather, and not at all during strong northerly or easterly winds.

Along the shore and on low rolling hills facing the harbor is the most con-siderable community on the island, consisting of a collection of summer hotels, a few dwellings, a church and several stores, and the whole place lies fully in view from the deck of an approaching steamer. It has a scattered-looking appearance. The only compact portion is a row of hotels and other buildings extending along shore from the landing to the Post-Office, the distance being less than half a mile. These buildings are on a low bluff, with a street inter-vening between them and its edge, while the shore in front is a gently shelving beach on which the fishermen haul up their boats, and at the foot of the bluff extending north from the landing are rows of fish sheds that are generally taken by visitors, at first sight, for bathing houses. Beyond the Post-Office, which stands on a miniature headland, the shore curves inward and the bathing beach properly begins. Three main roads lead out of this section, and they with their ramifications reach every portion of the island. Northward runs the Neck road leading to Sandy Point and light, a distance in this way of about six miles; directly across the island westward runs Main Street, between three and four miles in length, midway passing through the " Centre," the only other village on the island; southward High Street leads up the hills to the southern bluffs and the lighthouse, a distance of about two miles.

The bulk of the island is in the southern part, where the distance across is about four miles. From there it tapers gradually to a point at the extreme north. Southward the land slopes gradually upward from the harbor to a series of high, precipitous and picturesque bluffs, rising from 100 to 150 feet in height, which form the coast of the island in this direction. The faces of these bluffs are formed of clay, cut up into pinacles, headlands, precipices and slopes, while the shore at their base is strewn with boulders and rocks rounded by the ceaseless rolling of the waves. The effect on approaching these cliffs, as they are sometimes wrongfully called, is very unique. The greensward of the hills reaches to their edge, and in places the sea is not seen until the observer is on the brink, when, looking sheer downward for nearly two hundred feet, the sen-sation is as if one was suspended between sea and sky.

A portion of the southeast corner of the island is known as Mohegan Bluff, from the story that a party of the Mohegan tribe of Indians on an invad-ing expedition from the mainland were here penned up and destroyed by the island Indians, the Manissees. Near the edge of this bluff, which is about one hundred and fifty feet above mean low water, stands a fine government light-house, whose lantern gleams 204 feet above the sea. This lighthouse, one of

SCENES ON BLOCK ISLAND.

the best equipped on the coast, is a handsome brick structure erected in 1874 at a cost of $75,000, and contains a Fresnel cylindrical lens of the first order, which cost about $10,000. Almost on the edge of the bluff near the lighthouse are two powerful fog horns operated by small steam engines, which pierce the air with their shrill shrieks every half minute during the fogs which so frequently envelop the island. Returning from Mohegan Bluffs and the lighthouse "across lots" directly northward for the greater portion of the distance the harbor and hotels are in view, and on a nearer approach, especially if there are many vessels in the bay, the picture spread before the eye is one of the most beautiful to be had on the island. The bluffs between the lighthouse and landing gradually become lower, and form a succession of pleasing curves. About midway is a wild mass of rock projecting out a short distance into the ocean, and known as Old Harbor Point. On its south side is Pebbly Beach, a favorite resort for summer visitors, where are found in great profusion waveworn stones of every shape and hue.

The bluffs on the south side of the island reach their highest elevation about half a mile west of the lighthouse, attaining to a sheer elevation of 163 feet above mean low water. From there they gradually recede until at Black Rock Point and at Southwest Point, two miles westward, they are less than a hundred feet above the sea. The western shore may be said to begin here. The bluffs continue all along that side of the island, but they are low and sandy with much less variety than on the southern coast. The most westerly portion of the island is Dicken's Point, which has but a slight elevation, and is directly west across the island from Old Harbor Point, the distance being about three and a half miles, the greater breadth of the island.

Midway of the length of the island is Great Pond, which in comparison to the size of the island is an inland sea. The width of the island here is less than a mile and a half, and this pond in its broadest part stretches nearly from shore to shore, on the west a narrow strip of land, in no instance five hundred feet in width, being the only barrier between it and the ocean, while on the east it approaches within several hundred feet of Crescent Beach. This pond was formerly connected with the sea from the west, and was used in the early years of the century as a harbor by small vessels. A project is now on foot to again break through this beach, mainly to allow the pond to again become stocked with salt water fish. Great Pond is about a mile in width by a mile and a half in length.

Beyond the great pond the island extends northward for about two miles in the form of a narrow peninsula hardly more than a mile wide, and terminates in a long point to the northwest. This promontory from its character is called Sandy Point, and near its extremity is a stone lighthouse, built in 1867. It is the fourth lighthouse in this locality, the other three, the first of which was built in 1829, being rendered useless by the shifting sands on which they were located.

The surface of the island is almost wholly formed of hills and ponds. In every hollow is a sheet of water, which range in size from the great pond covering a thousand acres or more to little pools a few feet in circumference, and

THE OCEAN VIEW HOTEL. THE HARBOR AND THE BREAKWATER.

Nicholas Ball, Proprietor.   Marden & Cundall, Managers.

THE largest hotel on Block Island is the Ocean View. It is admirably situated on a bluff overlooking the harbor and the beaches and from its rooms and parlors magnificent views are obtained of the island and the ocean. It is acknowledged to be the palace hotel of Block Island. Its drainage is perfect. The house is fitted up with gas, electric bells. It has a magnificent music hall, with a theatrical stage, and during the season a fine orchestra plays on all suitable times and occasions. All these splendid opportunities for entertainment are utilized to the best advantage by a competent master of ceremonies. The table is strictly first class, a resident physician is always at hand, a fine livery stable is connected with the hotel, and a steam laundry is one of the necessary features. There is a U. S. cable office in the hotel, the rates to the mainland being only half a cent per word. The house and grounds are lighted with electricity. The guests who yearly frequent this hotel are a splendid class of people. For further information send for special hand book.

are so many in number that it would be a difficult task to count them. The principal large ponds are Chagum, Middle, Wash, Trim's, Harbor, Sands, and Fresh ponds. Probably some of these ponds are sustained by springs, but the most likely solution of their existence is found in the clayey character of the soil, which "holds the water like cauldrons," and thus retains the surface drainage from the frequent rains, while in summer they are protected from evaporation by the humid atmosphere and frequent fogs. Those along the shore are supposed to obtain their waters from the ocean by filtration through the sands.

The island is full of hills. The Rev. S. T. Livermore, its historian, gives the following graphic description of its remarkable appearance : "No person ever saw the surface of the ocean more uneven than is the land of Block Island. . . . Imagine several tidal waves, moving in nearly the same direction, from west to east, each rising about one hundred and fifty feet above the level of the sea, and their bases nearly touching each other ; and on the top, sides, and intervales of these, ' chop waves ' in every conceivable shape and position, covering completely the tidal waves ; and when the reader has done this, he has an outline of the view under the observer's eye who stands in a good light upon Beacon Hill." The last named elevation is the highest land on the island, being 211 feet above the sea level, and from its summit not only the entire island, its hills and ponds, can be seen, but the sea is visible on all sides except where the bluffs are highest at the southeast, and Long Island Sound, the shores of Connecticut, Rhode Island, and Long Island are plainly visible on clear days, the whole affording a truly magnificent prospect. Beacon Hill is about two miles west of the landing.

The numerous ponds, the abundant rains and fogs keep the island in a condition of beautiful verdure ; even during the sultry summer weather its hills are green and pleasant. Like Nantucket, Block Island is almost without trees, although traditions say that when first discovered by Europeans it was covered with forest. There is now no good reason to believe that trees would not grow in most of the sheltered valleys, and it is to be hoped that effort will be made to plant and cultivate them, as they would add much to the beauty of the already charming isle. The original forests were undoubtedly cut down and used for building material and fuel. From the time of their disappearance until about 1846 the fuel used on the island was peat obtained from many of the numerous ponds, where the vegetable deposit through long ages had formed into this material. But little is now used, although on the margins of many of the ponds the places where it was formerly cut can be easily discerned. Coal is now the principal fuel here, as elsewhere.

Near the geographical centre of the island and about a mile and a half by road westward from the harbor is "The Centre," a cross-roads with a few houses, a church, school, and the town house, a plain wooden building which also contains the "Island Library," a collection of several hundred volumes. The road to the Centre leads through pleasant farms, several of which have considerable orchards. Excellent views of the island's landscape are had, the whole surface being scattered with dwellings, so that there are really no desolate regions. Near the Centre are two quaint old wind-mills. The visitor who does not go beyond the harbor has little chance of observing the beauty of the island.

Notwithstanding the great exposure to the ocean breezes — in fact, because of it — Block Island is a delightful resort in summer. The climate is like that of Bermuda, the temperature rarely rising above 75 degrees, and being in the centre of conflicting ocean currents, its atmosphere is surcharged with ozone and other life-giving elements.

The island was formerly the scene of many shipwrecks, and many are the weird stories of wreckers that have here been given a "local habitation and a name." The most famous of these legends is that of the Palatine light, said to be a phantom ship, but probably some irradiation that passes over the surface of the deep. It was last observed in 1880 by Thomas Peace Hazard.

The government breakwater already mentioned consists of a huge wall of uncut stone projecting nearly fifteen hundred feet into the ocean. The work of building it was begun in 1871, and nearly every season since additional work has been done either in extending or repairing it. Previous to that time visitors to the island had to come ashore in small boats through the surf. The native Block Islanders were formerly very expert boatmen, as they had to navigate their boats through the surf every time they entered or left the water, and they developed a type of boat specially adapted to this trying service. This boat was small and light, sharp at both ends, and of a peculiar shape. Few of them are now in existence.

Crescent Beach, the magnificent bathing place, did not exist in its present form until after the great September gale of 1815, when the sea broke over, leveled a range of low sand dunes, and formed the existing beach. The sea in various parts of the island is continually encroaching on the land, the remorseless ocean is forever gnawing at the base of the bluffs, particularly on the south side, and frost and storm yearly tumble down thousands of tons to be swept away by the waves, thus moving the shore line landward every year. Hardly seventy years ago, while writing his famous Palatine letter to the Hon. S. L. Mitchell, of New York, Dr. Aaron C. Willey sat in his house less than five hundred feet northeast of the present Post-office, and looked out on the road between his house and the ocean. The road has disappeared and the site of the Willey House is now swept by the waves of the Atlantic more than two hundred feet from the land.

Block Island was first brought to the notice of the New England settlers by the murder of Captain John Oldham and his companions in 1636 by its savage inhabitants. On that account expeditions were fitted out from Boston by which the Indian inhabitants were punished and subdued, and the island then became the possession of Massachusetts, but was afterwards sold to private parties by the colony, and finally, in 1672, was duly incorporated as a Rhode Island town, and was named New Shoreham. The name perpetuates the memory of Adrian Block, an old Dutch navigator, who visited it in 1614. Verazzano, the Florentine navigator and explorer, saw it in 1524 as he passed along the coast, and he reported that it was full of hills and covered with trees.

Within the last fifteen years Block Island has been gradually coming into prominence as a summer resort, until at present it probably has a greater number of hotels than other any resort on the New England coast. Perhaps this statement ought to be qualified by saying that Narragansett Pier, with fewer hotels, has accommodations for a larger number of persons. Block Island, however, is as yet mainly a hotel resort.

One of the great attractions of Block Island is the fishing to be enjoyed off its shores or in the surrounding waters. About a third of the islanders are engaged in the fisheries, and the cod, mackerel, and swordfish are those chiefly sought for commercial purposes. The favorite sport of summer visitors is to fish for bluefish from a Block Island boat in the care of a hardy skipper, or better still to throw the line for sea bass from the foot of the bluffs on the south shore, where frequently very good catches are made. The ponds abound in fish, particularly Great Pond, and many of the summer visitors prefer this sport to the danger and disagreeable features incident to sea fishing.

A large proportion of the inhabitants, contrary to popular belief, make their living by farming, and a considerable area of the island is cultivated, some of the hills even to their summits. The sea-weed gathered on the shores makes an excellent fertilizer and is much used for that purpose. Large quantities of carrageen or Irish moss is gathered every season, principally on the west side of the island, and brings a good revenue to some of the islanders. There are no wild animals on the island, but many migratory birds make it a resting place at certain seasons of the year. Quite a number of sheep are kept by the farmers, and they form pleasing pictures grazing on the hill sides. Block Island mutton is famous for its flavor, which it owes probably to the excellent climate and fine grazing.

The population of the island in 1885 was 1,257, and of those about ninety per cent. were American born and all but 193 were born on the island. There are no poor on the island, and no almshouse. Nearly all the families own their own houses and land, and probably not more than five native families rent houses. The fisherman's property consists of his dwelling, a small piece of land for his garden, and his boat. This general ownership of their homes and lands has always made the islanders a peculiarly independent and genuinely democratic community, and as a consequence the standard of intelligence among them has been and is much in advance of the average rural population on the mainland.

There is during the summer a choice of three routes to reach Block Island: The Continental steamer leaving Providence at 9.00 A. M. connects at Newport with steamer *Geo. W. Danielson*, which leaves that port daily except Sundays for the island, at 12.30 P. M. and returning leaves the island at 8.00 A. M. The new steamer *Mount Hope* leaves Providence every Tuesday and Saturday at 9.00 A. M., and Newport on same days at 10.00 A. M., and also leaves Providence Sundays at 10.00 A. M.; returning, leaves Block Island same days at 3.00 P. M. The sea-going steamer *Block Island* leaves Norwich daily (except Sunday), at 8.15 A. M., New London at 9.30, touching at Watch Hill, arrives at the island at 12.30, and leaves at 2.00 P. M.

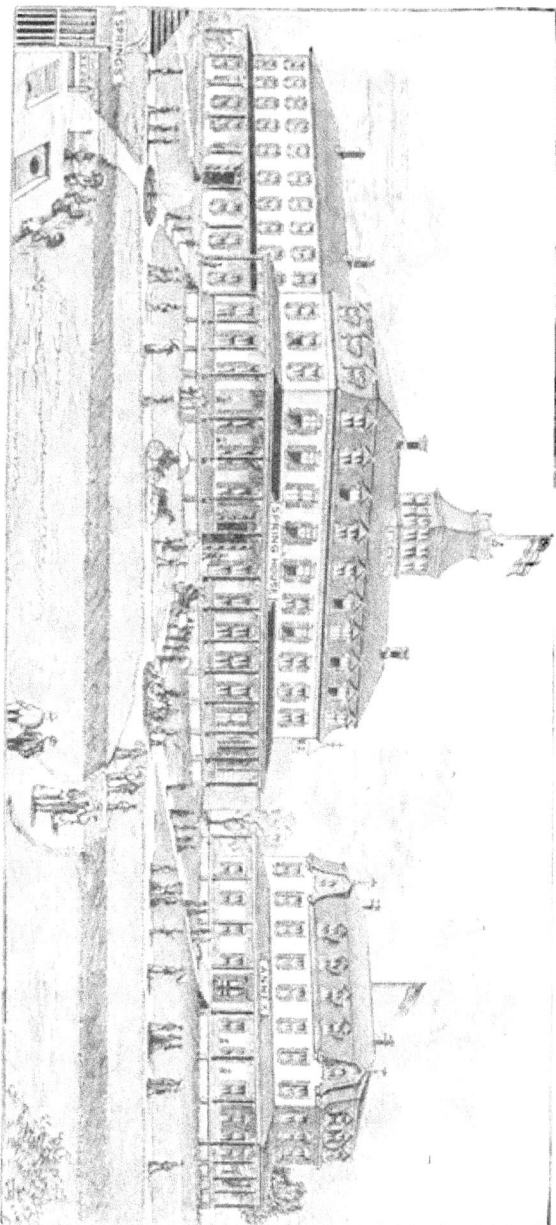

THE SPRING HOUSE AND ANNEX — B. B. MITCHELL, PROPRIETOR.

The original hotel at Block Island was the Spring House, established by its present proprietor, Hon. B. B. Mitchell, more than twenty years ago, when only two mails a week reached the island and the only means of communication with the mainland were the frail boats of the islanders. It was the foundation of the development of the island as a summer resort, and in spite of dull seasons and adverse circumstances the doors of the house have always been open. With the increase of summer business that in time came, accommodations had to be increased, until at present it consists of the old Spring House fronting east, the new Spring House fronting north, both forming one building, while in addition is the Annex, a good sized summer hotel in itself. These houses are situated on extensive grounds sloping down to the water's edge, and are elevated above the sea two hundred feet, while they are only a short distance from the landing. The proprietor, Hon. B. B. Mitchell, has largely assisted in developing the island as a summer resort, for besides his work in maintaining the Spring House, by his services in the Rhode Island General Assembly and his correspondence with public men, he has been largely instrumental in bringing about the construction of the breakwater and in introducing other improvements that have contributed so much to render the island popular. The house has all the modern conveniences, and is especially famous for its water supply which is obtained from the celebrated spring from which it takes its name, and which in fact first gave the impetus to Block Island as a summer resort. There are, in reality, two, differing radically in the quality of their waters, but both adapted for all purposes. Its ample grounds, fine location, pure and bracing water, conservative and careful management, all render this hotel one of the finest sojourning places on the island.

On an elevation overlooking the harbor, but a short distance from the landing, and reached by a short walk or drive is the Norwich House, which from its situation fully justifies its good name. From its piazzas the breakwater, the shipping, the village, and the hotels all lie at the spectator's feet, while a large portion of the island, its shores, hills, and ponds, are spread out to view. The house is surrounded by grassy slopes, thereby avoiding the flying sand that prevails near the highways. It is fitted up in a comfortable, commodious style, with modern conveniences. The terms are moderate, and every attention and courtesy is extended to the guests.

Near the landing, seated on the edge of the bluff, the street running on the landward side of it, is the Harbor Cottage, run by C. C. Ball, and one of the best appointed hotels in the place. For location and outlook it is unexcelled, and its table is well supplied, as Mr. Ball has his large store near by to draw from constantly.

THE HOTEL LIST.

BLOCK ISLAND.

Surf Cottage, Charles W. Willis; on bluff near bathing beach; 50 rooms. Rates from $10 to $15 per week; $2.50 per day.

Connecticut House, M. M. Day, 33 rooms. Rates $8 to $12 per week.

Woonsocket House, Almanza J. Rose; midway between steamboat landing and bathing beach; 50 rooms. Rates $2 per day.

Bellevue House, L. B. Mott; 20 rooms. $1.50 per day; $7 to $10 per week.

Block Island House, G. W. Conley, half a mile from landing; 30 rooms. $2, $10 and $12 per week.

Hotel Manisses, O. S. Marden; 75 rooms. Rates $2.50, $3.00, and $3.50 per day; $10 per week and upwards.

Highland House, D. A. Mitchell; 40 rooms. Rates on application.

Sea Side House, Captain Francis Willis, Beach Avenue; 20 rooms. $8 to $10 per week.

Pequot House, Thaddeus A. Ball, Main Street, near beach; 55 rooms. $9 to $15 per week; $2 per day.

Neptune Hotel, Wm. A. Durfee, 40 rooms. $2 per day; $10 per week and upwards.

The Adrian, Nathan Mott; 45 rooms. Rates on application.

Narragansett House, Reuben F. Randall; near wharf, 31 rooms. $9 to $14 per week; $2 per day.

Union House, Leander A. Ball; three minutes' walk from landing; 25 rooms. $2 per day.

Ocean View Hotel, Nicholas Ball, proprietor; O. S. Marden, F. C. Cundall, managers; 375 rooms. $1.50 to $5 per day; $21 to $35 per week.

Spring House, B. B. Mitchell; on heights overlooking landing; accommodations for 300 guests in large hotel and in an annex as large as ordinary hotel. Rates on application.

The Hygeia, C. H. Hadley, M. D., proprietor; S. A. Snow, manager.

National House, Ray G. Lewis; near post office, $5 rooms. $10 to $25 per week.

Harbor Cottage, C. C. Ball; at landing, 25 rooms. $10 to $12 per week.

BRISTOL.

Bristol Hotel, Martin V. Newton; 34 rooms. $2 per day.

BRISTOL FERRY, R. I.

Bristol Ferry House, Alfred Sisson; 35 rooms. $10 a week, single; $15 for two in a room.

CHARLESTOWN, R. I.

Ocean House, Peleg E. Sisson; northern shore of Pawawget or Charlestown Pond, Southern Rhode Island, 20 rooms. $7 to $8 per week.

CHARLESTOWN BEACH.

Ninigret House, H. W. Tuler. Furnishes table board for cottagers and others.

CUMBERLAND HILL, R. I.

Highland House, Mrs. George A. Jencks, about a mile from Manville; 14 rooms. $10 per week.

EAST GREENWICH.

Updike House, Nathaniel Carpenter, Main Street; 40 rooms. $2 per day.

Central House, Edwin M. Tilley; 81 Main Street, 17 rooms. $1 to $1.50 per day.

EAST PROVIDENCE.

Fyler's Cottage Home, E. W. Fyler; near steamboat landing; 20 rooms. $7 to $10 per week for one in room; $12 to $15 for two in room.

Silver Spring House, H. P. Bliss; Silver Spring, 3 miles from Providence; 20 rooms. $2 per day; $7 to $10 per week.

What Cheer House, Bullock's Point, Jas. E. Woodward; 50 rooms. $1 to $1.50 per day.

Riverside Hotel, George W. Paton; Lincoln Avenue, 50 rooms. $1 per day.

River View Park Hotel, Beverly J. Ring; Pomham Bluff; 25 rooms. $1 to $1.50 per day.

Ferry House, Emma A. Perry; Grant Avenue, accommodation for 30. $1 per day; $6 to $10 per week.

Camp White House, Alfred A. White; Riverside, 75 rooms. $1 to $1.50 per day.

FALL RIVER.

Commercial House, William L. Fish; 32, 32½ and 34 Second Street, near City Hall; 20 rooms. $1.50 to $2 per day.

Wilbur House, George E. Wilbur; 17 to 25 North Main Street, 75 rooms. $2.50 per day.

Narragansett Hotel, George F. Kingsley; 57 North Main Street; 50 rooms. $2 per day.

Mellen House, George Bowker & Co., North Main Street. Accommodations for 50.

Richardson House, A. C. Durfee; corner Main and Central streets; 100 rooms; European or American plan.

Park House, John West; 240, 242, and 244 South Main Street. European plan.

Evans House, W. C. Evans, 43 North Main, 28 rooms. $1.50 per day.

Vickery's Hotel, Charles P. Vickery, 7 North Main Street; 30 rooms. $1 per day.

JAMESTOWN.

Gardner House, Jamestown, opposite Newport; 20 rooms. $2 per day.

Bay View House, Charles T. Knowles, Jamestown, opposite Newport; 100 rooms. $12 to $15 per week; $2.50 per day.

Conanicut Park Hotel, O. C. Slader; 50 rooms. $2.50 per day; $9 to $15 per week.

LITTLE COMPTON, R. I.

The Sakonnet, J. L. Slocum, Seaconnet Point, 25 rooms and accommodations in Wilbur Cottage adjoining. $14 per week.

NARRAGANSETT PIER.

Revere House, F. P. W. Tefft, lessee; Ocean Road; 100 rooms. $3 per day.

Metatoxet House, John H. Caswell; 75 rooms. Double rooms $25 to $28, single $15 to $20 per week; $3 per day for one person.

Narragansett, Ezbon S. Taylor; Ocean Road; 40 rooms; $15 to $25 per week; $3 per day.

The Mount Hope, William G. Caswell; Ocean Avenue; 136 rooms. $3 to $4 per day.

The Mathewson, S. W. Mathewson; Ocean Avenue; 150 rooms. $4 per day. Special rate for week or month.

The Gladstone, W. A. Nye; 125 rooms. $4 to $5 per day; $20 to $35 per week single room; $30 to $45 per week double rooms.

The Rockingham, James G. Burns; corner of Main Street and Sea Side Avenue; 120 rooms. $3.50 to $4.00 per day.

The Atwood, James A. Tucker; 100 rooms. $3 and upwards.

Massasoit House, John Babcock; Mathewson Street; 70 rooms. $3 to $3.50 per day.

Atlantic House, S. T. Browning; 100 rooms. $2.50 to $4 per day.

The Delavan, J. O. Chandler; 57 rooms, and 6 in cottage. $3.50 per day for transients.

Ocean House, Geo. N. Kenyon; Caswell Street; 50 rooms. $3 per day; $14 to $17 single rooms, $22 to $25 double rooms per week.

Congdon House, David A. Segar; five minutes' drive from railroad station; 15 rooms. $10 to $20 per week.

Hotel Columbus, W. A. Nye; accommodation for 100 guests. $4 per day; $20 to $30 per week single room; $30 to $40 per week double rooms.

The Continental, A. F. Saunders; 120 rooms. $3 to $4 per day.

NEWPORT.

Ocean House, J. G. Weaver and Son; Bellevue Avenue; 300 rooms. $4 per day.

Brayton House, B. R. Brayton; 38 and 44 Pelham Street; 33 rooms. $2.00 to $2.50 per day.

The Aquidneck, L. F. Attleton; Pelham Street; 75 rooms. $2.50 to $4 per day.

Perry House, Henry Bull, Jr.; Washington Square; 100 rooms. $3 per day.

Pinard House, Arnaud Pinard; Bellevue Avenue, corner Bellwood Street; 22 rooms. $4 and $5 per day.

Germania Hotel, Richard Holzinger; State foot of Downing Street; 12 rooms. $2 per day.

Sherman House, M. E. Lewis; 108 Thames; 30 rooms. $1.00, $1.25, and $1.50 per day.

Cliff Avenue Hotel and Cottages, M. F. Messer; eight cottages on Cliffs; meals and service, and cottages in other parts city. Rates on application.

Clifton House, B. P. Cummings; 113 to 115 Bellevue Avenue; 33 rooms. $2.50 to $3 per day.

NORTH SCITUATE, R. I.

Moswansicut House, Henry Turner; on shores of Lake Moswansicut; 100 rooms. $7 to $10 per week.

NOYES' NECK, WESTERLY, R. I.

Chapman House, Harris P. Chapman, 2d; rooms in house and adjoining cottages. $1.50 per day; special rates to permanent guests.

PEACEDALE, R. I.

Peacedale House, Mrs. John Sykes; 25 rooms. $1 per day.

PAWTUCKET.

Benedict House, A. Franz Donath; corner Main and Broad Streets; 100 rooms. $2 per day.

Pawtucket Hotel, D. W. Bucklin; 23 Broadway.

PROVIDENCE.

Hotel Dorrance, George W. Cross; corner Dorrance and Westminster Streets; 200 rooms. European plan. $1.00 per day and upward.

Narragansett Hotel, L. H. Humphreys; corner Broad and Dorrance Streets; 300 rooms; rates according to location of rooms.

Hotel Perrin, Josiah B. Reed; 127, 129, and 131 Washington Street; 50 rooms. $2.00 per day.

Central Hotel, Hopkins & Sears; 6, Canal Street; 84 rooms; European plan. Rooms 50c., 75c., and $1.00 per day. American plan; $1.50 to $2.00 per day.

Music Hotel, Joseph S. Wheeler; 1 Aborn Street; 20 rooms. $1.00 per day.

Etna Hotel (formerly Freeman House), James S. Shattuck; 96 Union Street; 70 rooms. $1.50 per day.

Hotel St. George, Thomas Miller proprietor; F. T. Dodsworth, manager; 66, 68, and 70 Washington Street; 60 rooms. Special theatrical rates, $1.00 per day. Transient rates, $1.25 per day.

Hopkins Hotel, Truman A. Cunliff; 421 and 423 High Street; 50 rooms. $1.50 per day.

Mansion House, George R. Earle; 159 Benefit Street; 50 rooms. $1.00 to $1.50 per day; $5, $6, $7, and $8 per week.

Revere Hotel, Henry L. Carter; corner Pine and Dorrance Streets; 30 rooms; European plan.

Brucker's Hotel, P. Brucker, Sr.; 261 Westminster Street; 25 rooms. $2 per day.

City Hotel, 146 and 150 Broad.

Bijou Hotel, 110 Union, Matthew Barry.

Girard Hotel, E. W. Tinker, 51 to 58 Eddy.

WAKEFIELD, R. I.

Wakefield House, Jeremiah Briggs; 16 rooms. $2 per day.

Columbia House, George S. Holland, Jr.; 40 rooms. $1 to $2 per day.

WARREN.

Fessenden House, George L. Crump; corner Main and Croade Streets; accommodations for 50. $1.50 to $2 per day; $6 to $12 per week.

Cole's Hotel, Jeremiah Goff, Main, corner Joyce Street; 25 rooms. $1.50 to $2 per day; $6 to $10 per week.

WARWICK.

Apponaug Hotel, Apponaug, Geo. H. Clough; 25 rooms. $2 per day.

James Tinker's Hotel (Bank Cafe), Pawtuxet, Warwick side.

Warwick Neck House, B. S. Hazard; Warwick Neck; 40 rooms. Terms on application.

Oakland Beach Hotel, E. Stapton; 115 rooms, and one cottage with nine rooms. Terms on application.

Oakland Beach Farm House, Mrs. J. M. Phibbricks; 25 rooms. $2 to $4 per day.

Old Buttonwoods House, Albert Hopkins, at Old Buttonwoods Beach, Greenwich Bay; 24 rooms. $7 to $9 per week.

Buttonwood Beach Hotel, Mrs. Kate Brown, Cowesset Bay; 40 rooms. $2 to $3 per day.

Warwick Arms Hotel, Mrs. R. D. Goey, Rocky Point, $12 to $15 per week.

Cady's Hotel, River View, Mrs. T. N. Arnold, manager.

Bay Side Hotel, Thomas W. Gorton; 45 rooms; $17 to $30 for two persons per week.

WATCH HILL.

Atlantic House, O. S. Spencer; 80 rooms. $2 and $3 per day; $10 to $21 per week.

Plympton Bay View, and Dickens Houses, William Hill, all fronting on Little Narragansett Bay; 250 rooms. dining-room at Plympton. $3 in Plympton; $2.50 in Bay View; $2 in Dickens.

Larkin House, D. F. Larkin; 206 rooms; accommodations for 400 guests.

Narragansett House, N. E. Nash; 27 rooms. Reasonable, according to location.

Ocean House, J. F. Champlin; 100 rooms. $4 per day.

Peninsula House, Coates and Ockington; 40 rooms. Terms on application.

Watch Hill House, A. R. Hale; 165 rooms. $4 per day.

WESTERLY.

Dixon House, Chauncey W. Johnson; Broad Street; 125 rooms. $2 to $3 per day.

Leonard House, Charles Leonard, Main Street, 25 rooms. $1 to $1.50 per day.

Windsor House, Wm. N. Robinson, 58 High Street; 4 rooms. $1.50 per day.

WICKFORD.

Narragansett House, Henry S. Congdon; corner Wall and Main Streets; 17 rooms. $1 to $2 per day.

Cold Spring House, T. C. Peirce and C. P. Peirce; 51 rooms. $2.50 per day; $10 to $15 per week.

Bay View House, Daniel Lawton; 20 rooms. $7 to $10 per week.

WOONSOCKET.

Woonsocket Hotel, Cook, Mason & Co.; Market Square; 75 rooms. $2 per day.

Monument House, S. W. Elliott & Co.; Monument Square; 75 rooms. $2 per day.

Russell M. Joslin's

ⓒASH

MARKET.

Meats, Vegetables

—AND

Fine ⓒ Butter

At Low Prices and Warranted the Best.

PROMPT DELIVERY.

9 Richmond Street, - Providence, R. I.

MRS. P. C. HILLMAN,

INTELLIGENCE AGENCY

One Flight, Room 6,

ENTRANCES:

91 Westminster St., and 31 Exchange Place,

PROVIDENCE, R. I.

Elevator and Telephone

GELB & MOHN,

CATERERS,

ICE CREAM PARLORS,

197 Westminster Street,

Providence, R. I.

WILLIAM R. BROWN,

COSTUMES, REGALIAS, JEWELS, I. O. R. M. PARAPHERNALIA,

Gold and Plated Emblems,

Ribbon Badges and Rosettes, Constitutions and By-Laws, Ball Programmes, Tickets, Address Cards, all kinds of Society Printing. Write for prices

77 Dorrance Street, Providence.

PATENTS

U. S. AND FOREIGN.

JOSEPH A. MILLER & CO.,

SOLICITORS

AND

EXPERTS.

25 Butler Exchange,

PROVIDENCE, R. I.

Reports and Arguments furnished in Patent Litigation. Assistance and Counsel rendered as Experts in patent cases.

European, Canadian, and American Patents for Inventions, Designs and Trade-Marks procured promptly.

Researches made to determine the validity of American and Foreign Patents.

⇒The ◉ Sakonnet.⇐

LOCATION. The new Hotel, The Sakonnet, opened June 18, 1894, stands on a bluff on Sakonnet Point, Little Compton, R. I. Jutting out into the Atlantic on one side, and the Sakonnet River on the other, the Point is unsurpassed for grand and striking scenery, even amid a country famed as the finest in the state, and abounding in beautiful drives by forest, field and ocean.

A broad veranda extends entirely around the house, affording shade at all hours. From it may be seen the grounds, extending to the water's edge, the surf breaking on the rocks almost at the very door, the arrival and departure of the steamer not far away, and vessels passing near or out at sea. Facilities for surf or still-water bathing, also for boating and fishing are excellent.

ACCOMMODATIONS. The house contains 26 rooms, 15 of which are lodging rooms. On the first floor are Parlor, Sitting Room and two Dining-Rooms, each commanding a fine view of the ocean; a dressing room containing set bowls, etc., besides the Office, Kitchen and Butler's Pantry. The second floor consists of Bedrooms, ten in number, connected with the Office by Electric Bells. They are all light and airy, and overlook the ocean. A bath-room with all conveniences is on this floor, supplied, as is the Dressing-Room below, with hot and cold water. The third story contains five lodging rooms. The table will be provided with fresh eggs, milk, butter, poultry, and vegetables from the farmers in the vicinity. Horses and carriages for driving and accommodations for those owned by the guests may be had.

MEANS OF ACCESS. The Steamer *Queen City* leaves Providence and Sakonnet daily as per advertisement, except Sunday, connecting at Tiverton station with trains for Boston, Providence, and Newport. Carriages to and from trains can be furnished if desired. The steamer's landing is about a minute's walk from the house; her landing in Providence is very central.

All communications should be addressed to J. L. SLOCUM, Box 1,034, Providence, R. I.

STEAMER
⇒QUEEN CITY⇐

▽ ▽ ▽ ▽ ▽ ▽ ▽ ▽

Makes Daily Trips from Providence to Seaconnet Point, from May 1st to Oct. 1st, and balance of year Tri-Weekly.

THE sail down Narragansett Bay by this line is unsurpassed. Leaving the heat and dust of Providence behind, you are soon on the clear bright water, which wends its way to the ocean.

The cottages of the summer residents dot the shore on either side as you pass Silver Spring, Riverside and Nayatt on the one side, and Pawtuxet, Long Meadow, and Rocky Point on the other. After passing Nayatt, Warren comes in sight; then Bristol and Fall River. Sailing up Mt. Hope Bay, you pass Mt. Hope, celebrated in the early history of the state. After turning the northern extremity of the island of Rhode Island, you enter Seaconnet River and pass through the two bridges, and a short sail takes you by Fogland Point, and out where you can feel the gentle swell of the ocean, and soon arriving at Seaconnet Point where ample time is allowed for getting dinner, and for a drive or a bath.

What Cheer House

ᐅ-ᐊBULLOCK'S ❖ POINT.ᐅ-ᐊ

THE above house is located six miles from Providence, and it is a charming place to spend a little time by the sea-shore. The house will accommodate one hundred and fifty guests, and is conducted on the American plan, from $1.00 to $1.50 per day.

Connected with the house is a beautiful Pine Grove and a splendid Beach for Bathing; also a Dance Hall, the music for which is furnished by Vaughn's Orchestra.

Genuine Rhode Island Shore Dinners served daily, and a liberal discount from regular rates given to Sunday Schools and other Societies.

TOBOGGAN SLIDE, FLYING HORSES, BOAT SWINGS,

AND OTHER AMUSEMENTS.

J. E. WOODWARD, Proprietor.

PICTURESQUE NARRAGANSETT.

CAMPBELL & CO.,
Bicycles! Safeties! Tricycles!

Tandems, Stars, New Rapids, Quadrants.

BICYCLE REPAIRING AT REASONABLE PRICES.

SUNDRIES. SECOND-HAND WHEELS.

99 Orange Street, Providence, R. I.
BICYCLE REPAIRING A SPECIALTY.

W. II. DOUGHTY & CO.,
Manufacturers of and Dealers in

ICE CREAM

———AND———

✧HULLED CORN.✧

We use the best cream in the manufacture of our Ice Cream, no cheap stock used. Large or small orders delivered at short notice. Sunday orders a specialty. Sweet Cream constantly on hand. This season we supply Oakland Beach and Field's Point with our Cream.

Price off the team or at the Creamery, 40 cents per quart.

Price when delivered and packed, 50 cents per quart; $1.50 per Gallon; Large Orders, $1.25. Dishes and Spoons Free of Charge.

W. II. DOUGHTY & CO.,
NO. 79 FIFIELD AVENUE, - - PROVIDENCE, R. I.
TELEPHONE, 205-6.

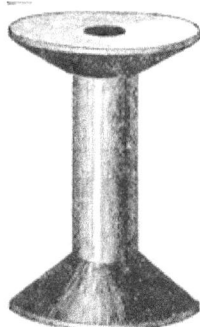

J. TRUMAN BURDICK. H. R. STODER

J. TRUMAN BURDICK & CO.,

⇒Real * Estate,⇐

All business relating to
the Sale, Rental, Insur-
ance, Care or Improve-
ment of Real Estate, carefully attended to.

Agents of EDWARD
BURGESS, Yacht De-
signer and Naval Archi-
tect.

FRANKLIN AND SPRING STREETS, NEWPORT, R. I.

ESTABLISHED 1850.

W. H. H. LAWTON,

(Successor to ISAAC LAWTON,)

—DEALER IN—

FRESH, SMOKED AND SALT

•• FISH ••

OF ALL KINDS.

OYSTERS, CLAMS, LOBSTERS,
QUAHAUGS.

22 & 24 LONG WHARF, NEWPORT, R. I.

CLARENCE A. HAMMETT,

323 Thames Street, Newport, R. I.,

Opposite Post-Office.

REAL ESTATE

—AND—

FINANCIAL AGENT

Deeds, Mortgages, Contracts, and all Papers
Neatly and Accurately Drawn.

Insurance Risks Placed with the Best Companies.

CHARLES T. STERNE,

—DEALER IN—

TOBACCO and CIGARS,

NEWSPAPERS, PERIODICALS, Etc.

No. 42 Washington Square, Newport, R. I.

NEW ENGLAND CONSERVATORY OF MUSIC

Franklin Square, Boston, Mass.

New England

Conservatory of Music

Franklin Square Boston

OLDEST IN AMERICA.

Has the largest and best equipped conservatory building in the world; the broadest curriculum of study; employs the ablest corps of teachers, and instructs the largest number of students.

The educational advantages of the Conservatory are grouped under the following schools :

1. A School for the Piano
2. A School for the Organ.
3. A School for Singing, Formation and and Cultivation of the Voice, Lyric Art, and Opera.
4. A School for Violin, Quartet, and Ensemble Playing. Orchestral and Band Instruments and Conducting.
5. A School for Harmony, Composition, Theory and Orchestration.
6. A School for Church Music, Oratorio, and Chorus.
7. A School for Training Music Teachers for Public Schools, etc.
8. A School for Tuning Pianos and Organs.
9. A School for Physical Culture.
10. A College of Music.
11. A School for Common and Higher English Branches, Latin, Italian, German and French Languages.
12. A School of Elocution and Dramatic Action.
13. A School of Fine Arts.
14. A Home for its Lady Pupils.

Instruction is given by ablest American and European artists and teachers, class and private lessons.

Students in any one school have the free advantages of all the schools, such as concerts, recitals, sight-singing and chorus practice, lectures, readings, etc., also use of large musical library. THE HOME is located in the heart of Boston, confessedly the musical, literary, and artistic centre of America. The beautiful park in front and the surrounding broad streets make it both healthful and delightful. It is splendidly equipped for both home and the schools, furnishing home accommodations for five hundred lady students, and class accommodations for three thousand lady and gentlemen students. It is supervised by the Director, Preceptress, Resident Physician, and Lady Teachers. The entire building is heated by steam and lighted by electricity. Opportunities here offered not surpassed by any similar institution in the world.

TUITION : $5, $10, $15, $20 and $25 per term. Board and Rooms $5 to $7.50 per week.

FALL TERM BEGINS September 13, 1888.

Beautifully Illustrated Calendar giving full information, sent free on application to

E. TOURJÉE, Director.

PICTURESQUE NARRAGANSETT.

Fall River and Providence Steamboat Company.

BLOCK ISLAND EXCURSIONS.

SEASON OF 1888.

STEAMER MOUNT HOPE,

Built by Montgomery & Howard, of Chelsea, Mass., (builders of the famous Steamers "City of Fall River" and "City of Brockton,") under the supervision of Mr. George Peirce, Supervisor of the Old Colony Steamboat Co., "Fall River Line." Machinery by W. & A. Fletcher Co., New York.

Extreme length, 200 feet; width, 34 feet; width over guards, 62 feet; depth of hold, 12 feet. Engine—Diameter of cylinder, 48 inch; stroke of piston, 10 feet. Feathering wheels.

The MOUNT HOPE is licensed to carry 2,000 passengers in the river service, and 1,300 in the outside service; is equipped with four metallic life boats, two life rafts, 2,000 block-work life jackets and six ring buoys.

THREE FULL LENGTH DECKS.

Leading from the Main Deck is the Ladies' cabin, beautifully upholstered and arranged with all the modern appliances for comfort and convenience. The Purser's Office is on the port side, also a coat or parcel room, arranged to receive small articles, wraps, etc. On the starboard side is the Gents' Wash Room and a new feature on Excursion Steamers—a Barber Shop. From the Main Deck leading to the Promenade Deck is an elegant Mahogany Stairway, ornamented and beautified by an immense plate glass Mirror, 8½ feet by 6 feet, which stands in a recess at the head of the Landing Forward from this deck is another grand Stairway leading from the Saloon to the Main Deck. Opening from the Saloon is ten (10) State Rooms, or cosy sitting rooms, all nicely furnished with Toilet Apparatus, Couches, Chairs and Electric Call Bells, all arranged to give a home-like appearance. From the Saloon or Promenade Deck is two stairways leading to the Upper or Hurricane Deck. From this deck the view is unobstructed. Nothing appears but the Pilot House and upper part of the Engine. All is carefully guarded by a setting rail both around the sides of the boat and around the engine. On this deck are the Life Boats and Rafts.

The Main Deck and Promenade Deck extend from stem to stern. The Hurricane Deck from stern to front of Pilot House. The Main Deck is arranged with seats around the sides and the Saloon around sides, ends and centres, all in Black Walnut. The Saloon Deck outside, and Hurricane Deck is also seated the entire length and width of the boat, and the entire seating capacity, with the 1,500 all new Brussels covered Camp Stools, is not less than 500 in excess of number of passengers allowed the steamer.

The boat is thoroughly and complete in all parts, is the largest carrying steamer of her length ever launched, was built especially for the outside excursion service, and is also very fast, averaging 16 miles an hour from Boston to Fall River in a southeast storm and on her trial trip.

Commencing Saturday, June 30, this Palatial Steamer will make Excursions from

PROVIDENCE AND NEWPORT

—TO—

◁BLOCK▷ ◁ISLAND▷

EVERY TUESDAY AND SATURDAY, AND FROM PROVIDENCE ONLY EVERY SUNDAY,

Leave Providence Tuesdays and Saturdays at 9 A. M., and Newport at 10.45 A. M. Leave Providence Sundays at 10 A. M. Returning, leave Block Island at 3 P. M., on all Days.

Excursion Tickets, Providence and Block Island, $1.00.   Newport, 75 cents.

CHILDREN UNDER 12 YEARS, HALF PRICE.

THE DELAVAN

◁NARRAGANSETT PIER, R. I.▷

J. O. CHANDLER, PROPRIETOR.

SEASON 1888.

Enters upon its Third Season under the management of its present proprietor.

THE TABLE

WILL BE SUPPLIED WITH THE BEST THERE IS IN THE MARKET.

The Post Office, Casino and Bathing Beach are only about three minutes' walk from the House.

The proprietor wishes to thank those who so liberally patronized him last season and hopes by studying the comfort of his guests to merit a continuance of the same.

The Pier is reached from New York via the Shore Line Railroad or by the steamer to Stonington, thence by rail to the Pier, or by Steamer to Newport, from Newport by Steamer. From Providence and Boston by the Old Colony and New York, Providence and Boston Railroads.

THE WATER USED IN THE HOUSE IS FROM THE GLADSTONE SPRING.

TERMS, $3.50 PER DAY

HOUSE LIGHTED BY ELECTRICITY. SUITABLE ARRANGEMENTS BY THE SEASON.

J. O. CHANDLER, PROPRIETOR.

COTTAGE TO LET.

NARRAGANSETT PIER

NAVIGATION LINE

FROM

NEWPORT to NEW YORK,

Via Narragansett Pier,

Commencing June 25, 1888.

STEAMER

HERMAN S. CASWELL,

LEAVES

Newport for New York at 7.15, 10.00 A. M. and 2.00 P. M., arriving in New York at 3.30, 4.30 and 11.00 P. M.

Local Time-Table.

Newport and Narragansett Pier.

Leaves Newport at 7.15 and 10.00 A. M., 2.00 and 5.15 P. M. Leaves Narragansett Pier 8.30 and 11.40 A. M., 3.15 and 6.30 P. M.

Regular Fare, - - - - - 50c.

Round Trip, - - - - - - 75c.

J. C. TUCKER, JR., Agent.

NARRAGANSETT PIER AND NEWPORT R. R.

To Narragansett Pier and Newport.

[June 25, 1888.]

ARCHIBALD MARTIN,

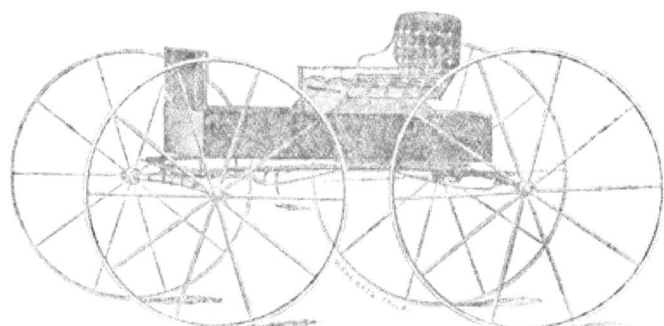

Carriage ✳ Depository,

165, 167 and 169 Pine Street, cor. Richmond,
PROVIDENCE, R. I.

Dealer in Fine Carriages, Harnesses, Etc.
CARRIAGE PAINTING and REPAIRING Neatly and Promptly Executed.
TELEPHONE CONNECTION.

PROVIDENCE ELECTROTYPING AND PLATING WORKS,

Manufacturers of

Jewelry Trimmings and Metal Art Work,

COPIES MADE FROM PATTERNS FURNISHED.

Gold, Silver, Brass and NICKEL PLATING, Oxydizing, Bronzing, Etc., also Polishing and Grinding.

No. 78 Friendship Street, Providence, R. I.

GEO. PRICE, Proprietor.

+Cigar and Tobacco Department.+

BABCOCK & BRIGHAM,

Wholesale Grocers,

93 and 95 DYER STREET, PROVIDENCE, R. I.

Largest Assortment of TOBACCO in the State.

Full Line of CIGARS from $12 to $100 per M.

"SUMNER" our leading 10c. Cigar.   "LINCOLN" our leading 5c. Cigar.

NEWPORT & WICKFORD

Railroad and Steamboat Company.

The only Rail Line between Newport and New York.   Express Trains, with elegant Drawing Room Cars between Wickford Landing and New York.

Tickets sold and baggage checked at Steamer Eolus, Commercial Wharf, and at Transfer Company's office, No. 4 Travers' Block, Bellevue Avenue, Newport.

Drawing Room Chairs and Sleeping Car Berths can be secured at company's office, Commercial Wharf.

[June 25, 1888.]

From Newport.

Leave.	A. M.	A. M.	A. M.	P. M.	P. M.	P. M.	P. M.	P. M.
NEWPORT		7 30	10 20	1 30		4 45	8 15	11 15
Wickford	5 35	8 31	11 20	1 52	4 37	5 47	9 17	12 27
Bellevue	5 50	8 55	11 35	1 55	4 40	5 50	9 20	12 29
Wickford Junction .. Arr.	5 42	8 40	11 50	2 45	4 45	5 55	9 25	12 30
Wickford Junction ... Lve.	5 43	8 43	11 56	2 45	4 49	6 0	9 28	5 02
Providence	6 50	9 15	12 10	3 15	5 35	6 40	9 55	5 35
Boston	8 15	10 50		4 30	8 00	8 00	11 00	7 00
Wickford Junction ... Lve.	8 45	9 38	11 46	2 05	4 57	6 28		1 25
Kingston	9 00	9 51	11 59	3 60	5 70			1 47
Westerly		10 25	12 30	3 3	5 44			2 06
New London		11 10	1 05	4 00	6 40	7 15		2 55
New Haven		1 10	2 55	5 55	9 00	9 40		4 35
New York	Arr.	3 50	4 30	8 00	11 05	11 00		7 00

To Newport.

Leave.	P. M.	A. M.	A. M.	A. M.	A. M.	P. M.	P. M.	P. M.
NEW YORK	11 30	5 00		8 00	10 00	1 00		6 00
New Haven	1 52			8 05	11 50	3 00		1 00
New London	3 30		7 15	10 05	1 05	1 30		3 10
Westerly	4 18	4 55	8 02	10 45	1 05	2 05	5 10	
Kingston	4 45	2 05	8 30	10 50	2 37	5 25	5 40	
Wickford Junction ... Arr.	5 09	2 05	8 10	8 40	11 20	2 45	4 29	6 05	9 25
Boston			6 50		10 00	1 00		
Providence	2 56		8 00	11 15	2 20	4 10	5 30	
Wickford Junction .. Arr.	4 29		8 45	11 00	2 55	5 05		
Wickford Junction ... Lve.	5 42	5 12	8 45	11 50	3 00	4 05	6 05	6 40	9 30
Bellevue		5 17	6 50	11 55	3 05	4 10	6 10	6 45	9 55
Wickford	5 50	6 25	6 55	11 55	3 04	5 00	6 15	6 20	9 38
NEWPORT	Arr.	6 20	6 35	7 05	1 00	4 10		7 00	7 00	10 00

Connections : —

At Wickford Junction, with New York, Providence & Boston Railroad.

At Providence, for Boston and Worcester.

At Kingston, for Peacedale, Wakefield and Narragansett Pier.

At Wood River Junction, for Hope Valley.

At Stonington, for Watch Hill and Stonington Line Steamers for New York.

At New London, for Norwich, Hartford, Springfield, Pittsfield, Albany and Saratoga, N. L. N. R. R.

At Saybrook, for Hartford, Connecticut Valley R. R.

At Bridgeport, for Great Barrington, Stockbridge and Lenox, Housatonic R. R.

C. U. COFFIN, Agent,
NEWPORT, R. I.

J. B. GARDINER, Supt.,
PROVIDENCE, R. I.

BLOCK ISLAND STEAMBOAT COMPANY.

NEW LINE BETWEEN PROVIDENCE AND BLOCK ISLAND, VIA NEWPORT AND CONTINENTAL LINE.

CARRYING THE UNITED STATES MAIL.

The New and Staunch Steamer

GEO. W. DANIELSON,

Captain Conley,

Is running daily, Sundays excepted, between Block Island and Newport, connecting with steamers of the Continental Line of Providence.

Leaving Block Island at 8 a. m., arriving at Newport in time to connect with the Continental steamer for Providence. Passengers for Block Island can take the steamer at Providence, arriving at Newport in time to connect with steamer to Block Island, which leaves Newport daily at 12.30 p. m.

All express matter for Block Island will be shipped by Earle & Prew's express; all freight to be marked "Block Island, via Continental."

WINTER TIME TABLE.

Leaves Block Island Monday, Wednesday, and Friday, 8.30 a. m.; returning, leaves Newport Tuesday, Thursday and Saturday at 12.30 p. m. Monday and Friday runs to Providence; returning 9.00 a. m. Tuesday and Saturday, stopping at Newport each way.

☞ On these trips steamer arrives at Block Island usually about 3.00 p. m., at Providence about 2.00 p. m.

❖Block Island House,❖

BLOCK ISLAND.

THIS hotel overlooks all others on the Island. From it the views of the ocean are magnificent. The distant shores of the Atlantic from Newport to Narragansett Pier, Point Judith and Watch Hill, afford the spectator a grand panoramic view of nature, land and water, while the nearer scenes at the harbor, of steamers, pleasure yachts and fishing vessels, arriving, discharging cargoes and passengers and leaving for various points please the eye with ever forming and dissolving views. The hotel is reached by a good road about half a mile from the landing, and a carriage for the conveyance of guests is in waiting on the arrival of the boat. The house is comfortable and home-like, and its table is supplied with vegetables fresh from the farm and garden belonging to the house.

CAPT. GEO. W. CONLEY, OF STEAMER DANIELSON, Proprietor.

NATIONAL ☙ HOUSE,
◁Block Island.▷

On the Bluff, fronting the harbor, is the National Hotel, a fine, large, four-story edifice with a French roof, and ample piazzas in front. It is a new house, opened for the first time this season, and contains fifty large, light and airy rooms, nearly every one of which looks out on the ocean. For convenience of location it is unsurpassed on the island, being only about two minutes' walk from the steamboat wharf, across the street from the Post-Office, a few steps from the U. S. Signal and Cable office, and near the Churches, principal stores and other public places. Crescent Beach, the principal bathing place, is only a short distance away, and a plank walk leads there from the hotel. The house has hot and cold water, and the latest improved sanitary and bathing facilities on each floor, while its drainage is absolutely perfect. The house is lighted throughout with gas, and every room is provided with electric bells. The table is supplied from one of the largest island farms, while by steamer supplies from the New York markets are daily received. With all of these conveniences and advantages the rates are reasonable, and as the house is under the direct control of its proprietor, Mr. R. G. Lewis, the best of service can with certainty be depended upon.

NEWPORT, R. I.

OCEAN HOUSE,

Address, J. G. WEAVER & SON, NEWPORT, R. I.; or J. G. WEAVER, JR., & Co., Everett House, Union Square, New York.

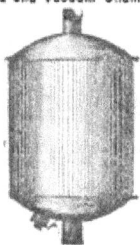

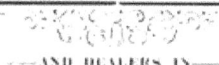

FOR MORE THAN HALF A CENTURY,

THE OLD UNITED STATES HOTEL,

OF BOSTON,

has maintained its RESPECTABILITY AND EXCELLENCE.

Originally the largest Hotel in Boston, it has been twice enlarged years ago, by the extensive wings on Kingston and Lincoln Streets, named respectively Oregon and Texas.

During the past five years it has been under the management of

Mr. TILLY HAYNES, of Springfield, Mass.

who has completely renovated, enlarged and improved the property, and last year added still another hundred rooms, by building across from Texas to Oregon.

Think of a Hotel from Texas to Oregon, and you will understand why this notice is written which is to say that the UNITED STATES recommends itself for its quiet, orderly management, and the notable character of its guests, its numerous public rooms and grand old parlors, broad halls and numerous stairways, while none of its 500 Guest Rooms are above the fourth floor.

These, with its very central location, its most excellent table, and moderate charges, recommend it to all who have once shared its hospitality.

Manufacturers of

SILVER AND GOLD PLATE

SALESROOMS, 37 UNION SQUARE,

NEW YORK.

What ⊚ Cheer ⊚ House,
"BULLOCK'S : POINT."

The above house is located six miles from Providence, and it is a charming place to spend a little time by the sea shore. The house will accommodate one hundred and fifty guests, and is conducted on the American plan, from $1.00 to $1.50 per day. Connected with the house is a beautiful Pine Grove and a splendid Beach for Bathing; also, a Dance Hall, the music for which is furnished by Vaughn's orchestra. Genuine Rhode Island Shore Dinners served daily, and a liberal discount from regular rates given to Sunday Schools and other Societies.

TOBOGGAN SLIDE, FLYING HORSES, BOAT SWINGS, and other Amusements.

J. E. WOODWARD, Prop.

THE LEADING PIANO-FORTES OF THE WORLD
—— ARE THE ——

SHONINGER PIANOS.

ESTABLISHED 1850.

Because they Are the Best Now Made. No Other Can Compete With Them. Will Sing Their Own Praise.

Facts which cannot be better demonstrated than by the use of these celebrated instruments, which have become so popular among the music-loving public.

The **Shoninger Grand Upright Cabinet Pianos** are constructed from the musician's standpoint as well as that of the mechanic, and are distinguished for their pure and resonant quality of tone, containing the greatest musical possibilities. As the best work and best material invariably insure the best results, the **Shoninger Pianos** stand pre-eminently in the front rank, having achieved the grandest success in musical science ever known to this soul-inspiring art, and are unsurpassed by any Piano Fortes ever made.

They have been pronounced by experienced connoisseurs to be the embodiment of perfection, and are especially adapted to withstand the SEVEREST CLIMATIC CHANGES, close attention being paid to this important feature.

EVERY PIANO FULLY WARRANTED.

In places where we have no authorized Agents we sell direct from the factory to the Consumer. A liberal discount allowed. ☞ Send for beautifully illustrated Catalogues and any desired information.

Highest Honors Awarded at the U. S. Centennial Exhibition at Philadelphia, 1876, Exposition Universelle de 1878, Paris, Rotterdam, 1883, and at State and Agricultural Fairs where our instruments have been exhibited. For full particulars address.

B. SHONINGER CO.,
NEW HAVEN, CONN., and 215 STATE ST., CHICAGO, ILL., U. S. A.

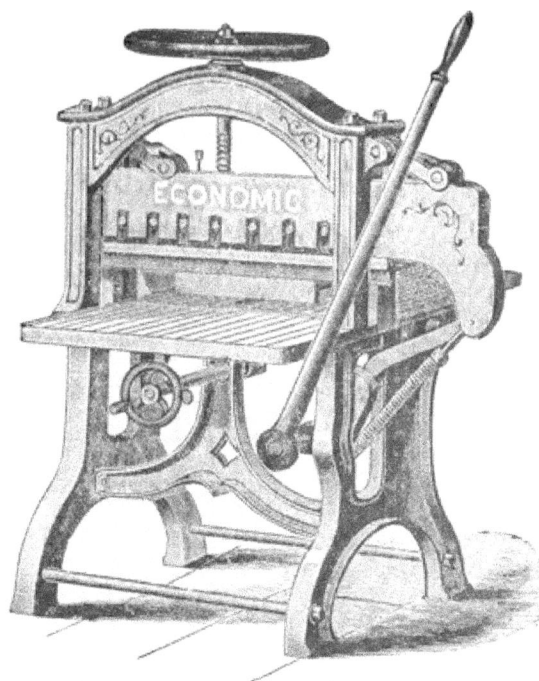

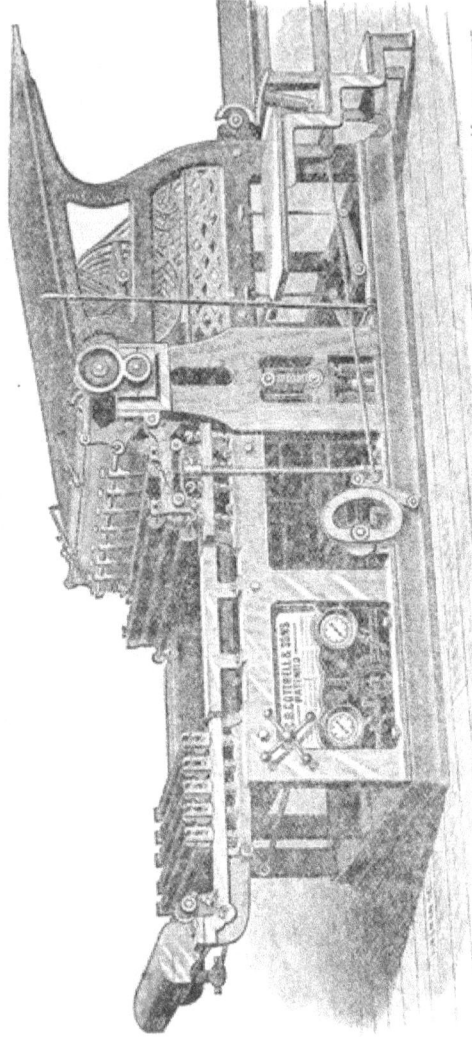

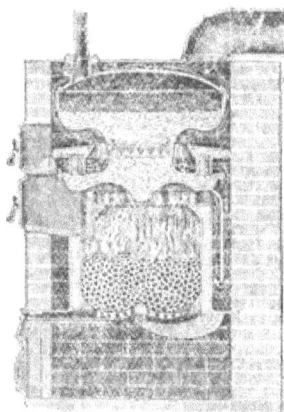

VIEW OF CAMP WHITE FROM THE BEACH

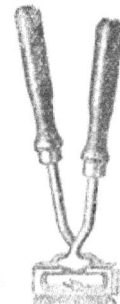

PRINCETON.

One of the most accessible and charming Mountain Resorts, not only in New England but in the whole country, is Princeton. The region of country known by this name is near the geographical centre of the State of Massachusetts, and in its limits is the grand old peak, Mount Wachusett, the crowning eminence of a belt of hills that extend across the State from north to south. It towers above the neighboring elevations and the surrounding country from 1,500 to 2,000 feet, while it is 2,480 feet above the sea level, and affords rare advantages in climate, scenery and healthfulness. Half way up the southern slope of the mountain, standing out on a projecting spur like a promontory, is the village of Princeton, and the chief hotels are all situated in the neighborhood. The Worcester division of the Fitchburg railroad runs through the town, five trains a day passing each way, and stages run from the station to the village and hotels, two miles or more away up the mountain roads, along which, as the tourist is whirled, delightful views of the mountain scenery are obtained. The view from the summit of the mountain extends over portions of the six New England States. It is claimed three hundred cities and villages can be distinguished, and the whole is a grand panorama of hills and valleys, forests and lakes. The elevation ensures clear air, free from fogs and mosquitoes, and in the hottest weather there is always a breeze. Princeton is 16 miles from Worcester and 47 from Boston.

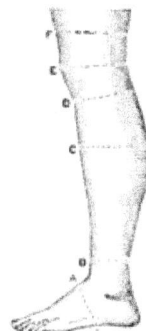